R109E.15

19R

THE NEW DALMATIAN

Ch. Green Starr's Colonel Joe
A record-breaking Group and Best in Show winner who has defeated more dogs than any other Dalmatian in the history of the breed.

THE NEW
DALMATIAN

COACH DOG – FIREHOUSE DOG

Alfred and Esmeralda Treen

New York

Macmillan General Reference
A Simon & Schuster Macmillan Company
1633 Broadway
New York, NY 10019

Library of Congress Cataloging-in-Publication Data

Treen, Alfred.
  The new dalmatian / Alfred and Esmeralda Treen.
    p. cm.
  ISBN 0-87605-134-4
  1. Dalmatian dog. I. Treen, Esmeralda. II. Title.
SF429.D3T74   1991
636.7'2—dc20   91-25459   CIP

10 9 8 7 6 5

Printed in the United States of America

Contents

About the Authors   vii

1. Origins of the Breed   1

2. Chronology of Ancestral Lore   9

3. The Coaching Dalmatian   25

4. The Firehouse Dog   35

5. The Dalmatian Comes to America   41

6. The Dalmatian Standard   51

7. Judging the Dalmatian:
   The Standard Revisited   59

8. Living with a Dal   77

9. Breeders' Practices   81

10. Background for Breeders   87

11. Progress in the Breed   97

12. Showing the Dalmatian   104

13. Obedience   107

14. The Dalmatian: Hunter,
    Herder, Coach Dog   121

15. Foundation Kennels   127

16. Present-Day Kennels   173

17. Around the World with the Dalmatian   197

18. The World Congress   215

19. Fun Things and Side Effects   219

20. Top Spots   227

21. The Dalmatian Fancy's Book of Records   231

    Epilogue   237

    Glossary   241

    Appendix   247

About the Authors

$\mathbf{A}$lfred and Esmeralda Treen have been Dalmatian afficionados for more than forty-five years.

Alfred has been judging Dalmatians since 1965. He now judges all Hounds, Toys, Nonsporting and most of the Terriers. He judged the national specialty of the DCA in 1970 and 1977 and in 1984 judged the special specialty held in conjunction with the AKC Centennial show. He has served the DCA as a governor, treasurer, vice president, and president, a member of the Standard and of the Education Committee. He served as a director of AKC for seven years, 1979–1985. He was president of the Waukesha Kennel Club for 30 years, a club which the Treens with the help of friends founded, and still serves the club as its Delegate to AKC. When living in Houston he was vice president of the Houston Kennel Club and when he moved to the St. Louis area he served as chief ring steward of the Mississippi Valley Kennel Club. At present he is on the Board of the Humane Animal Welfare Society of Waukesha County, the Board of Trustees of the Dog Writers' Educational Trust, and is a trustee of the Dairyland Greyhoud Park's charitable foundation.

Esmeralda Treen started judging Dalmations in 1969. In 1957 she became an obedience judge and continued in this segment of the sport until 1991. She is currently eligible to judge all Sporting breeds and all nonsporting breeds. She judged the DCA national specialties in 1973, 1979, and 1990.

In 1967 Mrs. Treen became co-editor of *The Spotter,* the DCA newsletter, and in 1971 turned it into a quarterly magazine that has received many awards from the Dog Writers' Association. In 1986 she received the D'Ambrisi Award from the Association of Obedience Clubs and Judges in recognition of her service to the sport.

Both Treens are members of the British Dalmatian Club, the Chicago Dalmatian Club, and were recently made honorary members of the Federacion Canofila Mexicana, the Mexican Kennel Club. Mrs. Treen is a member of the Dog Writers' Association. She also serves as a member of the Board of Visitors of the School of Veterinary Medicine of the University of Wisconsin.

The Treens have judged in 11 countries on 6 continents and in 46 of the 50 states.

1

Origins of the Breed

THERE is no "o" in "Dalmatian"! There are no Dalmatians in Dalmatia!

We believe it is important to start with the first things first. The spelling of the breed name should be correct: Dalmatian, not Dalmation! If you feel this is nit-picking and superfluous, believe it or not, some of the local breed clubs, many of the magazines published for the Dog Fancy and hundreds of people who have occasion to use the word misspell it frequently.

Dalmatian. It should be simple. The word is formed by adding a final "n" to the word "Dalmatia," the name of an ancient country now a province of Yugoslavia. Many people believe that the Dalmatian originated in Dalmatia and that is how the breed got the name. Many canine authorities place the origin of the dog somewhere around the Adriatic. While there is no absolute proof, this is probably where the forerunners of the breed emanated or developed. While it isn't literally true that there are no Dalmatians in Dalmatia, very few of these dogs exist in what is supposed to be their native land. Allegedly these are British imports or descendants of imports, and it is quite possible that the dogs did originate in that part of the world. The breed is believed to have come from somewhere near the Mediterranean or the Adriatic. There are various clues pointing to this as the original area, such as the discovery of the statue of a spotted dog in the Mycenae ruins mentioned in the *Penguin Book of Lost Civilizations*. This factor indicates that a dog similar in outline to the Dalmatian, and also spotted, did exist at a very early time in this area, although it may have been a spotted Mastiff.

Theories concerning the origin of the Dalmatian can spark endless discus-

1

Oil painting of boy on horseback with Dalmatian, from the collection of the late Mrs. George Ratner.

Famous Reinagle drawing of the Dal.

sions. For instance, the theory that the Dalmatian was the product of breeding the Istrian Pointer with the Harlequin Great Dane can evoke near shouting matches. It is well known that the Dane was not always as large a dog as we know him today. William Youatt refers to the Dalmatian as the "lesser Danish dogge." No less a breeder of Harlequin Danes than Antonia Pratt has reported that sometimes litters of Harls are born with rounded spots rather than the desired (in Danes) torn patches. This idea, however, was rejected vociferously by the Great Dane Club of America as being the worst sort of canard. It is up to you to decide if it could possibly be the origin of the Dalmatian.

As to why or how the breed was called Dalmatian, no one really knows. There are a number of theories, most of them quite logical, and anyone may believe any one of them. They are, however, still theories, not facts. Some of them have been around for a long while.

A young poet named Jurij Dalmatin (1546–1589), who lived in Serbia, another province of Yugoslavia, received some dogs from the Bohemian duchess Alena Meziricska Lomnice in 1573. In a letter to the duchess, Dalmatin wrote, "The interest in my Turkish-dogs grows in all Serbia. . . . I have presented several tens of them . . . these dogs are so popular that they call them by my name—Dalmatin. This new name is already more and more ingrained. . . ."

At the time Dalmatin wrote his letter about his "Turkish" dogs the entire area was under the domination of Turkey. The Turks overran the Balkans and pushed into Europe, where they were finally stopped by the Viennese in 1683. The Turkish rule of Bulgaria and other Balkan areas ended in 1827.

The name Jurij is another form of George, and Dalmatin is obviously a place-name, probably Dalmatia. In those years people did not have surnames. They had a first name and then something to distinguish them from all others with the same first name, either son of someone, or from a city, a village, a country or whatever. So Jurij, living in Serbia, was named Dalmatin because he came from that area. The word for the breed in Italy is "Dalmatina."

Certain theories as to why the dogs were called Dalmatians are so much conversation. We have read that the dogs were named Dalmatians because the spots resembled the bubbles in the volcanic rock found along the coast of Dalmatia. There is no volcanic rock along the coast of Dalmatia. The mountains are all layered limestone. It is true that spotty vegetation on some of the limestone mountains might give one the idea of spots, but that is too farfetched.

Dalmatians were called coach dogs long before they became known by the current name. According to the authority William Arkwright, the hounds were first in the development of the dog as we now know it. Then, through refinement in breeding, man developed the Pointer. Hunting dogs were important to put meat on the table. Arkwright also places the origins of the hounds and Pointers somewhere around the Mediterranean. He favors Spain because most writing indicates that hounds and Pointers were used there very early on.

Dalmatians do not exist in Dalmatia today. In 1930 the late Mr. Bozo Banac introduced Dalmatians to the country. He brought them to his home near

Dubrovnik from England in 1930. Locally they were referred to as the "English Dogs." Almost twenty-five years later someone visiting the lovely countryside discovered the last Dalmatian in Dubrovnik. He was descended from the "English Dogs" which Banac had imported. In the summer of 1977, we visited the old town of Dubrovnik. We did see one Dalmatian there. It was a young bitch owned by a man from Switzerland visiting Dubrovnik on his summer holiday. We also visited the island of Korcula but found no dogs there.

There are several serious breeders in Yugoslavia. They are located in Zagreb and Zupanja and they imported their breeding stock. Dalmatia is a region of Croatia, one of the six Socialist republics of Yugoslavia. Zagreb and Zupanja are situated in northern Croatia.

After the Trojan War, Achilles' son, Pyrrhus Neoptolemos, settled in Epirus where he either conquered or married into the family of an eponymous hero named Molossus. Molossus gave his name to the famous Molossian hounds of antiquity, which are mentioned in many classical works in Greek and Latin. These were a Mastiff type of dog.

Since Epirus, according to classical atlases, was the area immediately south of the Keraunian Mountains, directly east of Corfu, and the Roman Dalmatia was north of these mountains, it is possible that these dogs were taken into Dalmatia by the ancients. They were used as shepherd dogs and as dogs of war, guarding the mountains for their masters.

Harry Glover, the British authority, suggests that the Dal may have been confused with a spotted Mastiff, a larger, more powerful dog. His suggestion of the Mastiff type lends credence to the possibility that the spotted dog of Dalmatia is not a Dal at all but an Epirote or Molossian Mastiff.

The earliest known pictures portraying dogs that could be an original form of Dalmatians can be found in a fresco (circa 1360) in the Spanish Chapel of Santa Maria Novella in Florence. This church is under the Dominican Order of Friar Preachers, whose habits are white with black overcape. We shall never forget the smile on the face of the Dominican priest in the sacristy of that church when we asked where we could find the frescoes of the Spanish Chapel with the Dalmatians. His face lit up and he said, quite proudly, "Domini Canes!" The dog of God.

In the early days the church and the state were the institutions that controlled men's lives. The church came to be represented in painting and literature by various allegorical figures. We find symbolism in art throughout history. Somewhere along the line the black-and-white dog became the main representative of the church. This grew out of the Inquisition, that fearful state of affairs that held everyone in its thrall during the fifteenth century and into the sixteenth century. The order of the Dominicans was in charge of the Inquisition. So paintings, posters and other art forms used the Dal to represent the Dominican order. This has been considered an artistic and ecclesiastical joke through the years.

During the Cromwell years (1653–1658) in England, spotted dogs were

The Dalmatian dog pictured in *Dog in Health*.

Mr. Fawdry's Dalmatian dog Captain, a top winning dog in England.

used in antipapal tracts and leaflets as a symbol of Roman rule of the British church. Political woodcuts of that period can be found in the British Museum showing this, which tends to establish the breed in Italy at that time.

There is a mosaic frieze at the Church of Saint Francis, in Lima, Peru, that shows a Dalmatian. Based on the information provided by a tour guide and sent on by Benito Vila, we learned the tiles for the frieze were shipped from Spain to Peru in the late sixteenth century. It was not erected until 1620, because the viceroy had difficulty in locating anyone qualified to do the work. This is another instance of the white dog with black markings being used in an ecclesiastical setting, but this time in the Western Hemisphere.

It is difficult to say when the word "Dalmatian" actually came into use to describe the spotted dog we know. Thomas Bewick, in his first edition of 1790, shows a drawing of the dog and a description of the dog and it is clearly labeled "The Dalmatian or Coach Dog." Probably the first printed use in English of "Dalmatian" to designate our breed was in 1780, when a translation of Count de Buffon's *Natural History* was published in Scotland.

There is no mention of the Dal in *The Boke of St. Albans* (1480) and nothing in any of the published works on dogs written by Conrad Gesner (1587). Dr. Johannes Caius, who wrote *De Canis Britannicus Libellus* in 1560, later translated by Abraham Fleming in 1576 and called *Of English Dogges*, has a doubtful reference. Edward Topsell published a two-volume *Historie of Four-footed Beastes* in 1607, basing most of his knowledge on the Gesner and Caius and Fleming books. He did, however, state that the Italians were very pleased with a new variety of hunting dog, "especially the white and yellow spotted dogs."

The famous Dutch painter Gerard ter Borch painted a scene from the Congress of Munster in 1647. A detail of this painting shows the dauphin of France with his Dalmatian. The typical tricolor found in the old prints and paintings of the Dal is shown in a painting by Pieter Boel (1622–1674), which hangs in the Kennel Club on Clarges Steet, London. *The Hunting Party*, by Jan Fyt (1609–1661), includes a heavily marked Dalmatian type along with several spaniels and a Greyhound. *Hunting Dogs and Their Attendants*, painted by Francesco Castiglioni, probably about 1700, shows a Dalmatian trying to be a lapdog—something those of us who have had the breed will understand completely. That these dogs were favored by royalty is undeniable.

In the 1800s writers mentioned the dog frequently. Buffon, the great French naturalist, in 1772 proclaimed the Dal the Harrier of Bengal. He offered no proof of his statement. When we visited the Kennel Club in London, Commander Williams, upon finding out that we were doing research on the origins of the breed, stated, "Ours came from India!"

Many theories prevail on how the Dal could have migrated from the India area through Europe and to England. Some say that the Gypsies could have brought the dogs. The Gypsies, forced to migrate to the Middle East as early as the fifth century, established settlements in the Balkans and eastern Europe

A print of Spotted Dick from Hugh Dalziel's *British Dogs*.

An 1855 print of a Dalmatian dog from James Cowles Prichard's *Natural History*.

before the end of the fourteenth century. They came from the Upper Himalayas of northern India, where they had been part of a loose federation of nomadic tribes. In western Europe, Gypsy groups continued a nomadic life, their ranks being increased by migration from the Balkans as the Turks moved in late in the fifteenth century. They were hunters. They wandered through Europe as blacksmiths, horse traders and entertainers (musicians and fortune-tellers). Their true origin was unknown by medieval society. Whether they furthered the development of the Dalmatian because of the influence of their religious beliefs is pure speculation. White angels and black devils were featured in their doctrine of war between light and dark. There is a considerable bibliography of material on the migrations of the Gypsies, but it does not get into their dogs.

Perhaps the dogs migrated with the Roman legions. Caesar and Pompey fought their civil wars in the area now known as Yugoslavia. There were camp followers in Caesar's day, too, and perhaps spotted dogs.

Another theory concerning the name of the Dalmatian is an ecclesiastical one. There is a vestment, a tunic-type garment, beltless but with sleeves. Early ones were made of a soft white wool found on sheep from the mountains of Dalmatia. The garment has ornamental bands running from the shoulders to the lower hem. Many of these can be seen in the museums of the Vatican. As the church progressed in importance in the world, the Dalmatic, as this vestment is called, became more ornate. The ornamental bands became ermine. Weaving has always been an occupation in Illyria and Dalmatia. At one time the weavers of Illyria turned out the uniforms for the Roman army, as well as fabric for civilian use. Writing in *Black Lamb and Grey Falcon*, Rebecca West says, "No matter what bestial tricks history might be playing, there were always looms at work in Illyria."

Tying the Dalmatic vestment to the area of Illyria and Dalmatia is quite simple. In the Capitoline Museum in Rome, there is a statue of Augustus holding a shield that has a figure of an Illyrian wearing a Dalmatic. During the third century the pope dictated a rule that all martyrs would be buried in this type of garment. All deacons and officiating bishops in the Western church wear the Dalmatic and the monarchs of England also wear a Dalmatic at their coronation.

Is it possible that the ermine decorations on the Dalmatic reminded people of the spotted dog and thus the breed name came from a church vestment that apparently originated in Dalmatia, rather than because the dog originated there? It is impossible to prove.

2

Chronology of Ancestral Lore

In RESEARCHING canine history for clues of the Dalmatian's origin, we found that facts were few. Few written records in English on any subject exist earlier than the tenth century A.D. Dogs did not become subjects to write about until much later. E. Gwynne Jones, a British librarian, researched some 12,000 references to produce his *Bibliography of the Dog* (London, 1971). He located sources for 3,986 books published in the English language during the years 1570 through 1965. Only forty-one of these were produced before 1780, the year the term "Dalmatian" was printed in English, probably for the first time to designate a breed of dogs. It appears in a translation from the French of Buffon's *Natural History*. Among those forty-one, only one refers to a breed of spotted dogs.

In our search, we located eighty items with some bearing on the origin of the breed. Frequently, these were repetitious or in conflict. For the reader's interest we have listed some facts or quoted or summarized each writer's conclusions in the chronology and bibliography that follow.

3000 B.C.—"There is a coloured painting from the tomb of Redmera at Thebes which depicts the tribute from various parts of Asia. Eight dogs form part of the tribute, among them a greyhound, a mastiff, and a large spotted type not unlike the Dalmatian hound." H. Epstein, *The Origin of Domestic Animals of Africa* (Gwatkin, 1933–34).

Was the Dalmatian known in Egypt?

Needlework picture attributed to a member of the Juvenal family.

2000 B.C.—The Tablet of Antefaa II, from the tomb in the valley of El Assasif, includes four dogs complete with collars. William Youatt, *The Dog* (1847), describes one as resembling a Dalmatian. Edward C. Ash, *Dogs: Their History and Development* (1927), however, says, "It appears to me to be more of a great Dane and a mastiff cross than the famed carriage dog. It is significant that this type of dog is rarely, if ever shown in a hunting scene, suggesting that its main function was the guarding of property."

1700 B.C.—"I have seen at Tyrnia, the birthplace of Hercules, a fresco dating circa 1700 B.C. depicting a staghunting scene with a large number of dogs, clearly 'Dalmatians' though artistic license has given them red and blue spots." Vane Ivanovic, *Spots of News* (April, 1977).

1600 B.C.—"Spotted dogs were known and remarked upon in classical times, for mention is made of them by Greek and Roman authors, but unfortunately with insufficient detail to allow us to feel with any certainty that the dog mentioned as spotted was a Dalmatian. The discovery of a model of a dog of the Mycenae period of Grecian history shows that at that time, 1600 years B.C., a dog with round black spots had been noticed or was desired. This model, in terra-cotta, has upright ears, the body is white, marked with black spots, and to some extent conforming with the standard description of the Dalmatian." Edward C. Ash, *Dogs: Their History and Development* (1927).

1253—A report of a Dutch visit to Dalmatia describes dogs found there. It does not mention color or suggest a spotted dog.

1480—There is no mention of a spotted dog in Dame Julliana Berners's *The Boke of St. Albans*.

1570—"Recently (so fond are we all now of novelties), a new variety has been imported from France all white, with black spots; this is called the Gallican." Dr. Johannes Caius (Edward VI's physician), *De Canis Britannicus Libellus*. This Latin treatise may be the first mention in print of a breed of spotted dogs.

1576—"There is also at this day among us a new kinde of dog brought out of France (for we Englishmen are marvellous greedy gaping gluttons after novelties and covetous cormants of things that be seldome, rare, strange and hard to get). And they be speckled all over with white marble blew, which beautifies their skins and affoordeth a seemly show of comlinesse. These are called French dogs as is above declared already." *Of English Dogges*, translated from *De Canis Britannicus Libellus*, by Abraham Fleming, a student. Fleming's additions, which may be inaccurate, certainly confuse and suggest a roan spaniel or a belton setter. We do not know whether he actually saw a Gallican or was paid by the word like a scrivener and let his imagination have full play.

1587—*Historiae Animalium*, assembled by Conrad Gesner, included Dr. Caius's description of British dogs along with the sentence on the Gallican.

1607—"In Italy they make account of the spotted one, especially white and yellow for they are quicker nosed." Edward Topsell, *The Historie of Four-footed Beastes*.

Le Braque de Bengale. This is the name given by Buffon.

Spotted sporting dog trained to catch game.

1637—Aldrovandus, an Italian naturalist, captions an illustration, "A sagacious spotted dog for taking quail." Ash translates this differently, "Spotted sporting dog trained to catch game with English dog plant."

1653–1658—Antipapal tracts and leaflets in the British Museum published during the Cromwell period utilized spotted dogs as a symbol of Roman rule.

1772—A Dalmatian figure captioned "The Harrier of Bengal" in *Natural History*, by Count de Buffon (translated from the French by Barr), may be the first printed use of this term in the English language.

1780—"The hound, the harrier, the turnspit, the water-dog and even the spaniel, may be regarded as one dog. Their figure and instincts are nearly the same; and they differ only in the length of their legs, and the size of their ears, which, however, in all of them are long, soft and pendulous. These dogs are natives of France; and I am uncertain whether the Dalmatian dog, or, as it is called, the harrier of Bengal, ought to be disjoined from them; for it differs from our harrier only in colour. I am convinced that this dog is not an original native of Bengal, or of any other part of India, and that it is not, as has been pretended, the Indian dog mentioned by the ancients, and said to have been produced between a dog and a tiger; for it has been known in Italy above 170 years ago, and not considered as a dog brought from India, but as a common Harrier." Count de Buffon, *Natural History, General and Particular*, Vol. IV. Translated from the French and published in Scotland. This may be the first printed use in English of the term "Dalmatian" to designate a breed of dogs.

1780—Riedel shows a spotted dog marked English.

1790—"The Dalmatian, or coach dog, has been erroneously called the Danish Dog, and, by Mr. Buffon, the Harrier of Bengal; but for what reason it is difficult to ascertain, as its incapacity for scenting is sufficient to destroy all affinity to any dog employed in pursuit of the hare." Thomas Bewick, *A General History of Quadrupeds*. Possibly this was the first use of the term "Dalmatian" by a British writer to designate the breed. Bewick goes on to say, "It is very common in the country at present and is frequently kept in genteel houses, as an elegant attendant on a carriage, to which its attention seems to be solely directed. We do not, however, admire the cruel practice of depriving the poor animal of its ears, in order to increase its beauty."

1800–1803—"The common Coach Dog is a humble attendant of the servants and horses." Syndenham Edwards, *Cynographia Britannica*.

1803—The Dalmatian is listed as one of twenty-three known breeds of dogs in England. The Rev. William Bingley, *Animal Biography; or Anecdotes of the Lives, Manners and Economy of the Animal Creation arranged according to the System of Linnaeus*.

1804—"This particular race, of which so exact and beautiful a representation has been produced by the conjunctive efforts of the artists concerned, are by the earliest, and most respected writers, said to have been originally natives of Dalmatia, a district in European Turkey, bounded on the west by the Gulf of Venice; and from whence it is presumed, the breed was formerly transported to those countries, where by their prolific increase, they are now more universally known. Numerous as they become, and truly ornamental as they prove in the department to which they are so fashionably appropriate, less has been said upon their origin and introduction than upon any other distinct breed of the canine race.'' William Taplin, *The Sportsman's Cabinet.*

1820—"However he may have originated, he appears first to have been noticed in Dalmatia, a province of European Turkey, thence to have spread through Italy and the Southern parts, over most of the Continent of Europe, being generally esteemed a hound or hunting dog, notwithstanding his very universal different destination.'' John Scott, *The Sportsman's Repository.*

1829—"This dog has been erroneously called the Danish Dog by some authors, and Buffon and some other naturalists imagine him to be the Harrier of Bengal; but his native country is Dalmatia, a mountainous district of European Turkey. He has been domesticated in Italy for upwards of two centuries, and is the common Harrier of that Country.'' Captain Thomas Brown, *Biographical Sketches and Authentic Anecdotes of Dogs.*

1837—"Showy and interesting as it is, little that is interesting can be said.'' Thomas Bell, *A History of British Quadrepeds.* Pictured with a closed landaulette complete with coachman.

1839–1840—Colonel Hamilton Smith commented on the possibility that the coach dog was derived from an Indian breed "with a white fur marked with black spots, small half-dejected ears and a Greyhound-like form.'' A print from India is in his notes in *Naturalist's Library*, Volume 10, *Mammalia,* edited by Sir William Jardine. It is captioned "The Parent of the Modern Coach Dog.'' The dog in another illustration, called "Dalmatian or Coach Dog,'' is patched and carries its tail curved over the back.

1847—"The difference between these two breeds (The Great Danish Dog called also the Dalmatian or Spotted Dog) consists principally in size, the Dalmatian being much smaller than the Danish. The body is generally white marked with small round black or reddish brown spots. The Dalmatian is said to be used in his native country for the chace, to be easily broken and stanch to his work. He has never been thus employed in England but is clearly distinguished by his fondness for horses and as being a frequent attendent on the carriages of the wealthy. To that office seems to be confined, for its rarely develops sufficient sense or sagacity to be useful in any of the ordinary offices of the dog.'' William Youatt, *The Dog.*

1862—"Although Yougoslavia is considered by the F.C.I. to have been the original home of the Dalmatian, the breed has been developed and cultivated chiefly in England. When the dog with the distinctive markings was first shown in England in 1862 it was said to have been used by the frontier guards of Dalmatia as a guard dog. But nothing is definitely known about its origin. The breed has become widely distributed over the continent of Europe since 1920. Its unusual markings were often mentioned by the old writers on cynology.'' Dr. Erich Schneider-Leyer, *De Hunde Der Welt* (1960), translated from the German by Dr. E. Fitch Daglish, *Dogs of the World* (1964).

1867—First edition of *Dogs of the British Islands*, a series of articles and letters reprinted from "Field," by Dr. John Henry Walsh, otherwise known as "Stonehenge," mentions neither the Dalmatian nor the Danish dog.

1872—"I am at a loss when I try to trace the breed to its source. By French writers it is called 'Le Braque de Bengale,' and so Buffon named it. In 1556 a print was published at Cadiz of a recently-imported Indian dog, somewhat intermediate in shape between the Greyhound and the Southern Hound, light and strong in frame, deep in the chest, shorter in head than the Greyhound, with small, half-falling ears. This dog was white, and entirely covered with small black spots. It was conjectured that it belonged to a breed possessed by the Mohammedan princess of the west coast, and without much doubt it was the parent of our present—or past—Coach Dogs. These facts, and a figure of the imported dog, will be found in the tenth volume of the 'Naturalist's Library,' nearly word for word as I have quoted them." Rev. Thomas Pearce ("Idstone"), *The Dog.*

1879—"The origin of the Dalmatian is quite as obscure as that of other breeds. . . . I think it reasonable to assume that he is a native of Dalmatia, on the eastern shores of the Gulf of Venice. This does not militate against the idea suggested by the motto at the head of the chapter ('A newe kind of dogge brought out of Fraunce, and they be speckled all over with white and black.'—Dr. Caius), which I have taken from Caius, that we had the dog from France." Hugh Dalziel, *British Dogs.*

1883—Stonehenge (John Henry Walsh), under a chapter heading, "The Dalmatian and Danish Dogs," concludes his description of the Dalmatian with "he has been long employed in England to accompany our carriages as an ornamental appendage, but this fashion has of late years subsided. Hence he is commonly known as the 'Coach Dog' but in his native country is used as a pointer in the field, and is said to perform his duties well enough.

"The small Danish dog is smaller than the Dalmatian, but being spotted in the same way, and characterized by the same fondness for horses, they are generally confounded under the term 'Coach Dog.' ''

1883—"In many of his points he pretty closely resembles a large Bull Terrier, but in head he is more like the Pointer." Gordon Stables, *Our Friend the Dog.*

1891—"The Dalmatian, or Coach Dog, came from the Province of Dalmatia, in the southern part of Austria, bordering on the northeast shore of the Adriatic Sea, and from this province it derives its name. It is known in France as the 'Braque de Bengale,' and is there supposed to be an Indian variety." Major T. J. Woodcock, *The American Book of the Dog*, edited by G. O. Shields ("Coquina").

1894—"There is little doubt that our modern 'coach dog' originally sprang from Dalmatia, a province in the southern part of Austria, hence his name, but from there he might have gone over to Spain, or perhaps, in the first instance some Spaniard might have sent him out to Dalmatia, where the enterprising inhabitants soon claimed him as their own. However, it does not matter much what country first gave him birth.'' Rawdon B. Lee, *A History and Description of the Modern Dogs of Great Britain and Ireland (Non-Sporting Division)*.

1897—''Records of the sixteenth century describe such a dog as belonging to Spain. The latest authentic trace is to Denmark, where it was used for drawing carts. Resembles the pointer in form.'' H. W. Huntington, *My Dog and I*.

1901—''. . . probably indigenous to Dalmatia, a province of Austria, but records of the XVI century describe such a dog as belonging to Spain. The latest authentic trace is to Denmark, where it is used for drawing carts. It very much resembles the pointer in form.'' H. W. Huntington, *The Show Dog*.

1903—''The origin of the Dalmatian is not quite as obscure as that of many other breeds. There appears to be no valid reason to reject the origin suggested by his name, and, with no arguments against it that bear investigation, and suggestions to the contrary appearing to be mere fancies unsupported by proof, it is reasonable to assume that he is a native of Dalmatia, on the eastern shores of the Gulf of Venice, where, we have been assured, by some of the older writers on dogs, this variety has been domesticated for at least two hundred years.'' C. H. Lane, *British Dogs*, edited by W. D. Drury.

1904—''As to the dog's origin there seems to be no precise data or information, but there is little or no doubt that he comes from Dalmatia, on the eastern shores of the Gulf of Venice.'' Theo Marples, *Show Dogs*.

1904—''A good deal of uncertainty as to the origin shrouds the undoubted antiquity of the Dalmatian dog. It has had attached to it in different countries and at different times such irreconcilable localisation as the Danish dog and the Bengal Harrier! Buffon presumed it to be an offshoot of the French Matin, transported to the northern latitude of Denmark; Dalziel thinks it reasonable to assume its native home was Dalmatia, on the eastern shores of the Gulf of Venice. . . . Having thus drawn the track of the Dalmatian across two continents, from Copenhagen to Calcutta, I leave the choice of allocating its place of nativity to the wisdom or fancy of the reader.'' Herbert Compton, *The Twentieth Century Dog (Non-Sporting)*.

1905—''It is more probable that this variety of dog originally came from Dalmatia in the south of Austria, though there is nothing, so far as our knowledge goes, in proof of this.'' Frank T. Barton, *Non-Sporting Dogs—Their Points and Management*.

1905—''It is passing strange how such a man as Buffon came to name the Dalmatian the Bengal Harrier, and Youatt was as bad when he lumped him in with the Great Dane—the Danish dog, as he was called at that time—as only differing in size. The Dalmatian is a dog of ancient lineage and with as straight a record as almost any dog. He was the hound that came from Dalmatia, and there is little reason to doubt that he was of the same class of hound that the pointer emanated from. Even to this day they have very much in common, in appearance, habits and disposition, and the Dalmatian is by no means a bad shooting dog, when any attention is paid to his training.'' James Watson, *The Dog Book*.

The Dalmatian from a study by
Thomas Brown, 1829.

A comparison of the Dane and the Dal.

A typical Dalmatian from the
American Book of the Dog,
1891.

1907—"Of the antecedents of the Dalmatian it is extremely hard to speak with certainty. . . . The earliest authorities agree that this breed was first introduced from Dalmatia, and it has been confidently asserted that he was brought into this country purely on account of his sporting proclivities." F. C. Hignett, *The New Book of the Dog*, edited by Robert Leighton.

1907—"A great deal has been written on this old breed as to its native land, some writers claiming it a Danish dog, others going so far as to describe it as the Turkish breed. However, there is no question in my mind but that Dalmatia, on the eastern shores of the Gulf of Venice, was the native home of this sporty breed." D. C. Sands, Jr., secretary of the Dalmatian Club of America, *Dogs*, edited by G. A. Melbourne.

1907—"Very little is known of the origin of this dog or what country first gave him birth." H. Fred Lauer, *The Dalmatian or Coach Dog*.

1908—"The Dalmatian—formerly known as the Carriage Dog; vulgarly as the Plum Pudding Dog—is of very ancient lineage. Regarding the origin of the breed, Buffon considered it an off-shoot of the French Matin; Youatt connected it with the Great Dane. In the writer's opinion, the dog probably originated from the same class of hound as did the Pointer. The earliest writers, including Dalziel, almost unanimously hold that the breed was introduced from Dalmatia—hence the name." Hebe Wilson-Bedwell, *The Kennel Encyclopaedia*, edited by J. Sidney Turner.

1927—"According to old records, his native country is Dalmatia, a mountainous district on the Adriatic coast. He has been domesticated in Italy for upwards of two centuries and is the common harrier of that country." Mrs. Fred Kemp, *Pedigreed Dogs as Recognized by The Kennel Club*.

1927—"Many places, far apart, have been the supposed native land of the 'Dalmatian,' 'Carriage Dog' or 'Plum Pudding Dog,' but Dalmatia is the country which most writers claim to be the correct one. . . . It is a curious fact that no information can be gathered from the people of Dalmatia as to the origin of the dog in their country." Franklin J. Willock, *The Dalmatian*.

1927—"That the Dalmatian is an Italian breed we find supported in later times. During the stormy period of Cromwell's power, when anti-Roman Catholicism was rampant, many illustrated leaflets, often extremely vulgar, show Roman Catholicism depicted in the shape of a Dalmatian dog of the very same type as such dogs are today." Edward C. Ash, *Dogs: Their History and Development*.

1931—"Originally a product of Dalmatia, the breed was first introduced to these shores on account of their sporting proclivities, as they were capable of doing a good day's work in the field; although we find they at all periods prefer feathered to ground game, and though taking little notice of hares, would be happy working with the sportsman when pheasants and partridges were about." Arthur Craven, *Dogs of the World*.

1931—"The name, appearance and original vocation of Dalmatians have given play to various witticisms, some calling them Damnation Dogs, Carriage

Dogs, Spotted or Plum-pudding Dogs. Attempts have been made, without being convincing, to divorce them from their association with Dalmatia, the pre-War province of Austria bordering the eastern side of the Adriatic. One writer in 1843 endeavoured to show their connection with the Bengal Harrier, whatever that was. . . . In the absence of any better evidence I think we are safe in assuming that the breed did come from Dalmatia or neighbouring regions, and that it was used there and in Italy to do the work of pointers." A. Croxton Smith, *About Our Dogs, The Breeds and Their Management.*

1931—"Its origin is uncertain. It probably came from Italy. It is very unlikely that it originated from Dalmatia. Travellers who visited Dalmatia make no mention of any such dog. In 1253 a Dutch traveller visited the country and describes, amongst other things, the dogs he saw there as large, powerful dogs, that pulled carts, and were used by the sportsmen to face bulls and bait lions. It is certain that if white dogs covered with spots existed in the country they would have been mentioned and described, for the Dalmatian is not a dog that can be passed without notice. Later works, giving the experience of travellers and describing the country, the people, and the natural history, make no mention of such a breed of dogs." Edward C. Ash, *The Practical Dog Book.*

1932—"While it is generally conceded that the Dalmatian originated in Dalmatia—a rugged, mountainous 5,000 square mile part of Yugo-slavia on the Adriatic coast—from the following varied accounts of the writers accepted as the authorities of the seventeenth and eighteenth centuries it will be seen that the evidence in support of this supposition is neither based on definite facts nor is it in any way so conclusive as to establish the matter beyond doubt.

"What little data there is available is tantalisingly conflicting and in some cases is obviously mere conjecture on the part of the authors. The 'lifting of copy' being as rife then as it is today, it is not surprising to find that they stole each other's opinions or 'facts' without crediting the source, and expressed them with enthusiasm and embellishments as their own. In this way any early sign-post which may, in the light of latter-day investigations, have pointed the right direction has been lost.

"Even so, it is upon such writings that the declared origin of many of our present-day breeds is founded, for the investigator who endeavours to trace their ancestry beyond 150 years or so soon finds himself enveloped in a veritable sea of confliction and lost in a cloud of obscurity." James Saunders, *The Dalmatian and All About It.*

1933—"No one seems to know when the breed began. There was once a story that he was part tiger and came from Bengal. That was a pretty idea but a poor invention. Far more plausible was the idea that he lived in Denmark and worked for the peasants as a draught-dog, but that theory has not much value, the dog used in Denmark being the harlequin Great Dane, which, being also spotted, no doubt was confused with the Dalmatian. Then, of course, we have the story that he came from Spain. Perhaps he did come that way sometimes with cargoes of brandy or wine, or precious metals. The only thing we know is that he has always been called the Dalmatian and he probably came direct from that part of Southern Europe. Possibly wandering gipsies brought him, as he seems to have been almost as valuable as a dancing bear in the way of amusing the squires and yokels of Britain and extracting gifts from the people who had money to give away. Once the gipsies, who roved all over Europe, learned that there was a trade to be done in these dogs, there would be a supply to meet the demand, and we know that even to-day there is a trade in horses carried on by gipsy tribes in parts of Europe and Asia.

"The curious thing is that the Dalmatian, so far as we know, is not the common dog of any country, so we have no evidence of that kind as to his place of origin." Rowland Johns, *Our Friend the Dalmatian.*

1934—"The origin of the Dalmatian is very uncertain; but there is one fact which stands out clearly. The breed has been known in England for over two hundred years at least. At the second recognized dog show held in this country, in 1860, only five breeds were scheduled. One of these was the Dalmatian. This is their first authentic appearance as a show dog.

"As far back as 1790, however, Dalmatians were mentioned in contemporary literature, and they also figured in early heraldry. One theory suggests that they originated in Dalmatia and were imported into this country during the eighteenth and nineteenth centuries by the gentlemen of the period who were making the 'Grand Tour.' They found them useful as guards as well as being ornamental. If this is their true origin it is curious that no trace of them remains in Italy. Another suggestion is that they were used as gun-dogs in Spain, but there seems little corroboration of this theory." Walter Hutchinson, *Hutchinson's Dog Encyclopedia.*

1935—"It is fair to imagine that the first of the distinctly spotted dogs came from Dalmatia, a country situated along the eastern Adriatic Coast, Europe." Freeman Lloyd, "Dog Breeds of the World," *American Kennel Gazette* (March 1).

1935—"Nor can I understand the why and wherefore of this handsome dog's name, for when I was in Bosnia I made inquiries of natives, familiar with Dalmatia, and none seemed to have heard of the dogs in question, being indigenous to, or inhabiting, that country." Harding Cox, *Dogs of Today.*

1940—"The Pointer, who is the dog most like him and probably related to him, is a product of Spain, which is a great way from Dalmatia, and his traditional masters the Gypsies, know no homeland." Arthur Roland, *The Story of Pedigreed Dogs.*

1942—"The Dalmatian is truly a dog of mystery. Not only is its origin completely unknown, but even its birthplace is in dispute. Part of this confusion as to the original home of the breed may be due to the fact that the Dalmatian has been a favorite with gypsies. A wanderer like its Romany masters, it has been seen and known in various localities, but not located in any particular place. It is said that the breed originated in Dalmatia, a province of Austria on the eastern shore of the Adriatic. There is, however, no definite proof of this." Edwin Megargee, *Dogs.*

1945—"apparently indigenous to Dalmatia but not found there in any substantial strength . . . in fact quite a different type to the Dalmatians of Britain and the USA . . . originally used as a gun dog in the Balkans and Italy, then as a guard against highwaymen in France about the middle of the seventeenth century, and introduced from there into England at the end of the eighteenth century." Clifford L. B. Hubbard ("Canis"), *The Observer's Book of Dogs*.

1945—"This is another dog of questionable origin. He is considered to be indigenous to Dalmatia, but the breed was frequently found in the company of gypsies who roamed the Balkans." Felice Worden, *The Sketch Book of Dogs*.

1947—"The plum-pudding dog, Bengal harrier, Dalmatian, or as it is better known perhaps, 'the carriage dog,' is an old variety. Its name, 'Dalmatian,' is a mystery . . . there is considerable evidence that the Dalmatian was an Italian variety." Denlinger, *The Complete Dalmatian*.

1948—"That they are a very old breed is beyond question . . . It is usually assumed that these dogs came from the country after which they are named, on the eastern shores of the Adriatic and in Italy they have been used for doing the work of pointers." Sigma, *The Book of the Dog*, edited by Brian Vesey-Fitzgerald.

1948—"The origin of the breed is obscure, as is its early history. Early references to the Dalmatian suggest it was a type somewhere between the Pointer and the so-called Lesser Danish Dog; Buffon described a spotted dog of similar size but called it the 'Bengal Harrier' (which was quite a safe title in the days when knowledge of dogs was so scant). Taplin considered it a relation of the Great Dane. From the author's researches, however, the Dalmatian appears to be a descendant of the Istrian Pointer which may at some past date have had a little Great Dane blood introduced to give depth of muzzle and tone to the colour; the Istrian Pointer is remarkably like the Dalmatian except that the markings are not in uniform spots nor so dark in color. It is well known that the Dalmatian was used as a gun-dog in Italy, Austria and other countries which dabbled in the affairs of Dalmatia, and not until about 1665 does any evidence appear of it being used in its now traditional role of coach dog." Clifford L. B. Hubbard, *Dogs in Britain*.

1957—"The origin of the Dalmatian is still obscure despite very many attempts at research into his early history. Practically all the early writers on dogs were completely confounded when dealing with this breed while the majority cribbed from each other and got into deeper messes by coining new names for the breed in support of their theories. A lot of trouble has resulted from these old names for the breed especially as they were for the most part names like Bengal Foxhound, Great Danish Dog, Lesser Danish Dog, Bengal Harrier, Spotted Dog of Holland, and so on . . . The 'Old English Hound' is yet another breed mentioned as ancestor (the claim that Dalmatians were used to hunt in packs has been given as support for this). However, summing up I feel we are on quite the safest ground for the time being (for there is still much to learn of this breed) if we regard the basic stock from which the Dalmatian is descended as the Istrian Pointer (Istrianer Braque), himself carrying the blood of mid-European Pointers, and the old small type of Harlequin Great Dane." Clifford L. B. Hubbard, *The Dalmatian Handbook.*

1957—"There is no official record for the first introduction of the breed." Brian Vesey-Fitzgerald, *The Domestic Dog: An Introduction to Its History.*

1958—"The early history of the Dalmatian has been traced, and closely linked to the gypsies of central Europe. As far as they wandered so did their dogs.

"The most likely site of origin of the breed was probably the small province of Austria known as Dalmatia, and the breed has been known as a Dalmatian for at least 200 years." Evelyn Miller, *Dalmatians as Pets.*

1958—"No compelling evidence proves that the Dalmatian coast was his first home, nor can any other region boast his birthplace. . . .

"Some authorities think he sprang from spotted dogs of ancient India. Others say Egypt of the Pharaohs, Italy or what is today Yugoslavia. All admit the mystery surrounding his name. Perhaps easiest to believe is the idea that he first showed his telltale spots among bands of gypsies roving the Balkans." National Geographic Society, *Man's Best Friend.*

1959—"The spotted 'coach dog' has been a close companion of men and horses as far back as our historical records go. . . . Ancient Egyptian paintings show a dog with a white coat and the distinctive black spots following a chariot, and during the centuries when man traveled by coach the Dalmatian is found running along with the carriage, usually trotting under the front or rear axle or between the horses.

"The Dalmatian was an early favorite with wandering Gypsy bands, who spread the breed throughout Europe. He received his name from the province of Dalmatia in Austria, where he was once bred on a large scale and where the breed was standardized to the present size and coloring." Arthur Liebers, *How to Raise and Train a Dalmatian.*

1961—"The origin of the Dalmatian is shrouded in mystery. He has been traced back hundreds of years, but no particular country or place can be pinpointed as the site of his genesis." Evelyn S. Nelson, *Pet Dalmatian.*

1962—"The actual place or country of their origin is wrapped in mystery. It would seem that the most probable explanation is that several countries and perhaps as many distinct types of dogs have contributed in the past to their make-up." Catherine Gore, *Dalmatians.*

1963—"There are almost as many marks of interrogation in the history of Dalmatians as there are spots on the dog's body. The one thing that appears to be clear is that the breed has no definite connection with Dalmatia, although there may be a link with Italy.

"The suggestion that the Dalmatian may be of Italian origin rests largely on a painting of two typical Dalmatian heads by one of the Castiglione family and the fact that under Cromwell's regime in this country, the breed appears to have been a symbol of popery. The latter fact, however, does make it plain that these spotted dogs were known in this country in the seventeenth century." S. M. Lampson, *The Country Life Book of Dogs.*

1964—". . . an ancient breed and we do not know its original home. Unlike so many modern breeds it is in no way man-made. It has come down to us as a heritage from the past, an original breed with its elegant shape and spectacular markings as curious and striking in their way as the stripes on the zebra.

"Many and varied theories about the origin of Dalmatians have been put forward but . . . little reliable evidence exists for any of them. . . . This dog may have survived almost unchanged from the dawn of history." Eleanor Frankling, *The Popular Dalmatian*, revised and reprinted in 1969 as *The Dalmatian*, with the 1964 history repeated.

1968—"Dogs of the pointer type are of very ancient lineage. Today they are distributed throughout mountain areas between northern India and western Europe. Such are the dogs of the gypsy caravans and the Dalmatians—one distinctive breed of pointer—supposed to have been brought with the gypsies from India to Dalmatia, whence they reached Britain in the eighteenth century." Richard and Alice Fiennes, *The Natural History of Dogs*.

1970—"It may be that when the gypsies of India migrated to Europe, they took the animal from place to place, roving over the Balkans and settling temporarily in Dalmatia, a province of Austria. The gypsies made numerous uses of the breed, with bird hunting its main occupation." Beth Brown, *Dogs That Work for a Living*.

1971—"The most likely theory about the origins of the Dalmatian we know today seems to be that the breed was developed as a mid-European hunting dog. The name would seem to imply that they came from Dalmatia, now part of Yugoslavia; there is little evidence to support this, but we do know that a spotted dog very much resembling the Dalmatian has been widely distributed throughout Europe for the last four hundred years or more." Betty Clay, *The World Encyclopedia of Dogs*.

1971—"The Dalmatian, as the name implies, comes from Dalmatia, on the Adriatic coast. Even so, it is a breed which flowered in Great Britain in those now far-away times when the English aristocracy was expected to indulge in bizarre eccentricities.

"It is believed that specimens were brought back during the grand tours of Europe which were then a feature of the lives of upper-class Englishmen. They soon put the dog to work: it was to adorn their stately processions by horse and carriage. This the Dalmatian did by trotting with the entourage." Maxwell Riddle, *The International Encyclopedia of Dogs*.

1973—"Many authors have written about the origins of this dog but very few are in agreement. His name should indicate his origin but this is not the case. The breed appears to be quite ancient, since the friezes discovered in Greece and the Middle East dating back to remote periods show dogs similar in lines and coat to the present Dalmatian.

"Some authorities think that he came from Denmark, a theory supported by the fact that he is called Dane in some countries. He is quite prevalent today in Denmark. Buffon believes that he is descended from the Mastiff which after having passed from England to Denmark and then to warmer climates, presumably produced the Turkish Dog. Besides these theories there are many others, all different, all somehow plausible, but none certain, while Angliola Denti di Pirajno, a well-known expert on the breed states: 'The hypothesis which seems to rest on the most solid base indicates that the Dalmatian has an Eastern origin.' " Fiorenze Fiorone, *The Encyclopedia of Dogs.*

1973—"Despite his name, no trace of him has been found in Dalmatia. He is a dog of very ancient origins. One finds him represented on ancient Egyptian bas-reliefs and on Greek friezes. He was not classified as a breed, however, until the eighteenth century when a very similar but now extinct breed, the Bengal gundog, was recognized in England." Gino Pugnetti, *The Great Book of Dogs.*

1977—"The breed is quite an ancient one, and it has been suggested that it was originally a guard dog, and even a war dog in Dalmatia or Croatia, though there is a possibility that here it was being confused with the spotted German Mastiff known at one time as the Tiger Dog, which was a hunting and fighting dog. . . . In Dalmatia where these dogs are said to have originated they were probably a small version of the spotted or harlequin Great Dane, and probably these were later crossed with Pointers to reduce the size and improve the markings." Harry Glover, compiler and editor, *A Standard Guide to Pure-bred Dogs.*

1977—"I myself come from Cartat in Dalmatia. My family, and in particular my step-father, Mr. Banac, a shipowner, were often asked about Dalmatians by visiting English friends. None of us knew of the origins of Dalmatian dogs. We then introduced Dalmatians to Dalmatia in the early thirties. Dr. Frankling has referred to this in her book.

"There are dogs in our part of the world to some extent similar, short-haired pointers you could call them, occasionally with well defined black spots on a gray ground, not what one might call convincing evidence of the Balkan origin of Dalmatians." Vane Ivanovic, *Spots of News*, British Dalmatian Club.

1988—"Despite its name it is unlikely that this dog is a native of Dalmatia. It is believed by some to have its origins in the East—a direct descendant of the now extinct Hound of Bengal—and by others to be a native of Denmark, where it is found in large numbers and known also by the name of Small Dane." Maurizio Bongianni and Concetta Mori, *Dogs of the World.*

3

The Coaching Dalmatian

T HE DALMATIAN has had the knack of improving without changing. While it has lost the opportunity and joy of running with the carriage, the coach and four, the tallyho and the fire engines, it still has the desire. It is still built to run hard for long distances. It may be the only true coach dog. At any rate, it is the only dog that was traditionally bred and trained to run with the horse-drawn vehicles.

When it has the chance, it is still delighted to go with the horses. It may hock with a mounted horse, lead or follow a vehicle, or run under an axle. Historically, the Dalmatian is under the front axle, the closer to the horses' heels the better.

Coaching has been the Dal's accepted role for more than three hundred years. In his *Dogs in Britain* (1948), Clifford Hubbard says, "Not until about 1665 does any evidence appear of it being used in its now traditional role of coach-dog. By 1670 it was certainly used in France as an accessory to travel by coach, and was invaluable as a guard against highwaymen."

That the Dalmatian considers guarding its owner's property part of the job of coaching is made clear in Major T. J. Woodcock's article in 1891: "A good Coach Dog has often saved his owner much valuable property by watching the carriage. It is a trick of thieves who work in pairs for one to engage the coachman in conversation while the other sneaks around in the rear and steals whatever robes and other valuables he can lay his hands on. I never lost an article while the dogs were in charge, but was continually losing when the coachman was in charge."

At seven months of the age Coachman's Courbette and Coachman's Croupade wait patiently for Bill Fetner to harness the horse before going for a coaching drive.

Mrs. Reeves and the late Lloyd Reeves out for a morning ride.

COACHING STYLES AND PREFERENCES

Woodcock also tells us, "In training for the carriage, it is usually found necessary to tie a young dog in proper position, under the fore axles, for seven or eight drives before he will go as required. Some bright puppies, however, require little or no training, especially if they can be allowed to run with an old dog that is already trained."

A research team from Harvard University in 1940 found that the tendency to run under a vehicle or to follow a horse was inherited but that it differed from dog to dog as to the exact position preferred if the dog had a choice. In their study of inheritance of position preference in coach dogs, Clyde E. Keeler and Harry C. Trimble worked with a large kennel of Dalmatians that for more than twenty-five years had trained Dals to follow horses and run under carriages. They reported:

> This training usually began shortly after the dogs were six months old. In the beginning a pup would be taken out with its collar fastened to that of a trained dog and the pair led behind the carriage at gradually increased rates of speed. In most instances the leash could be omitted in a short time and the neophytes then were permitted to seek the particular position which suited them best. It has been observed throughout this long period that dogs did have individual preferences for particular positions and that they always sought those same places.
>
> Dogs of the Dalmatian breed have definite differences with respect to the eagerness with which they follow horses and carriages. Since approximately 70 per cent of the animals tested chose those positions which entitled them to be rated as "good" coaching dogs, it is evident that this trait is well intrenched in the breed.
>
> Two of the dogs in the colony which were classed as failures from the coaching standpoint were also described as "man-shy." This description suggests the possibility of some relationship between natural timidity and poor coaching ability.

The study reached three conclusions. First, Dalmatian dogs trained for running beneath carriages have individual preferences for distance behind the horses. Second, something connected with these preferences appears to be inherited. Third, it is possible that "bad" coach following may be an expression of general timidity. The last may be one of the reasons shyness is considered a major fault in the Dalmatian Standard.

In "Teaching a Dalmatian to 'Coach,' " an article in *Country Life in America* (1911), Eleanor Walton Yates quotes a Dalmatian Club of America (DCA) member who has driven with Dalmatians both here and in England:

> I find the most practical as well as the best English custom is for the dog or dogs to run directly under the front axle near the horses, but always clear of the horses' heels. Running between two horses and under the pole, the dog takes many chances and does not look as well as under the axle, when the trap is high enough to allow it. The dog must follow the pace of the horse and stick there. He must stay under until his master or the groom alights, unless he is trained to jump in the trap and keep watch over the robes, whip, etc.

Mr. J. Sergeant Price, the pioneer of the Dalmatian interest in this country, gives about the same version, and he has used these dogs under single, double, and four-in-hand traps.

In judging, dogs are allowed 75 points for ability to keep with the trap, 25 points counting toward their trueness to standard.

Running underneath the vehicle, or "coaching" as it is called, seems to be a characteristic formed by heredity in a Dalmatian, as most of them take to this place themselves. Even puppies when only a few months old will go under the trap with little training, and being kept with the horses all the time and going with the team, will soon find their way up behind the horses' heels where one would think it impossible that the horses would not strike them on the head with their hoof every step they take. They delight to go fast—the faster the pace the better they seem to enjoy it. While most Dalmatians take to coaching themselves, others are like black sheep in a flock and will never learn.

EARLY DAL ROAD TRIALS

One of the rules compiled by the DCA Road Trial Committee of 1912 stated "that a four-wheel, one-horse trap should be used, and that the dog should travel with her shoulders under the front axle." This was an interesting development since pictures of the results of 1910 and 1911 road trials show Dalmatians running under a two-horse, single-axle trap.

At the close of World War II people were anxious to resume their normal activities, and these included dog shows. However, the clubs that sponsored the shows were not all ready to resume giving shows and so there were not quite as many for the first several years of peace. They were hard to get to, many people having disposed of their automobiles, and it was an expensive hobby.

Some Dal fanciers wanted to get back in the swim of competition and so revived the road trials that had been held in the past using driving horses and vehicles for the dogs to coach with. Now the trials were planned without vehicles.

Mrs. Alfred Barrett and Mr. and Mrs. Lloyd Reeves revived the sport in the New England area. Mr. Reeves rewrote the road trial rules to be used on horseback instead of in a riding vehicle and the trials were held.

Mr. and Mrs. Meistrell held a road trial on Long Island. While both trials seemed to be most successful they were not continued, probably because of the great expense. Conditioning of the dogs and horses was time-consuming and expensive for the exhibitor, who either had to hire a horse at hourly rates for training and on the day of the show or transport his own mount to the show site and condition both horse and dog for the trial.

In order to have a successful trial the judges and the stewards needed two horses each since they were riding thirty miles in following the exhibitors and moving along at a brisk pace most of the way.

At the trial on Long Island, held at Rice Farms in Huntington, the course

Participants in a Dalmatian road trial held in the late 1940s.

Painting of Mrs. Paul Moore.

was ten miles and circular, starting and finishing at Rice Farms polo field. The foot judge checked dogs at the start and finish; a mounted judge and steward rode along with each entrant. These last two alternated so that the horses could be rested in between.

Along the course were signs marked with the pace at which the rider was to go. The requirements included walk, trot, canter, and hard gallop, with the dogs off lead, at the horses' heels throughout. The course went through sections of wood, high grass, open fields, across a main highway (a sit-stay was ordered before crossing the road) and past a farm yard with chickens, cows, goats and a noisy but unaggressive farm dog. The course started on the polo field and ended there with a hard gallop past the foot judge, the dog still heeling.

The cost of the horses, the rental of a van to transport the horses and various other expenses were borne by the Great Neck Dog Training Center. No entry fee was charged at this trial as it was an experiment.

The road trials in New England following the war were conducted along lines that had been set before the outbreak of hostilities. These road trials were designed to award points and a Road Trial Championship of Record would be awarded to a dog that acquired ten points. The championship stakes would count whether the stakes were open or member stakes.

The distance of the trials was set for:

1 day   15-mile puppy trial
2 day   25-mile derby trial (25 miles each day)
3 day   25-mile all-age trial (25 miles each day)

There were two judges on foot and one mounted judge. The mounted judge started riding with the first handler. Handlers were staggered at ten-minute intervals. The mounted judge rode for about ten minutes with each handler. The foot judges were posted at the most difficult sections on the trial so that they could observe the dogs under the hardest working conditions. When the last dog passed the unmounted judges, they were picked up by automobile and taken ahead to another point of the trial where the first handler was about to pass.

Much of the outline of the road trial rules was based on foxhound trials and information was available from a prominent Master of Fox Hunt (MFH) in the area.

The trials were run in Dover, Massachusetts, one time but abandoned because of the obvious disadvantages outlined above.

REVIVING ROAD TRIALS

Linda Myers, a Dal breeder and horse fancier, decided to try to give something back to the breed by reviving the road trials. Forrest Johnson, the owner of Croatia Dalmatians and a former president of the DCA, sent her a copy of the original rules. After studying them, Mrs. Myers felt that if road trials were

Road trial participates, RT 1989.

Best in Show and National Specialty winner Ch. St. Florian Pisces Jordache calls upon Carriage for Hire "Your Carriage Awaits" to show off his coaching abilities. This dog is owned by Linda Fish of Pisces Dals and handled by Bill McFadden, shown enjoying a leisurely ride.

to be an ongoing performance event for Dalmatians the rules would need to be augmented. Prospective trial hosts would need a clear picture of how to organize a road trial, and prospective competitors would need a list of what would be required of them and their dogs. These requirements were to be practical, demonstrating not only the "speed and endurance" called for in the Standard but the basic skills that the dogs would need to be safe and pleasant escorts as well.

Linda Myers studied the AKC's "Rules Applying to Registration and Dog Shows" and "Obedience Regulations," discussed them and the original road trial rules with such knowledgeable fanciers as Marilyn Suthergreen, Betty Garvin, Sue MacMillan, Cathy Murphy, Forrest Johnson, Linda Fulks, Meg Hennessey and Janet Ashbey and then sought input from three previous road trial participants, Wendell Sammet, Lois Meistrell and Mrs. Lloyd Reeves. The rules were reviewed and revised with the help of these people.

Robert McKowen, vice-president of Performance Events at the AKC, was helpful and encouraging. In addition to supporting existing performance events, such as hunting tests, Mr. McKowen has been encouraging new events for other breeds.

After Mrs. Myers completed her work on the revised rules, she persuaded the Puget Sound Dalmatian Club to offer a road trial. It was held in Woodinville, Washington, in September 1989—the first road trial in forty years. Robert McKowen cut the ribbon at the starting line to signal the revival of the Dalmatian road trials. The dogs were worked on a 12.5- and a 25-mile course. Beth White, Melody Dalmatians, was the mounted judge and Charles Cyopik, Country Road Dalmatians, was the course judge. Dr. Dennis O'Callahan, assisted by Jennifer Gasseling, was the start/finish veterinarian, while Dr. Michael Bellinhausen was the midpoint veterinarian.

Three teams were entered for the twenty-five-mile course. Each rider was permitted as many as six Dals on a team. In this competition seven dogs were entered: four with one rider, two with another and the third competitor had one dog. Each rider was accompanied by a mounted escort.

The competitors were spaced at thirty-minute intervals. They were first checked by the veterinarian and then taken to the starting line, where they rode out with the mounted judge. Each entrant was required to do a recall, hock exercise, hock past an oncoming distraction and a long/sit wait. Following these exercises the team was permitted to ride the rest of the course. On the trail the course judge conducted the speed exercise, requiring each exhibitor to gallop his horse and demonstrate his dogs' ability to keep up. The dogs and horses were checked for soundness by the midpoint veterinarian. Upon completion of the course the start/finish veterinarian again checked the dogs and horses for soundness.

Four teams were entered in the 12.5-mile course and seven dogs were involved. The same exercises were required of them.

Those in attendance felt the road trial had been a huge success. Competitors included Deana Karst, Linda Myers, Judy Butts, Sybil Paquette, Bunny

Primacio and Caroline Banks. Although the feeling was that all participants were winners, Caroline Banks and Fantasy Freckled Miss, CD, were the first-place winners in the 12.5-mile course and also High in Trial; Linda Myers and Hushabye Lacy were the first-place winners in the 25-mile course.

The DCA has appointed a road trial committee to support the revival of the trials. The national club is offering Road Trial Recognition Award certificates to all Dals who compete in road trials. Several groups are looking into hosting road trials and plans are under way to offer the trials in conjunction with the DCA National Specialty to be held at the Kentucky Horse Park in Lexington in 1993.

Answering the alarm

4

The Firehouse Dog

IT WAS EASY for the Dalmatian to earn the nickname "Firehouse Dog." He moved into the firehouses with the horses. Coach dogs readily became firehouse dogs in America as the man-drawn volunteer fire brigade pumpers and hose carts became horse drawn. The breed's built-in love for horses made it a natural. While other breeds and other animals also became firemen's pets and mascots, the more colorful spotted dogs that ran ahead to clear the way became traditional features of city life.

This was particularly true in New York City, where Captain Joseph C. Donovan was a Dalmatian breeder and delighted in furnishing a pup to a new fire station or one without a mascot. On at least one occasion a New York fire fighter showed a winning Dalmatian at Madison Square Garden. This was Bessie of Engine Company No. 39 at the 1910 Westminster Kennel Club show. She was particularly fond of Lieutenant Wise, who called her a natural-born mascot. He said, "By instinct she would run ahead of the horses whooping it up and getting people out of the way for us."

Kate Sanborn, who interviewed Wise in 1916 for her book *Educated Dogs of Today*, seemed to think Bessie knew what her boss was talking about as she got up and put her head near his hand. Both of them had been transferred to Murray Hill, Flushing, soon after the mechanization of Engine Company No. 39. Wise told her:

> She knows I'm talking about her. If I died suddenly she would be in an awful fix. She'd keep looking for me. When we were at headquarters with three fine horses and plenty of work, she always followed me home on my day off. I was living up in the Bronx then and of course had to ride. Bessie would not stay in the engine

Mike of New York Fire Company No. 8

house but would run after the car I had taken. Finally I got a street-car pass for her and I guess she is about the only dog in this city that could hop on and off a car without causing trouble with the conductor. Her fire department badge, a little brass helmet swinging from her collar and her pass from the Street Railway Company made her safe. She knew the right corner as well as I did and traveled the line alone if by any chance she missed me. Her son Mike has the pass now.

I'm afraid she is the last of the mascots. The companies that have been motorized find their dogs will not run ahead of the gasoline engines and trucks. They miss the horses and I guess are afraid of the machine.

Bessie would always follow me into a burning building in the old days and stay one floor below the fighting line, as the rule required. We had to establish that rule for fear a dog might cause a man to stumble if retreat was ordered. Bessie, I think, knew as much about the risks we ran as we did, but she stuck to the rules and always waited a floor below the men handling the nozzles.

Bessie's career had been doomed for a long time. When the first motorcars appeared on the roads in 1892 there was a cloud cast on the occupational future of the coach dog and the horse. Kate Sanborn reported, "For five and a half long years Bessie cleared the crossing at Third Avenue and Sixty-seventh Street for her company, barking a warning to surface-car motormen, truck drivers, and pedestrians, and during all that time she led the way in every one of the average of forty runs a month made by No. 39. Then like a bolt from the sky the three white horses she loved were taken away, even the stalls were removed, and the next alarm found her bounding in front of a man-made thing that had no intelligence—a gasoline-driven engine. Bessie ran as far as Third Avenue, tucked her tail between her legs and returned to the engine house. Her heart was broken. She never ran to another fire."

At the time Bessie was shown at the Garden, the Westminster Kennel Club offered a special class for Dalmatians, dogs and bitches, owned by members of the New York Fire Department. The results of the show indicate that first place was won by Mike, owned by Dan M. Lynx, breeder-owner. Bess, owned by Lieutenant Wise, was second. Smoke II, owned by Hook & Ladder No. 68, came in third, and another Bess, owned by Pierre A. Debaun, was reserve.

As fire-fighting equipment became mechanized in the early 1900s, many Dalmatians adapted to a less strenuous but still exciting role of riding to the scene of a fire on the equipment or staying on guard at the station.

Today this modest role as mascot to fire fighters continues. Occasional news reports from many parts of the United States feature some aspect of the Dalmatian linked with the firehouse. Sparky, the Dalmatian wearing a fireman's helmet, is the usual symbol of Fire Prevention Week. He is well known to schoolchildren in this country, as he is found on posters and in coloring books.

Many firehouses use Dalmatians in teaching safety to schoolchildren, and firehouses in many areas of the country still keep Dals as mascots. These dogs have been trained to show how children should act if they are caught in a building that is on fire. Perhaps the most famous one is Cee Kay Becky Thatcher, UDTX.

Cee Kay Becky Thatcher, UDTX, the Springfield, MO, Fire Department mascot.

Becky Thatcher's badge and proclamation making her the official mascot.

Happily known throughout the Springfield, Missouri, area as Becky the Firedog, her picture has been used on billboards, on TV and on posters that have been handed out to all schools.

The fire fighters at Becky's station built a miniature hook and ladder truck that is known as Charlie's Angel. It is taken to the demonstrations on a trailer and used to show the schoolchildren all the types of equipment fire fighters use when fighting fires. Becky demonstrates how to crawl in a smoke-filled room and how to roll over to put out flames if one's clothing is burning. She rides the fire trucks to the fires but stays on the truck out of the way.

Becky received a certificate making her the official mascot of the International Association of Fire Fighters, Local No. 152. She also has her own fire fighter's badge. In addition to going to schools as a certified therapy dog, Becky also visits patients in rehabilitation centers, nursing homes and hospitals. She is welcomed wherever she goes. Her proud owner is Carolyn Krause.

Old-fashioned horse-drawn fire engine pumper escorted by Dalmatians.

No picture of Mount Vernon is complete without dogs.

40

5

The Dalmatian Comes to America

WHILE we do not know of the earliest date that a Dal was brought to this country, we do know George Washington bred coach dogs. We located two items that indicate this.

First, in a letter to his nephew, George Augustine Washington, August 12, 1787, George Washington wrote, "At your aunt's request, a coach dog has been purchased and sent for the convenience and benefit of Madame Moose: her amorous fits should theretofore be attended to, that the end for which he is sent may not be defeated by her acceptance of the services of any other dog." The original letter is in the Library of Congress collection.

Second, the Alderman Library at the University of Virginia has Washington's *Ledger B*. In it on August 14, 1787, he notes the amount he paid for the coach dog—fifteen shillings. The purchase was apparently made in Philadelphia and charged to his cash account. Unfortunately, he did not note the name of the dog's original owner.

According to the *Oxford Dictionary of the English Language,* no one used the term "Dalmatian" until 1824. We know this is in error, as we found that the first edition of Bewick published in 1790 uses the term "Dalmatian" and shows a picture of a Dal.

The first Dalmatian to be registered by the American Kennel Club was known as Bessie, 10519; whelped October 1887; owned by Mrs. N. L. Harvey, they shall go by the first conveyance that offers as they are already purchased agreeably to Mathews directions. — The hinges you will receive in a bundle with the wimble bit agreeably to your Aunts request in a former letter. — If the wimble bit (which is a complete one) is given to Mathew take a mem°. of the number and quality of the pieces & make him sign it for I have suspicions that many of my tools are converted after a while to the uses of themselves & called their own

At your Aunt's request a Coach Dog has been purchased and sent for the conveniencee, & benefit of Madame Moose; her amorous fits should therefore be attended to, that the end for which he is sent may not be defeated by her acceptance of the services of any other dog. —

With respect to the money which has been called for by the Directors of the Potomk. Company, the treasurer must wait till I return. and this cannot be considered as any great indulgence as I have always been punctual hitherto in my payments. — As I did not advise to the annual meeting of the Comp.y myself & did not receive your intimation of it till it was too late I could not appoint a substitute in time & must for these reasons be excused. —

If Fairfax does not chuse to stay on his present lay, he must go. — I like him very well, but I do not chuse to give away my substance to Overlookers; who I am sure cannot make so much in any other way. — He cannot I should think have forgot, that his wages were only £30 a year & that it was my own act to add ten pounds more, long after the Bargain was made, merely on acct. of the trouble he would have with the fishery. —

If Mr. Lund Washington wants Dows money he must have it, but really I see no more than the man in the moon where I am to get it to pay my Taxes &c. &c. &c.a. if I have made no Crop, & shall have to buy Corn for my people

You must endeavour to get stuff for the Venitian blinds — one ready made goes by the

George Washington's letter.

San Francisco, California; recorded as white, black and tan; breeder and pedigree unknown.

We also know that after the time of General Washington the Dalmatian or coach dog didn't disappear from America. In Alistair Cooke's great book, *America*, can be found a picture of Southern slaves and bales of cotton they have picked. Lying at their feet is a dog that is definitely a Dalmatian. The general use of cameras seems to have developed about the time of the Civil War.

In writing of Strawberry Mansion, the stately white house that stands above the Schuykill River in Philadelphia, Joan Church Roberts, in an article in *Architectural Digest*, traces the history and development of the house. The established date of its beginnings is 1797–1798, when the central portion of the house was named Summerville. It was built by a brilliant Quaker lawyer, Judge William Lewis. Judge Lewis lived in the home until his death in 1819.

In 1821 the property was sold at a sheriff's sale and was purchased by Joseph Hemphill, also a lawyer. Mr. Hemphill had two sons, Alexander and Coleman. The Hemphill family lived there for about ten years—and it would seem that they lived extremely well. Coleman Hemphill "built a race track, raised Dalmatian dogs, and grew strawberries from 'roots imported from Chile.' " Coleman had very little interest in business pursuits. His father, in partnership with William Ellis Tucker, was involved in a china factory in Philadelphia where they produced Tuckerware, and he refused to become interested in the business. There is a story to the effect that Coleman brought his Dalmatians into the showrooms at Seventeenth and Chestnut streets, turned them loose and the dogs managed not to leave a single complete unbroken set of china.

THE DCA IS FORMED

Few people today would know the name of Alfred Maclay, yet he was the first president of the Dalmatian Club of America. Harry T. Peters, father of the well-known and popular multi-Group judge, Harry Peters of New York, was the first vice-president. J. Sergeant Price, Jr., was the secretary-treasurer. Mr. Price remained a member of DCA until his death.

The original group of enthusiastic breeders started meeting in 1904 and organized the club in 1905. There were twenty-six members in the club's roster, including Howard Willets, Joseph B. Thomas, Jr., Mrs. C. F. Denee, Percy Drury, H. Fred Lauer, Dr. Henry Jarrett and Rachel Holmes. H. Fred Lauer is remembered for having written the first book about the breed published in the United States. Copies of this original book (really a pamphlet by today's standards) are quite rare and exceedingly valuable on the antique book market.

In 1913 a young lady, Flora McDonald, joined the club. Mr. Peters had moved up to president; Arthur Whitney was vice-president and Theodore Crane was secretary-treasurer. Mr. Maclay was the delegate to the AKC. Mr. Crane retired from the office of secretary-treasurer in 1915 and Miss McDonald was named to the post, a job she held until her death in January 1967. Miss McDonald later became Mrs. Leonard W. Bonney.

Another name change took place among the early members. Miss Holmes became Mrs. Fay Ingalls, which name is probably remembered by some of the people now active.

Early kennel names which appear in extended pedigrees of most of the dogs being shown at the present time include Gladmore (Franklin J. Willock); Head of the River (Mrs. Sanger); Tally Ho (Mrs. Bonney); Borrodale (Mrs. Gladding); Cress Brook (A. E. Bonner); Four-in-Hand and Le Mel (Leo Meeker); Tattoo (Mrs. Pauline Orr, later Mrs. Hohmiller); Rabbit Run (Mrs. Reeves); Sarum (Mrs. Maurice Firuski); Lorbryndale (Robert Byron); Walls (Mrs. Evelyn Wall); Strathglass (Hugh Chisholm); Stock-Dal (Sidney C. Stockdale); Whitlee (Jean Whiting Verre); Hackney Way (Dr. and Mrs. Zane Feller); Whiteside Sioux (Mrs. Wilbur Dewell) and Regal.

In the late 1930s we find Roadcoach (Mary P. Barrett); Tomalyn Hill (Evelyn Nelson White); Gren (Mrs. Wiseman); Reigate (George and Mary Leigh Lane, and Mrs. Close); Williamsview (William Hibbler); Kingcrest (Dr. and Mrs. George King); Sitts-In (Rudolph L. Sittinger); Dalquest (Marjorie Van der Veer) and Green Star (Dr. and Mrs. David G. Doane).

World War II placed a damper on dog activities for obvious reasons. Many shows were canceled during the war and many of the great Dals were sent off to do their duty in the wartime effort. In the late 1940s another group of people came into the picture. We were introduced to Quaker's Acre, Ard Aven, Coachman, Colonial Coach, Pryor Creek, Dalmatia, Williamsdale, Dal Duchy, Rovingdale, Oz-Dal and Braintree. Many of the older kennels dropped out of sight while still others continued to breed and show. The Valley Kennels became a well-known name. When Mrs. Ratner (then Sue Allman) purchased a fine dog from Roadcoach Kennels, breed history was made. The dog was named Roadcoach Roadster. He was campaigned in a new and vigorous way, which brought fame to the dog, to In the Valley Kennels, to Roadcoach Kennels and to the breed.

The line of succession in the presidency of the Dalmatian Club of America shows that Mr. Whitney succeeded Mr. Peters and was followed by John C. Weekes. A few years later Franklin J. Willock became the president. When Mr. Willock retired Mrs. Alfred E. Barrett (Roadcoach Kennels) accepted the office and served for nineteen years. She was succeeded by Evelyn S. Nelson. Within the last thirty years we have had a number of people at the helm. They include William W. Fetner, Jr. (Coachman), William Hibbler (Williamsview), Dr. David G. Doane (Green Starr), Alfred E. Treen (Pryor Creek), Robert Migatz, Dr. N. Sidney Remmele (Tuckaway), John A. Austin (JaMar), Richard Heriot (Caravan), Forrest Johnson (Croatia), Dr. Charles Garvin (Korcula), Mrs. Alan Robson (Albelarm) and Mrs. Ray Baley (Firesprite).

The Dalmatian painted by Edward Megargee

Ch. Windholme's Market Rose

The original rules of DCA limited the membership to fifty people. This was changed in 1937 because of the growing interest in the breed. The interest was sustained and furthered by the hard-working Mrs. Hohmiller and Mr. Willock. Mrs. Hohmiller was the first *American Kennel Gazette* columnist for the club, although Mrs. Bonney wrote a number of a early columns for the magazine.

In the early days of the Dal in the United States the largest and apparently the most important kennel was Gedney Farms, White Plains, New York, owned by Howard Willets. Another important breeding kennel was Halnor Kennels, Oak Ridge, Virginia, owned by Mrs. C. Halsted Yates. Mr. Willock's kennel, Gladmore, was among those of prominence. It was through Mr. Willock's efforts that the DCA started specialty shows, the first one being held in 1926. Most of the entries were from his kennel, Mrs. Sanger's Head of the River and from the well-known Tally Ho Kennels of Mrs. Bonney. These people urged others to whom they had sold puppies to enter and make this a gala affair. A Mrs. West (later Mrs. Austin) had the honor of being the judge of the first DCA National Specialty. The national scope of the club was actually limited to the eastern seaboard. Shortly thereafter a breeder in the Michigan area became very active. Cress Brook Kennels is still to be found in many of today's pedigrees.

The DCA sponsored at least two road trials for coaching Dals. The first was at Wissahicock Kennel Club and the second was held at the York, Pennsylvania, show. Fred Lauer's description of the trials indicates that most Dals still carry the coaching instinct. Lauer gives detailed information on the method of training dogs to coach. And we well remember the story of the Fetners, Coachman Kennels, St. Louis, receiving delivery of a newly refurbished vehicle, a gig, and deciding to try it out with their driving horse. They hitched up the gig and off they went for a drive in their immediate area. Suddenly they were aware that they were not alone. Coaching as though she had been trained to do it was a six-month-old puppy, Coachman's Quadrille, who had been curled up on the patio when they took off with the gig and the horse. Oddly enough, this bitch soon to become a champion had the call name of ''Gig.''

In the late 1930s obedience was introduced to the sport of dogs and among the most prominent in our breed to participate in the Obedience Trials were the Meistrells. Lois and Harland trained their dogs well and seemed to win the trials with increasing regularity until the war brought a stop to it. They donated their dogs to the war effort, were active in Dogs for Defense and helped to train dogs for the canine units.

The first Dal to receive a CD title was Meeker's Barbara Worth. The first CDX, UD and TD was Io, owned by Harland Meistrell. The first bench champion to win a CD was Ch. Byron's Penny, owned by Robert Byron. The first champion CDX Dal was Mrs. Bonney's Tally Ho's Black Eyed Susan. Ch. Duke of Gervais, owned by Maurice Gervais, was the first champion UD in the breed. The first liver Dal to win in obedience was Virginia Prescott's Roadcoach Cocoa, UD.

46

THE GROWTH OF THE BREED

The year 1950 is about the time that the breed started to proliferate. Oddly enough, a statistical study in 1978 indicated that the percentage of Dalmatians being registered, shown and bred had remained approximately the same as in 1950 in ratio to the overall number of dogs being registered, shown and bred because the entire Dog Fancy has had such extensive growth.

When DCA allowed its membership to be opened to more than fifty members the increase was very slight. As recently as the 1960s the figures of 150 to 170 remained the top of the membership. By the end of that decade the number had grown to about 180. At this time the DCA lists more than 1,000 members.

The Dal Standard has certainly changed since the beginning of DCA and the showing of the breed. Mr. Lauer in his book *The Dalmatian*, 1907, talks about the color in Dals. Having expounded on the number of black ears on Dals, black at birth, he states:

> The reason we do not often see the jet black ear (the ear that was black when born) at a show is, that as a rule this dog is mostly too dark and poorly marked for a show dog and the owner does not show him. When you get a good spotted eared dog he is usually very lightly spotted over the body. A very good spotted dog in body has seldom a good spotted ear. How many litters are born in which there are not from one to four of the puppies with one black ear, or both, or with blotches on the face over the eye? Not many I presume. Therefore, I have no objections to the black ears, and we should not penalize a dog for black ears nor for tan spots on the legs and cheeks, for these we know to have been proper Dalmatian colorings from the very first of our information regarding the breed up to the time the English Clubs were started and there is no reason why the change has been made.

Mr. Lauer has art on his side to prove his statements. One of the earliest prints of a Dal obtainable shows a Dalmatian with a distinct brown patch on its face.

Another reason for the solid or poorly marked ears is probably the old custom of cropping the Dals' ears. The ears were not cropped in the fashion of a Doberman, Boxer, Schnauzer, etc., as we know the process today. Instead the ears were cut off next to the head. There was a good reason for this. Being used as a guard dog with the coaches, the Dalmatian was subject to attack by wild animals and other dogs and the ear simply made a good place to grab. Without the ear leather the Dalmatian had less vulnerable areas to offer an attacker. The famous Reinagle print of the Dalmatian shows a dog without any ear leathers.

In the early stages of development in this country the markings were not considered so terribly important by the exhibitors. Pictures in Lauer's book show dogs that would, today, be sold as pets and would never see the inside of a show ring. Refinement of our spotting patterns have been an evolutionary process. Today we see beautifully marked animals. And with the emphasis on markings accounting for 25 percent of the Standard, we also see some very unsound, poor types being named winners because they have such great spotting patterns.

By 1963 a check of the Dalmatian kennels advertising in the dog magazines showed Maranan, Tandem Acres, In the Valley, Sachsedals, Long Last, Dalwyck, Reigate, Greeneland, Blackpool, Crown Jewels, Hay Hill, Rustic Rail, Dal Haven, Tara Lou, Coachman and Castle Coach. Coachman, Long Last, Blackpool, Crown Jewels and Maranan are still among the kennels actively breeding.

In recent years the catalog of the National Specialty show has a list of kennel prefixes with the names and addresses of the owners, when that information is available, and the word "inactive" following the prefix if that kennel is no longer in existence. This has become an important feature of the catalog. At the DCA specialty show held in California in July 1978, there were more than 500 kennel names listed. Of those, 210 were founded in the last seven years. Some of them have had great success in the ring and others are simply names of kennels and owners.

Early on, the Dalmatian Fancy was concentrated on the East Coast, principally in New York and New Jersey, but extending from southern New England south to Virginia. The relatively few prominent breeders and the limited number of dogs shown in the breed tended to create a Dalmatian gene pool that produced dogs fairly similar in type. As the breed grew in popularity, Dalmatians began to appear in other parts of the country. Prominent local breeders developed. Other gene pools flourished. Availability in the various regions often prevailed over scientific breeding. Local winners became popular sires. Regional characteristics developed. Knowledgeable judges could almost be sure what part of the country a particular exhibit came from. This was not always complimentary.

PUBLICATIONS ON THE DAL

Fortunately several factors developed that tended to improve the situation. More information became available within the Dog Fancy as the number of publications increased. "Where Fanciers Gather" in the AKC *Gazette* spread information from member specialty (parent) clubs that was thought to be authentic and of worthwhile importance. Over the years the Dalmatian Fancy was represented by breed columnists Pauline Orr (later Mrs. Hohmiller), Mrs. L. W. Bonney (1927), Franklin J. Willock (1930), Evelyn Nelson (later Mrs. Gerald T. White) and currently Betty (Mrs. John P.) Garvin. Commercial aviation, air freight and the interstate highway system made it easier to visit prestige shows and to ship bitches to studs that hopefully might improve a breeder's line.

For many years *The Spotter* was a typewritten newsletter sent to the Dalmatian Club of America membership occasionally. An inquiry as to its schedule in 1953 brought back the response, "It is published whenever the editor accumulates enough material to make it worth mailing." In 1967, when Esme was asked to become its coeditor, she did it on the basis that it would be published quarterly. In 1971 it became a magazine, complete with articles, pictures, breed statistics and advertising. The current editions carry advertisements from a large number of breeders who show excellent dogs that have either finished championships or obedience titles and of which the owners and breeders are very proud.

In addition to *The Spotter*, the Dalmatian Fancy now has another magazine devoted to the breed, *The Dalmatian Quarterly*, published by Hoflin Publishing Ltd. It was started in spring 1987 and has achieved great success. It is an entirely different format from *The Spotter* and offers different features. The initial issue carried a wonderful interview with Bill Hibbler of Williamsview Kennels. Bill has been breeding Dalmatians for the past forty-five years and is one of the most knowledgeable breeders in the United States.

Janet Ashbey (Sugarfrost), Jean and Bill Fetner (Coachman), Dr. Remmele (Tuckaway), Susan Brooksbank (Bearded Oaks), Elaine and Paul Lindhorse (Centurion) and Chris and Mike Jackson (Long Last) are among those who have been featured in recent interviews.

CLUBS

Considering the size of the United States, it was natural that as Dalmatians became popular in given areas regional clubs would develop. These clubs provide opportunities to discuss and learn about the breed. They hold matches and specialties and engage in breed education and other activities to further the breed. Some are involved in rescue work. Currently there are thirty-eight of these active local clubs. Twenty of them have been recognized by the American Kennel Club; nineteen are licensed to hold specialty shows at which championship points may be awarded and one is eligible to hold sanctioned matches under AKC rules. The other eighteen are in various stages of growth and development. The following is a list of the active clubs.

AKC LICENSED

    Chicagoland Dalmatian Club
    Dalmatian Club of Detroit
    Dalmatian Club of Greater Atlanta
    Dalmatian Club of Greater Indianapolis
    Dalmatian Club of Greater New York
    Dalmatian Club of Greater Phoenix
    Dalmatian Club of Greater St. Louis
    Dalmatian Club of Las Vegas
    Dalmatian Club of Northern California
    Dalmatian Club of Southern California
    Dalmatian Club of Southern New England
    Dalmatian Organization of Houston
    Davenport Dalmatian Club (Iowa)
    Delaware Valley Dalmatian Club

Greater Pittsburgh Dalmatian Club
Greater Twin Cities Dalmatian Club (Minnesota)
Greater Washington Dalmatian Club (D.C.)
Puget Sound Dalmatian Club
Western Reserve Dalmatian Club (Ohio)

AKC SANCTIONED

Mount Hood Dalmatian Club (Oregon)

DEVELOPING

Cascade Dalmatian Fanciers
Central Carolina Dalmatian Club (North Carolina)
Central Maryland Dalmatian Club
Central States Dalmatian Association (Missouri)
Cumberland Valley Dalmatian Club (Tennessee)
Dalmatian Association of Lincoln & Omaha
Dalmatian Club of Alaska
Dalmatian Club of Mid New Jersey
Dalmatian Club of San Diego County
Dalmatian Organization of Tulsa
Greater Denver Dalmatian Club
Greater Sacramento Dalmatian Club
Mid-Connecticut Dalmatian Club
Mid-Florida Dalmatian Club
Narragansett Bay Dalmatian Club (Rhode Island)
Pine Tree Dalmatian Club of Maine
Sierra Hills Dalmatian Club
Tidewater Dalmatian Club (Virginia)

6

The Dalmatian Standard

THE FUTURE of any breed depends upon many individual decisions by breeders, exhibitors and dog show judges. Their benchmark is the Standard, once known as the Standard of Perfection. The Dog Fancy established the written Standard as the official basic description of the ideal dog in each breed. A Standard is intended to outline ideal goals for breeders, give judges a guide to selecting the best quality present in the show ring and assist potential buyers in deciding upon a breed and then selecting a satisfactory dog of their own. In the United States each Standard is drafted by the parent club of the breed and approved by the American Kennel Club.

The current Dalmatian Standard is the result of more than one hundred years of discussion, debate, drafting and redrafting. The British Standard, made official in 1890, was used in America until the formation of the Dalmatian Club of America. By February 2, 1905, the DCA had published a booklet presenting the "Points of the Dalmatian." The Standard recommended by the newly formed club was basically the British Standard of 1890 modified slightly to tighten some wording. The paragraph labeled "General Appearance" was placed at the end just before the Scale of Points.

Somehow, without any fanfare, by 1913 the Dal's height was specified as between nineteen and twenty-three inches and the weight difference between dogs and bitches was eliminated. The Standard remained unchanged until 1950.

On July 11, 1950, the American Kennel Club approved an addition to the Standard on Gait and changes in the Scale of Points to accommodate this. Ten points were assigned to Gait; to accomplish this, five were taken from Legs and Feet and five were taken from Color and Markings. The new paragraph read:

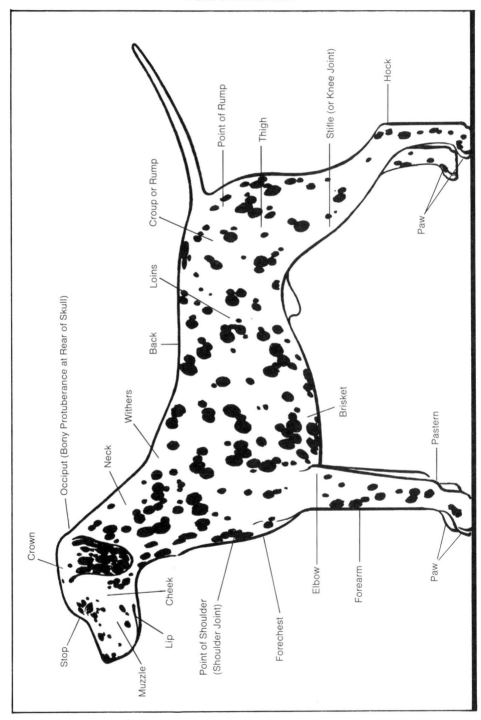

Points of the Dalmatian

Gait—Length of stride should be in proportion to the size of the dog; steady in rhythm of 1-2-3-4, as in the cadence count in military drill. Front legs should not paddle nor should there be a straddling appearance. Hind legs should neither cross nor weave; judges should be able to see each leg move with no interference of another leg. Drive and reach are most desirable.

An attempt to disqualify dogs taller than twenty-three inches at the withers was not approved by the AKC in 1950. At that time an ad hoc committee of three did the measuring when a dog's height was challenged. This did not always work smoothly. The AKC looked with great disfavor upon adding a disqualification in any breed Standard that might lead to unpleasant incidents during its administration in the show ring. Also at that time the AKC was not convinced that greater height would endanger the future of the breed.

Twelve years later the DCA membership voted to approve several additions and modifications to the Standard to overcome problems encountered in the ring and in the whelping box. The General Appearance section was moved to the front paragraph and the phrases "poised and alert . . . free of shyness . . . intelligent in expression" were added. Other additions were made to highlight faults. There was also some tightening of language to make the Standard more useful to newcomers to the breed. The AKC position had changed and for the first time faults and disqualifications were identified. The specified disqualifications were: any color other than black or liver, any size over twenty-four inches at the withers, patches, tri-colors and undershot or overshot bite. The proposal was submitted to the American Kennel Club, published in the *Gazette* and on December 11, 1962, was approved by the AKC board of directors.

The 1962 Standard continued in effect for nearly twenty-seven years. A proposal by the Standard Committee to change the Standard was returned to the committee by the membership in 1975. The following year the committee was restructured and instructed to clarify the description of the patch and the gait. While a proposed revision achieved a favorable vote by the membership in 1981, it received less than the two-thirds majority that the American Kennel Club had long held necessary to change a breed Standard.

The current Standard was approved by the American Kennel Club on July 11, 1989, and became effective September 6, 1989.

Official Standard for the Dalmatian
Effective September 6, 1989

General Appearance—The Dalmatian is a distinctively spotted dog; poised and alert; strong, muscular and active; free of shyness; intelligent in expression; symmetrical in outline; and without exaggeration or coarseness. The Dalmatian is capable of great endurance, combined with a fair amount of speed.

Deviations from the described ideal should be penalized in direct proportion to the degree of deviation.

Size, Proportion, Substance—Desirable height at the withers is between

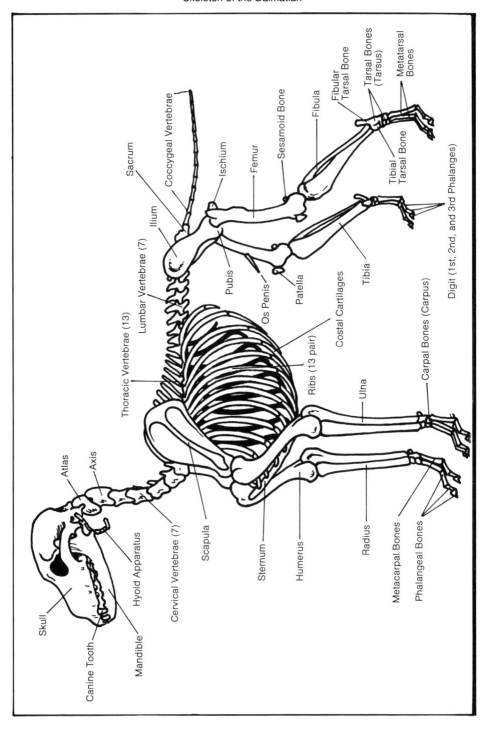

19 and 23 inches. Undersize or oversize is a fault. Any dog or bitch over 24 inches at the withers is disqualified.

The overall length of the body from the forechest to the buttocks is approximately equal to the height at the withers.

The Dalmatian has good substance and is strong and sturdy in bone, but never coarse.

Head—The head is in balance with the overall dog. It is of fair length and is free of loose skin. The Dalmatian's expression is alert and intelligent, indicating a stable and outgoing temperament.

The eyes are set moderately well apart, are medium sized and somewhat rounded in appearance, and are set well into the skull. Eye color is brown or blue, or any combination thereof; the darker the better and usually darker in black-spotted than in liver-spotted dogs.

Abnormal position of the eyelids or eyelashes (ectropion, entropion, trichiasis) is a major fault.

The ears are of moderate size, proportionately wide at the base and gradually tapering to a rounded tip. They are set rather high, and are carried close to the head, and are thin and fine in texture. When the Dalmatian is alert, the top of the ear is level with the top of the skull and the tip of the ear reaches to the bottom line of the cheeks.

The top of the skull is flat with a slight vertical furrow and is approximately as wide as it is long. The stop is moderately well defined. The cheeks blend smoothly into a powerful muzzle, the top of which is level and parallel to the top of the skull. The muzzle and the top of the skull are about equal in length.

The nose is completely pigmented on the leather, black in black-spotted dogs and brown in liver-spotted dogs. Incomplete nose pigmentation is a major fault.

The lips are clean and close fitting. The teeth meet in a scissors bite. Overshot or undershot bites are disqualifications.

Neck, Topline, Body—The neck is nicely arched, fairly long, free from throatiness, and blends smoothly into the shoulders.

The topline is smooth.

The chest is deep, capacious and of moderate width, having good spring of rib without being barrel shaped. The brisket reaches to the elbow. The underline of the rib cage curves gradually into a moderate tuck-up.

The back is level and strong. The loin is short, muscular and slightly arched. The flanks narrow through the loin. The croup is nearly level with the back.

The tail is a natural extension of the topline. It is not inserted too low down. It is strong at the insertion and tapers to the tip, which reaches to the hock. It is never docked. The tail is carried with a slight upward curve but should never curl over the back. Ring tails and low-set tails are faults.

Forequarters—The shoulders are smoothly muscled and well laid back.

The upper arm is approximately equal in length to the shoulder blade and joins it at an angle sufficient to insure that the foot falls under the shoulder. The legs are straight, strong and sturdy in bone. There is a slight angle at the pastern denoting flexibility.

Hindquarters—The hindquarters are powerful, having smooth, yet well defined muscles. The stifle is well bent. The hocks are well let down. When the Dalmatian is standing, the hind legs, viewed from the rear are parallel to each other from the point of the hock to the heel of the pad. Cowhocks are a major fault.

Feet—Feet are very important. Both front and rear feet are round and compact with thick, elastic pads and well arched toes. Flat feet are a major fault. Toenails are black and/or white in black-spotted dogs and brown and/or white in liver-spotted dogs. Dewclaws may be removed.

Coat—The coat is short, dense, fine and close fitting. It is neither wooly nor silky. It is sleek, glossy and healthy in appearance.

Color and Markings—Color and markings and their overall appearance are very important points to be evaluated.

The ground color is pure white. In black-spotted dogs the spots are dense black. In liver-spotted dogs the spots are liver brown. Any color markings other than black or liver are disqualified.

Spots are round and well defined, the more distinct the better. They vary from the size of a dime to the size of a half-dollar. They are pleasingly and evenly distributed. The less the spots intermingle the better. Spots are usually smaller on the head, legs and tail than on the body. Ears are preferably spotted.

Tri-color (which occurs rarely in this breed) is a disqualification. It consists of tan markings found on the head, neck, chest, leg or tail of a black- or liver-spotted dog. Bronzing of black spots and fading and/or darkening of liver spots due to environmental conditions or normal processes of coat change are not tri-coloration.

Patches are a disqualification. A patch is a solid mass of black or liver hair containing no white hair. It is appreciably larger than a normal sized spot. Patches are a dense, brilliant color with sharply defined smooth edges. Patches are present at birth. Large color masses formed by intermingled or overlapping spots are not patches. Such masses should indicate individual spots by uneven edges and/or white hairs scattered throughout the mass.

Gait—In keeping with the Dalmatian's historical use as a coach dog, gait and endurance are of great importance. Movement is steady and effortless. Balanced angulation fore and aft combined with powerful muscles and good condition produce smooth efficient action. There is a powerful drive from the rear, coordinated with extended reach in the front. The topline remains level. Elbows, hocks and feet turn neither in nor out. As the speed of the trot increases, there is a tendency to single track.

Temperament—The temperament is stable and outgoing, yet dignified. Shyness is a major fault.

Dalmatian movement

General Appearance 5
Size, Proportion, Substance 10
Head 10
Neck, Topline, Body 10
Forequarters 5
Hindquarters 5
Feet 5
Coat 5
Color and Markings 25
Gait 10
Temperament 10

               Total 100

DISQUALIFICATIONS

Any dog or bitch over 24 inches at the withers.
Overshot or undershot bite.
Any color markings other than black or liver.
Tri-color.
Patches.

Approved July 11, 1989
Effective September 6, 1989

7

Judging the Dalmatian: The Standard Revisited

THIS CHAPTER might be called "What the Standard Means" or "Interpreting the Dalmatian Standard" or "Understanding the Dalmatian Standard." The Standard defines those characteristics that distinguish the Dalmatian from all other breeds. In their quest for quality, it is hoped that Dalmatian breeders, exhibitors and judges will frequently revisit the Standard to enlarge or refresh their understanding of the characteristics of the Dalmatian.

In 1987 the American Kennel Club launched a program to work with the various parent clubs to standardize the format and the language of the breed Standards so that judges could more easily find specific items. The AKC adopted the same format used in the 1980 edition of *The Dalmatian—Coach Dog—Firehouse Dog*. The various sections were placed in about the same sequence that a judge would use when examining a dog.

Throughout the rest of this chapter, the revised Dalmatian Standard is presented section by section, followed by the authors' comments. These comments are intended to give some background and insights that will be helpful in understanding what a Dalmatian is supposed to be.

General Appearance—The Dalmatian is a distinctively spotted dog; poised and alert; strong, muscular and active; free of shyness; intelligent in expression; symmetrical in outline; and without exaggeration or coarseness. The Dalmatian is capable of great endurance, combined with a fair amount of speed.

Developed as a coach dog, the Dalmatian ideally is an active, medium-sized dog with a happy, alert and intelligent manner. It is sound and symmetrical. Its important characteristics are its colorful appearance, friendly manner and the ability to move well and with grace, yet displaying the potential stamina to keep up with the horses for long periods of time.

Other than color and markings, there are no features that are peculiar to this breed. Ideally, the Dalmatian is just under twenty-three inches at the withers and about as long (front of chest to back of rump), usually slightly longer than tall. The coat is pure white highlighted with black or liver (brown) round spots from a dime to a half-dollar in size, evenly distributed over the body. The topline is level, the chest deep and the tuck-up moderate. The tail is long enough for the tip to reach the hock joint. It is carried straight back with a slight curve upward. The shoulders slope moderately. The forelegs are strong and straight, the hindquarters well muscled and the hocks well let down. The feet are small and compact. The Dalmatian moves smoothly, in a rhythmic fashion—much like four-four time in music—and gives the impression that it could continue all day.

> Deviations from the described ideal should be penalized in direct proportion to the degree of deviation.

The approach to judging should be positive. Look for quality, as defined in the Standard. The Dalmatian should be judged as a coach dog and deviations that suggest another breed are violations of breed type. A Pointer outline, a Bull Terrier front or a Foxhound tail are extreme examples. Judging is a search for the ideal, and the farther any part is from the perfection specified the more serious the fault.

> *Size, Proportion, Substance*—Desirable height at the withers is between 19 and 23 inches. Undersize or oversize is a fault. Any dog or bitch over 24 inches at the withers is disqualified.
>
> The overall length of the body from the forechest to the buttocks is approximately equal to the height at the withers.
>
> The Dalmatian has good substance and is strong and sturdy in bone, but never coarse.

The British Dalmatian Standard's section on *size* starts: "Overall balance of prime importance, but the ideal height to be aimed at is. . . ." This certainly hints that height is not the only factor in the size of this symmetrical breed. Length of body; size of rib cage, head and neck; bone and muscle all contribute to the impression of size. The Dal is a medium-sized dog. Bigger is not better. Once it ran beneath the whiffletree or the axle. There "big" could be "bad," with the vehicle beating or rubbing off its hide as they passed over irregular road surfaces. Maybe that is why some ran in front of, alongside or behind the conveyances.

As early as the 1940s there was concern in the United States that Dals were getting too big to be considered coach dogs. Others were too small. In 1962 a

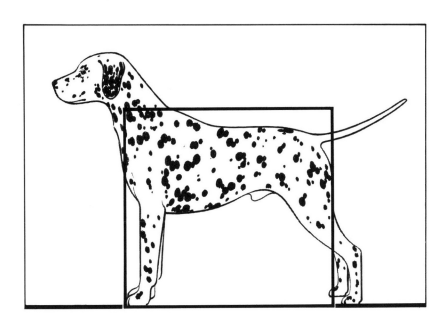

Proportion and shoulder layback

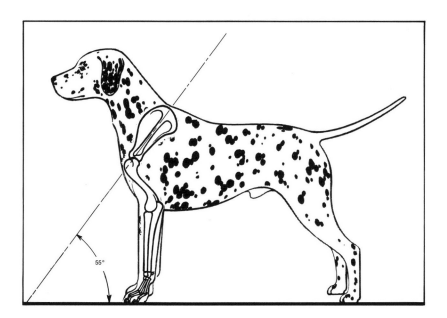

55°

61

fault was established for undersize or oversize dogs—under nineteen inches or over twenty-three inches—and any size over twenty-four inches at the withers was designated a disqualification from the show ring.

Other breeds also have size disqualifications. In the show ring, if another exhibitor protests the size of a Dalmatian or if the judge believes that a dog may be too tall, the judge sends for the AKC-approved official measuring instrument called the wicket. This is then set for twenty-four inches. The handler puts his dog in a show pose and the judge brings the wicket forward over the back and lowers it to the withers. If both feet of the wicket rest on the ground or floor the judge marks his book "Measured in" and the dog is judged. If the wicket rests on the dog's withers but both ends do not touch the floor the dog is dismissed from the ring and the judge marks his book "Measured out—disqualified."

The influence of *sex* is not mentioned in the DCA/AKC Standard. However, the Standards used in Canada, England, Mexico and other Federacion Cynologique Internationale (FCI) countries specify the ideal height of the bitch as one inch shorter than that of the dog. Some breeders, exhibitors and judges like bitches to be feminine. Others (excluding these authors) prefer "doggy" bitches. In the United States, personal preference has a wide swing, as the breed Standard allows a range of four inches in the desirable height, plus an additional inch before disqualification.

> *Head*—The head is in balance with the overall dog. It is of fair length and is free of loose skin. The Dalmatian's expression is alert and intelligent, indicating a stable and outgoing temperament.

In saying "of fair length" the Standard means "beautiful to the eye; of pleasing form or appearance." The Dalmatian is not a "head breed" but the *head* must be in proportion to the rest of the dog. It is a simple, clean-looking head, smooth and free of wrinkle.

Experimental breeding, most of it 100 to 150 or more years ago, left some unwanted recessive traits in many breeds, including Dalmatians. We see these reminders of other breeds occasionally in the heads of Dalmatians. A great depth from the point of the nose to the underjaw says "Mastiff." A full, square jaw says "Great Dane." A muzzle tilted so that the nose is slightly higher at the tip than where the muzzle joins the topskull says "Pointer." A head tending to an oval or egg shape says "Bull Terrier." Fortunately, these traits are seldom seen. Hopefully, specimens with these characteristics are not used in breeding. They rarely win in the ring under a knowledgeable judge.

> The eyes are set moderately well apart, are medium sized and somewhat rounded in appearance, and are set well into the skull. Eye color is brown or blue, or any combination thereof; the darker the better and usually darker in black-spotted than in liver-spotted dogs.

The Standard is fairly clear on *eyes*. One might miss the possibility that a Dal may have one brown and one blue eye or even an eye with both colors. This

Good head

Too throaty

Snipey muzzle

happens occasionally. It happens in human beings, too. If it does not spoil the dog's expression there is no problem.

Previous to 1962 the Standard stated, "Wall eyes are permissible." This raised the issue of whether a blue-eyed Dalmatian was a second-class dog. The answer was "No!" Blue was accepted along with black and brown. But in other countries, including Canada, Mexico, England and the sixty-seven FCI countries in Europe, Asia and the Americas, blue eyes are considered a serious fault. Many do not agree. As far back as 1954 the foremost British Dalmatian authority, Dr. Eleanor Frankling, wrote, "It seems likely that the factor for blue eyes is fairly widely distributed among dogs of today. In most parti-coloured breeds such eyes are not considered a fault. They are not faulted in American Dalmatians, and although they are frowned on here, I personally think it is rather a pity, for a bright blue eye is by no means unattractive."

Abnormal position of the eyelids or eyelashes (ectropion, entropion, trichiasis) is a major fault.

These problems are rarely found in the ring. Evidence of corrective surgery calls for disqualification under AKC rules.

The ears are of moderate size, proportionately wide at the base and gradually tapering to a rounded tip. They are set rather high, and are carried close to the head, and are thin and fine in texture. When the Dalmatian is alert, the top of the ear is level with the top of the skull and the tip of the ear reaches to the bottom line of the cheek.

Few comments are necessary on *ears* except to confirm that when alert their base is level with the topskull. Flyaway ears are not typical or desirable. Ears must hang close to the sides of the head. Ear leather is thin and fine in texture and preferably spotted. Are black ears considered patched? Not if broken—that is, if some white hair is visible to indicate overlapping spots.

The top of the skull is flat with a slight vertical furrow and is approximately as wide as it is long. The stop is moderately well defined. The cheeks blend smoothly into a powerful muzzle, the top of which is level and parallel to the top of the skull. The muzzle and the top of the skull are about equal in length.

Viewed from above, the outline of the Dalmatian's *head* appears almost pear shaped, with the *topskull* and *muzzle* about the same length. The topskull is nearly as broad as it is long with a slight center groove starting at the occiput, coming down the stop between the eyes and extending onto the muzzle to the nose leather. Viewed in profile the topskull is nearly flat.

The *stop* is not a pronounced feature, but rather a subtle rise where the muzzle blends into the upper head, further emphasized by the groove and by the position and shape of the well-developed arches over the eyes. From the side, toplines of the skull and the muzzle appear approximately parallel. The muzzle's underline tapers from the nose to the skull, but the muzzle should never appear pointed or snipey.

> The nose is completely pigmented on the leather, black in black-spotted dogs and brown in liver-spotted dogs. Incomplete nose pigmentation is a major fault.

The *nose* is fully colored to match the spots, as are the eye rims. Butterfly and flesh-colored noses both result from a lack of pigmentation. Some breeders and breeder-judges consider it unforgivable to take a Dalmatian with either fault into the show ring.

> The lips are clean and close fitting. The teeth meet in a scissors bite. Overshot or undershot bites are disqualifications.

This disqualification for improper bites was added in 1962. Previously the Standards had not mentioned teeth. *Lips* are to be the same color as the spots.

To summarize, the head is nicely balanced with a spacious skull and a powerful muzzle. The muzzle is never weak or pointed. The lips are clean and dry. There are no flews or dewlaps.

> *Neck, Topline, Body*—The neck is nicely arched, fairly long, free from throatiness, and blends smoothly into the shoulders.

The *neck* arches forward gracefully from the shoulders. While many Dalmatians have been trained to hold their head high in the ring, normally when the dog is running free the head is thrust forward and is only slightly higher than the topline. A dog shown on a tight lead with the head pulled back so that the neck is like a stovepipe rising from an old-fashioned base burner is badly handled. If one were to extend a line along the front leg from the foot upward it would emerge well behind the head. The neck is moderately long and blends smoothly into the back and shoulders.

> The topline is smooth.

A word about the anatomy of the *topline* is in order as a frame of reference. "Topline" is defined in the dog glossary of *Dog Standards Illustrated* (Howell Book House, 1976) as the "Backline profile of dog from top of skull to tail base." Its structural components are (1) seven cervical vertebrae (neck), (2) thirteen thoracic vertebrae (back), (3) seven lumbar vertebrae (loin) and (4) the sacrum, which with the ilium forms the croup. The coccygeal vertebrae continue from the sacrum to form the tail.

> The chest is deep, capacious and of moderate width, having good spring of rib without being barrel shaped. The brisket reaches to the elbow. The underline of the rib cage curves gradually into a moderate tuck-up.

The *chest* should be viewed from three vantage points. From head-on one can see that it is deeper than it is wide and that it is well filled. From above one can see that it is wider at the shoulder than at the loin. From the side the forepart

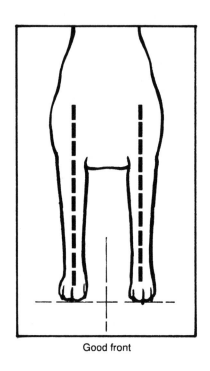

Good front

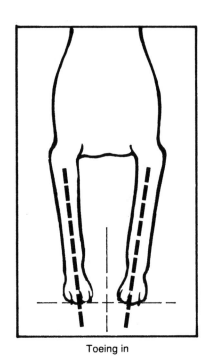

Toeing in

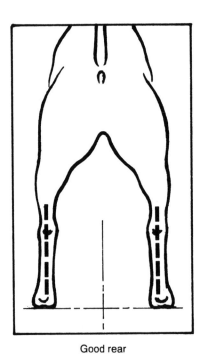

Good rear

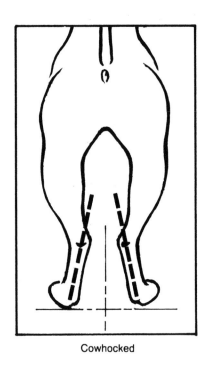

Cowhocked

of the chest is only slightly visible in front of the forelegs, but the lower portion of the chest (brisket) extends to or below the dog's elbow.

The degree of roundness of the *ribs* is not great enough to form a barrel- or even an egg-shaped chest cross-section. This would interfere with the set-on of the shoulders and would limit movement. It is a vertical oval tapering down to the brisket.

Only a moderate *tuck-up* is expected. The Dalmatian requires plenty of lung room. The bottomline slopes upward gradually from midchest to the end of the ribs. A ''herring-gut'' bottomline that slopes up steeply from the front of the chest does not provide a large enough chest cavity to enable the Dal to do its job.

> The back is level and strong. The loin is short, muscular and slightly arched. The flanks narrow through the loin. The croup is nearly level with the back.

The *back* is relatively smooth and level but not necessarily flat. This is true whether we use the dog glossary definition that identifies the back as ''that part between withers and set-on of tail along the vertebrae'' or the old-time breeders' definition that limits the back to the area over the rib cage. To the latter we add the ''coupling'' (loin area) and the croup or rump to complete the horizontal portion of the topline. If the components are properly constructed and the muscles in good condition, the topline from the withers to the onset of the tail remains fairly level whether the dog is moving or standing.

The *loin* is strong and, as it is in most breeds, slightly arched. Looking down at the dog's back one can see that the sides through the loin area are not as far apart as on the chest or the croup. The *croup* is rounded.

> The tail is a natural extension of the topline. It is not inserted too low down. It is strong at the insertion and tapers to the tip, which reaches to the hock. It is never docked. The tail is carried with a slight upward curve but should never curl over the back. Ring tails and low-set tails are faults.

The *tail* is important to the overall picture of a balanced Dalmatian. It extends back naturally from the topline, curving upward only slightly. Proper length can be determined by seeing if the tip will reach the hock.

The tail is strong at the base and tapers gradually. It is not curled. If the base of the tail is set much below the level of the topline it spoils the Dalmatian's appearance. So does a vertical tail or one carried over or curled over the back. When moving, the tip is rarely held higher than the head.

> *Forequarters*—The shoulders are smoothly muscled and well laid back. The upper arm is approximately equal in length to the shoulder blade and joins it at an angle sufficient to insure that the foot falls under the shoulder. The legs are straight, strong and sturdy in bone. There is a slight angle at the pastern denoting flexibility.

Good *shoulders* are important if the Dalmatian is to move efficiently. The angle of the scapula (shoulder blade) determines the extent of the reach. Visualize a line projected along the spline (ridge) of the shoulder blade to the ground.

The sloping shoulder produces a greater range of movement than does the vertical one. Theoretically, since "oblique" means an angle not vertical to or horizontal to the plane of reference, in this case the surface on which the dog stands, the optimal or ideal angle could be forty-five degrees from horizontal. The ideal has never been determined. Shoulders close to ninety degrees produce poor movement. The best-moving dogs obviously will have shoulder blades that are less than ninety degrees from the horizontal, but no one is sure how much less.

The optimum forty-five degrees has been quoted by dog writers over a long period of time as producing the proper movement. However, this statement has not been made or verified by an authority with standardized research data to support his or her conclusions. From observation in and out of the ring we get the impression that shoulder layback on most well-moving dogs is apt to be within the range of from sixty-five degrees from the horizontal down to fifty degrees and that forty-five degrees might be a worthy goal—or merely a bit of dog fancy folklore.

Coming down the leg, the upper arm (humerus) is normally joined to the shoulder blade at a ninety-degree angle. Usually slightly shorter than the shoulder blade, it permits the lower legs to drop vertically so that the foot is directly under the center of the shoulder blade. Viewed head-on, the legs are straight and parallel. The elbows are close to the body. From the side there may be a slight bend at the *pastern*. The Dalmatian's pasterns are flexible for a smooth gait and short for endurance.

> *Hindquarters*—The hindquarters are powerful, having smooth, yet well defined muscles. The stifle is well bent. The hocks are well let down. When the Dalmatian is standing, the hind legs, viewed from the rear, are parallel to each other from the point of the hock to the heel of the pad. Cowhocks are a major fault.

Since both drive and reach are essential to good movement, the *hindquarters* must be in balance with the forequarters. The *stifles* must be moderately well bent and the thighs well muscled for the Dalmatian to maintain its ability to move with the horses. The *hocks* are low (well let down) for endurance. They are perpendicular to the ground when the dog is standing naturally or in a show pose. When the dog is seen from the rear, the centerline of each leg is straight. Hocks that turn inward toward each other are a serious weakness, particularly considering the Dalmatian's principal purpose.

> *Feet*—Feet are very important. Both front and rear feet are round and compact with thick, elastic pads and well arched toes. Flat feet are a major fault. Toenails are black and/or white in black-spotted dogs and brown and/or white in liver-spotted dogs. Dewclaws may be removed.

The *feet* are tight and round, small and catlike. The Dalmatian does not need the additional leverage of long harelike feet for a speedy start, as this would waste energy. Large, spread-out feet would also be inefficient. The pads are tough and thick and should never be flat. Because more than half of the Dalmatian's weight is carried by the forequarters, the front feet are larger than the hind feet. Feet point straight ahead.

The *toenails* should be kept short. Long nails tend to make the feet splay. Long nails also cause dogs to develop weak pasterns and poor gait. To avoid stepping on the long nails, the dog rocks its weight back and this causes it to go down on his pasterns.

> *Coat*—The coat is short, dense, fine and close fitting. It is neither wooly nor silky. It is sleek, glossy and healthy in appearance.

The *coat* should be of uniform texture as described, with two possible exceptions. The hair on the ears is shorter, softer and more silky in texture than the rest of the coat. If the dog is patched the texture of the patch will match that of the ears.

The coat is a good indicator of a dog's health and condition. It should be clean and free from blemish. Dalmatians should not be in the ring unless they are in good condition. While there have been no scientific studies completed that would substantiate this, there seem to be some isolated genetic families and/or diet patterns that produce an excessive amount of skin problems in a few dogs.

> *Color and Markings*—Color and markings and their overall appearance are very important points to be evaluated.
>
> The ground color is pure white. In black-spotted dogs the spots are dense black. In liver-spotted dogs the spots are liver brown. Any color markings other than black or liver are disqualified.
>
> Spots are round and well defined, the more distinct the better. They vary from the size of a dime to the size of a half-dollar. They are pleasingly and evenly distributed. The less the spots intermingle the better. Spots are usually smaller on the head, legs and tail than on the body. Ears are preferably spotted.
>
> Tri-color (which occurs rarely in this breed) is a disqualification. It consists of tan markings found on the head, neck, chest, leg or tail of a black- or liver-spotted dog. Bronzing of black spots and fading and/or darkening of liver spots due to environmental conditions or normal processes of seasonal coat change are not tri-coloration.

The key to a nicely marked Dalmatian is an even, pleasing distribution of spots. Too few or too many spots spoil the picture, as do large blank areas without spots (which breeders sometimes refer to as "white patching"). Heavily marked dogs frequently have concentrations of overlapping spots on their neck and shoulders. There should not be too many places where large numbers of spots overlap. A confluence of spots is unsightly and might be mistaken for a patch by an unknowledgeable judge, although patches are relatively easy to distinguish.

> Patches are a disqualification. A patch is a solid mass of black or liver hair containing no white hair. It is appreciably larger than a normal sized spot. Patches

Coins illustrating range of spot sizes

Heap of coins

A patched Dalmatian

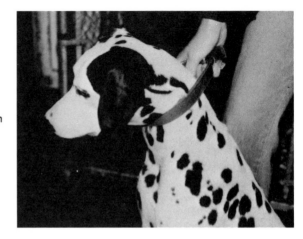

are a dense, brilliant color with sharply defined smooth edges. Patches are present at birth. Large color masses formed by intermingled or overlapping spots are not patches. Such masses indicate a cluster of individual spots by its uneven edges and some white hairs scattered throughout the mass.

Describing a *patch* so that someone not in the Dalmatian Fancy can readily visualize one and instantly recognize the presence or absence of one isn't a simple task. The description should create a picture in a person's mind that contrasts an unfortunately overmarked Dal with a patched one. These images are analogous to a table with a handful of coins spilled on it versus a table with a puddle on it created by a bottle of ink being tipped over.

In the first image, some of the coins may overlap. This does not create a patch. It is more like a confluence of spots, each one at least partially discernible. The area covered has irregularly scalloped edges and usually includes some white hair that partially defines the edges of some of the overlapping spots.

Contrast this with the smoother outline of the puddle or patch. The patch has no indication of spots or partial spots. There is an absence of white hair within the area covered. Typically the hair within the patch is shorter, finer and softer than the other hair on the animal being evaluated.

With these features firmly in mind, a judge from outside the Dal Fancy is equipped to recognize the presence or absence of patches as quickly as a breeder. How does a breeder learn to recognize a patch? It is present at birth and all too easily recognized as a black or brown blot on a pure white puppy. Dalmatian puppies are several days old before their spots begin to appear.

Gait—In keeping with the Dalmatian's historical use as a coach dog, gait and endurance are of great importance. Movement is steady and effortless. Balanced angulation fore and aft combined with powerful muscles and good condition produce smooth efficient action. There is a powerful drive from the rear, coordinated with extended reach in the front. The topline remains level. Elbows, hocks and feet turn neither in nor out. As the speed of the trot increases, there is a tendency to single track.

Gait is best evaluated at a slow trot. It should be free from sidewinding (crabbing). The spine should point in the direction the dog is going.

The dog's gait in the ring is the judge's test of balance and soundness. Going away, the legs should move in parallel, the rear legs tracking the forelegs. The judge should not see cowhocking, crossing over or spraddling. Coming back, the legs should be seen coming down straight with no paddling, weaving or out-at-the-elbows or out-at-the-shoulders movement visible. Side movement should display balance along with ample reach and drive. A short mincing side gait denotes straight shoulders and lack of rear extension. A Dal that minces can hardly move with the horses for long periods of time.

Temperament—The temperament is stable and outgoing, yet dignified. Shyness is a major fault.

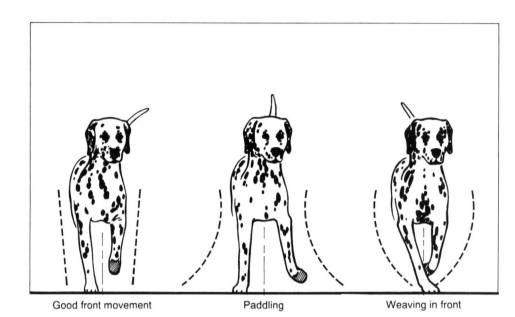

| Good front movement | Paddling | Weaving in front |

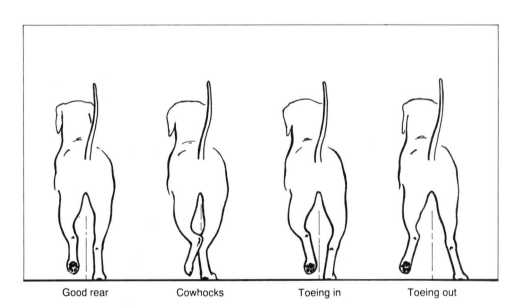

| Good rear | Cowhocks | Toeing in | Toeing out |

Good front movement

Good movement going away

Good side movement

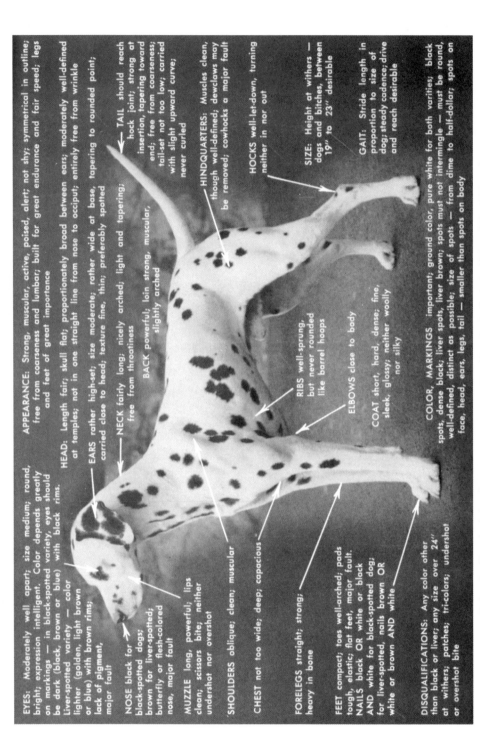

Dalmatian Standard visualization reprinted from *Dog Standards Illustrated* (Howell Book House).

The above phrases are not taken directly from the Dalmatian Standard, but rather indicate what the Standard implies.

A well-bred Dalmatian has a stable *temperament* that makes it a good companion. Aloof, yes. Shy, no. A Dalmatian should be eager, warm and friendly once its preliminary suspicions have been satisfied.

For many years Dalmatians were bred to be guard dogs. They ran with the coach or carriage to ward off wolves and highwaymen. They protected their master's belongings from thieves while he was dining at the inn. They still fancy themselves to be guard dogs when a stranger appears at the door, but when a member of the family makes the caller welcome, so do they.

A Dal should be neither shy nor aggressive. Good breeders breed for stability. The American Kennel Club expects a judge to dismiss from the ring any dog in any breed that shows any signs of viciousness. This is a rare problem in Dals.

Dogs exhibiting shyness or a streak of viciousness are eliminated from breeding programs so that only puppies of sound temperament are produced. These puppies will hopefully receive enough socialization during their first seven to ten weeks of life to enhance their ability to accept human as well as canine friends. A well-bred Dalmatian is intelligent and perceptive, and its behavior should make it trustworthy around unattended young children.

Breeders and judges need to pay serious attention to temperament. At home the Dalmatian should be the careful guard, the sensible, friendly companion. In public places it walks calmly at its master's side, accepting whatever praise or interest is expressed in its colorful appearance with wagging tail. In the ring a Dalmatian should be calm and alert, exhibiting stability and poise. A judge will do well to pass over an excessively exuberant dog or a shy one that is difficult to examine.

SCALE OF POINTS

General Appearance	5
Size, Proportion, Substance	10
Head	10
Neck, Topline, Body	10
Forequarters	5
Hindquarters	5
Feet	5
Coat	5
Color and Markings	25
Gait	10
Temperament	10
Total	100

The *Scale of Points* demonstrates that 75 percent of the emphasis of the Standard is on the Dalmatian as a whole and only 25 percent is on its color and markings. Gait and the physical features that control the Dal's movement total 45 percent, so they are extremely important.

Any dog or bitch over 24 inches at the withers.
Overshot or undershot bite.
Any color markings other than black or liver.
Tri-color.
Patches.

All faults and disqualifications mentioned in the Standard are genetically undesirable in breeding. There are six other disqualifying items common to all breeds of dogs. These require disqualification under AKC rules and are not listed in the specific breed Standards. A dog that is blind, deaf, castrated, spayed or that has been changed in appearance by artificial means except as specified in the Standard for its breed, or a male that does not have two normal testicles normally located in the scrotum will be disqualified.

Certainly a judge penalizes for faults but does not judge by them alone. He or she looks for quality. The serious breeder breeds for quality and avoids a breeding that would involve using two dogs with the same fault, whether that fault is dominant or recessive. Honest breeders plan breedings to eliminate inherited faults from their litters. They work to replace weak features with strong ones to improve the quality of their lines.

A good definition of quality is found in Howell's *Dog Standards Illustrated*: "*Quality*—an air of excellence, combining breed characteristics and including soundness and harmony, making the animal an outstanding specimen of the breed, both standing and in motion."

8

Living with a Dal

ANYONE contemplating buying a Dalmatian puppy should be aware of a number of things concerning these dogs. It is always a good idea to learn as much as possible about any breed before acquiring a puppy.

A good Dal puppy will grow to a sturdy, well-muscled dog, one that is able to keep going on the road or in the field for hours on end. The dog will have a trusting attitude toward you, its master, and will present a reserved manner toward strangers. After it has been introduced to the stranger it will be friendly and loving. Some Dalmatians smile. It is necessary to determine that the dog is smiling and not snarling. The entire attitude of the smiling Dalmatian is quite different from that of a dog who is daring you to approach one step nearer. The uninitiated person may be unable to tell the difference and thus will fear your dog. The Dalmatian has great ability to guard and protect its own property. It was bred to guard. It is willing to learn if you don't push it. Pushed, it can seem quite stupid. It will become a member of your family, so it behooves anyone acquiring a puppy to train it properly. It cannot know what you want it to do unless you teach it.

Training a Dalmatian for Obedience work is a little more strenuous than training it to be a good house dog. Many organizations offer puppy kindergarten classes that will introduce your dog to other dogs and to simple behavior patterns—all of which are useful in the home.

Training a Dalmatian for Obedience will require a good deal more time and effort but can be extremely rewarding. After you have trained your dog in obedience, you may want to enter Obedience Trials. If you have purchased a ''show prospect'' Dalmatian, you should attend conformation classes as well as

Dr. Michael Manning exercising puppies.

Breakfast with Brewster.

obedience classes. Some training clubs use the conformation showing as another obedience exercise, changing collars and teaching the owner how to present the dog in the breed ring. Other clubs offer either breed or obedience showing, requiring you to go to two different classes. Whichever you choose, you will have a great deal of fun showing your Dal in obedience and/or conformation. Rules governing the sport of showing and regulations covering Obedience Trials can be obtained at no cost by writing to the American Kennel Club, 51 Madison Avenue, New York, New York 10010. The instructors at the classes you attend can advise you about where and how to enter your dog. The sport of showing dogs can become a great family hobby, one in which every member of the family is involved. It is an activity that affords a great deal of friendship with many people from different parts of the country and can become a lifelong hobby.

When you acquire your puppy you will want to establish certain patterns in its life. Start as soon as possible to make a habit of these things so that as your dog grows it will expect them.

Grooming a Dalmatian is the simplest thing in the world. If you have a pet Dalmatian the important thing is to keep it brushed. Dalmatians shed. Some people believe that only the white hairs are shed, never the black or liver. Actually, this is simply myth. The shed hair just seems to be all white because the darker hairs rarely show on clothing, furniture, etc. A jokester once quipped that "Dalmatians shed only twice a year, every morning and every night!" Brushing will keep the shedding down.

If you are preparing the dog for the show ring you will want to trim its whiskers, "pants" and tuck-up. The entire idea is to give it a smooth outline. Scraggly hairs left on the outline of the rear legs and the tuck-up and some "moles"—those funny little growths found on all dogs—spoil the appearance.

Running a dog on concrete at all times will spoil the development of the foot. A good type of kennel run surface is pea gravel. This seems to make the foot arch well and stay tightly knit. The only danger of using pea gravel is that some dogs will eat it.

Toenails should be cut on a regular basis whether the dog is a pet or a show prospect. If the nails are allowed to grow long, the feet can splay. A tight, catlike foot is most desirable and long nails will prevent this type of foot development.

In cutting toenails, if you start the process at an early age and do it regularly you will not have problems. Putting the dog up on a grooming table or something higher than it is used to will help in making it behave for the cutting process. The quick is retractable and keeps moving back when the nails are properly cared for. Have a container of ferric subsulphate powder handy to stop bleeding if you cut too deep. To smooth the nails some people use a sandpaper disk on the end of a power hair clipper. Some people have found that a wood rasp makes a good file.

Other than giving your dog a bath from time to time with a quality dog shampoo, brushing it well and keeping it in good health so that it is not plagued by skin problems, there is little more to do than to train it to show well.

In training your dog, when you move it around on a loose leash and stop it, at least one foot will be in the correct position. With much effort and practice you should be able to walk it into a show pose and, with the use of a little liver for bait, keep it showing well. Wag your hand in front of it and say, "Wag your tail." It won't take long before a wag of your hand will produce a wag of its tail. Dals look better with the tail moving than just hanging at half-mast.

Exercise is important. If at all possible, move your dog for a mile or so each day at a given pace. Determine which speed shows your dog's movement to best advantage by having someone else move the dog for you at various speeds. Then work at that pace each day. Too fast for you to keep up? Try using a bicycle.

Swimming is good for the Dal, but you have to be careful not to overdo this form of exercise. Loaded shoulders can be the result.

There are many ailments that can befall all dogs, including the Dalmatian. The Dal is subject to skin troubles that crop up from time to time. Much of the pinking that occurs on Dals is diagnosed as skin allergy. Many people refer to this as "grass allergy." Whatever causes the rash or pinking probably has more to do with the general metabolism of the dog than with grass.

When you notice this sort of rash occurring on your Dal, get a fungicide lotion from your veterinarian to put on it. Scratching the lesions—and surely the dog is going to scratch an itch—can cause a fungus to start in the skin and this will then spread over the dog's body and make the skin condition much more difficult to control.

Also check your dog's diet. John Lowery of the Dalmatian Research Foundation developed a rice diet that is very good for those dogs who tend to have skin problems. This diet is not difficult to prepare and the dogs seem to love it. A recipe and instructions can be obtained by writing to the secretary of the Dalmatian Club of America.

The Dalmatian has a urinary system that is rare in canines. The Dal is the only breed of dog whose urine stops short of forming urea or allantoin and produces, instead, uric acid. This peculiarity is thought to be one of the causes of bladder and kidney stones in Dalmatians. Too many dogs are lost to this condition. Sometimes a stone will be lodged in the urethra and cause great pain. Other times "gravel" will be passed in the urine. Sometimes, in acute cases, the stones will pile up and completely block the passage from the bladder; this situation will require surgical removal of the stones.

Again, the rice diet is of help in maintaining a healthy animal. Massive doses of vitamin A are frequently prescribed to keep the epithelial tissues healthy. The bladder is lined with these tissues. Use of Allopurinal in treatment of dogs subject to stones has had some success.

Much research is being done in these areas and it is hoped that a cure will be found in the near future.

9

Breeders' Practices

$\mathbf{T}$HERE ARE certain practices common among the ethical breeders of all breeds of dogs. These cover breeding, selling and showing, and have been developed as unwritten laws to protect both buyer and seller.

A bitch should not be bred before the age of one year or after the age of eight years. A male should not be used at stud under the age of nine months. A registration application showing the age of the stud to be less than this will probably be questioned by the American Kennel Club. The bitch should not be bred more than every other season.

Before going into the breeding aspects of the sport of dogs it is advisable for the breeder to become familiar with the breed Standard and understand what he is doing. Breeding pet stock is not in the best interest of any breed. Pet buyers should be encouraged to have their puppies neutered. The breeder should explain to the puppy buyer the faults of the animal and why it should not be used in a breeding program. Anyone who intends to breed should buy top-quality "show stock," study pedigrees, compare his own dog to the dog he plans to use in the breeding, avoid common faults and be prepared to cull when the puppies arrive.

It is considered proper for the bitch to "visit" the stud dog. Two breedings about twenty-four to forty-eight hours apart are the custom. Some stud owners prefer one breeding and feel that is sufficient. It is the custom, too, to offer a repeat breeding for no cost if the bitch fails to have a litter. One puppy constitutes a litter. However, most stud dog owners will allow a repeat breeding in the case of a single puppy in the litter. Many stud dog owners will allow a repeat breeding if the bitch is so unfortunate as to lose a litter after it has been whelped. The stud fee pays for the stud service only. It does not guarantee puppies. The proven

Ch. Melody Up Up and Away, CD, with puppies

Puppies at three weeks

male covers the bitch. If the bitch is a proven bitch there should be puppies.

Before selling puppies, the breeder should have had them checked for worms, wormed them if necessary and given them either temporary or permanent DHL inoculations, depending upon the advice of the veterinarian. Puppies should not be sold under seven weeks of age. According to dog behaviorists the forty-ninth day is the ideal time for a puppy to move into its new home. Earlier than that the puppy is still in need of its dam and littermates.

All Dalmatian breeders should make sure that the homes to which their puppies are moving are suitable. Small children can be cruel to dogs without meaning to be, and parents must be aware that the dog should have some protection from them. A fenced yard is a plus, but an unfenced yard is not necessarily an insurmountable drawback if the new owners are responsible people and are prepared to take on the care and training of the pup.

The buyer should be given a return privilege written into the sales agreement. A limited amount of time should be specified so that the new owner may have the puppy inspected by his or her own veterinarian. This practice should be encouraged. There should be a written bill of sale signed by the breeder and the buyer. This should contain the name of the sire and the dam, their AKC registration numbers, date of whelping, color of puppy and any other pertinent information either party specifies and both agree to. If the litter has been registered, a registration application should be given the buyer along with the bill of sale. If the dog has been individually registered, the registration certificate, duly signed, is given along with at least a three-generation pedigree of the pup.

Dalmatian puppies that are born ''patched'' should not be sold. However, if one is sold it should be without registration papers and with agreement to neuter the animal. The new owner should receive a bill of sale with these facts stated in writing, which both buyer and seller should sign.

A patched Dalmatian has its patch at birth. This is a large area of solid color, black or liver, that can be seen while the puppy is still wet and does not disappear when the coat dries. The pigment remains. Tiny touches of color on the ear, toes, nose, etc., are not to be confused with a patch. The color in a patch is intense and uniform. The texture is quite velvety in the adult dog as the patch, soft and silky like the rest of the puppy coat, does not change when the puppy matures. Sometimes spots will run together. These can be distinguished from patches because of the white hairs that intermingle with the black or liver spots that have run together.

Perhaps the most discouraging thing is to find a deaf puppy in the litter. Fate seems to enjoy making the best puppy in the litter, the one with the best markings, the best movement, etc., the deaf pup. It is heartbreaking as there is nothing that can be done for this pup. The best course is to have the veterinarian put the puppy down.

There is a deaf gene in Dalmatians. Deafness can be tested in the puppies at about four weeks of age. The test should be repeated at five and again at six weeks to be sure. Generally, if a puppy is deaf the evidence will appear by that time. Occasionally a puppy will lose its hearing at a later time, but this is not usual. Of course, a deaf puppy cannot be sold. Most people euthanize them. However, many research studies are being done on the problem of deafness and a puppy could make a contribution to one of them.

A puppy sold as a "show" prospect offers another situation that both the buyer and seller must consider. When the dog has reached maturity, if it has developed any disqualifying faults, the buyer should receive as rebate a portion of the purchase price, thereby bringing the cost of the puppy down to the level of the pet prospect. This, of course, is an item to be included in the sales agreement. Generally the buyer does not wish to give up a dog he has had for a year or more, but since the dog did not live up to its promise as a show prospect, he should not have more than a pet price invested.

Too often we hear of a breeder who advertises extensively and who represents every puppy sold as a "show dog." This is rationalized on the basis that the only requirement for a dog to be classified as a show dog is eligibility to be registered with the AKC as purebred and having no disqualifying faults. It may still lack quality.

Unfortunately, there have been cases where inferior dogs have been campaigned to their championship even though originally these dogs were sold as pet quality by knowledgeable breeders who believed them not worthy of competing for a title. All too frequently because of advertising and other promotion such dogs have sired many litters and left their less-than-desirable mark on the breed.

Most dog fanciers are in the sport as a hobby and few, if any, actually make or attempt to make money from their dogs. Most dog fanciers who have been in the sport for a number of years are willing to help novices with advice and physical aid—if the novice will accept it. Too often the novice, after obtaining his show dog and breeding one litter, sounds as if he "wrote the book." This attitude causes old-timers to resent the newcomer. Those novices who listen and ask questions will learn a great deal from those with more experience. There are no stupid questions.

Besides asking old-timers, newcomers can also read and study. The following suggested basic reading guide offers much useful knowledge:

Alston, G. G. with Vanacore C. *The Winning Edge: Show Ring Secrets.*
American Kennel Club. *The Complete Dog Book.*
Brown, Curtis and Thelma. *The Art and Science of Judging Dogs.*
Carlson, D. G., and Giffin, J. M. *Dog Owners Home Veterinary Handbook.*
Dangerfield, Stanley, and Elsworth Howell, eds. *International Encyclopedia of Dogs.*
Fiennes, Richard and Alice. *The Natural History of Dogs.*
Gaines Dog Research Center. *Basic Guide to Canine Nutrition.*
Little, Clarence C. *The Inheritance of Coat Color in Dogs.*
Lyon, McDowell. *The Dog in Action.*
Onstott, Kyle. *The New Art of Breeding Better Dogs.*
Pearsall, Margaret E. *The Pearsall Guide to Successful Dog Training.*
Pfaffenberger, Clarence. *The New Knowledge of Dog Behavior.*

Vanacore, C. *Dog Showing: An Owner's Guide.*
Whitney, Leon F. *How to Breed Dogs.*
Willis, M. B. *Genetics of the Dog.*

Videocassette programs of considerable value are:

American Kennel Club. *Dalmatian.*
Dalmatian Club of America. *A Review of Color in the Dalmatian.*

Dalmatian puppies at eight weeks

Ch. Pryor Creek's Tuxedo Satin with day-old litter

Dinnertime

10

Background for Breeders

REGISTRATION wasn't nearly as important in the early part of this century as it is today. Until the early 1950s it was possible to register dogs solely by virtue of their wins. The requirement was ten championship points acquired. These would allow a dog or bitch to be entered in the stud book. Later this was changed to fifteen championship points, or a championship.

One of the most prominent lines in the breed came from some of this unregistered-type stock, Reigate. Ch. Reigate's Lady Culpepper and Ch. Reigate's Lady Fauquier were litter sisters out of an unregistered bitch named Jo and sired by Freckles, who was also unregistered. Freckles's dam and Jo's dam were the same, Betty, an unregistered bitch. Freckles's sire was Cress Brook Pepper, owned by George W. Cutting and bred by A. E. Bonner. Jo's sire was Skipper, unregistered, as were his parents, Tom and Star. Betty's sire was Nip, an unregistered dog but her dam was Borrodale Witch, bred and owned by Mrs. John R. Gladding.

Ch. Reigate's Lady Culpepper's claim to fame is the fact that she is the dam of Ch. Reigate's Bold Venture. This great dog is in the pedigree of many of the leading dogs of today. He had one blue eye, perfectly acceptable even in those days.

Until 1962 there wasn't a single word in the Dalmatian Standard concerning the dog's bite. We have watched the judging at many Specialties and many other Dalmatian classes where the judges never looked at the mouths. The first judge we saw do so was Derek Rayne back in the late 1950s. When asked why he checked bites since the Standard didn't cover it, he replied that a dog with a bad bite was an unsound dog and he wouldn't put it up. A bad bite has been a disqualification since 1963. From time to time puppies will be born with a bad bite and the breeders are hard put to tell where this is coming from. Those of us who have Bold Venture in the background of our pedigrees can stop wondering. His dam, Lady Culpepper, was badly undershot! This information comes from correspondence with Mrs. Close, who showed the bitch to championship for her in-laws, George and Mary Leigh Lane, owners of Reigate Kennels. Correspondence with Mrs. Close has revealed much of what is in the past of many of the great ones, and what many people thought of some of the greats and near-greats in the breed.

Of course, Lady Culpepper was not the only Dalmatian to have a bad bite. But since her son was a great sire and appears in so many extended pedigrees, she has been singled out as a culprit.

IMPORTING

Importing stock can be a risky business. It can improve a breeding program or wreck it with new problems. A breeder should have a reason. The import should be able to make a contribution to the breeding program. The breeder had better know what he is looking for in an import. Just because a dog comes from overseas does not necessarily make it great. One must take into consideration the genetic background of the dog, the good points and faults and make sure that the breeding would be a good one. Naturally, at one time importing was a necessity. Now, it probably isn't. Get from most of the good English bloodlines can be found in the United States.

Another important thing to remember when importing from England is that there is no size disqualification there. The English dogs tend to be larger. The spotting patterns, however, seem to be better.

Early imports that had a great deal of influence on the breed after World War II include the dogs that Leo Meeker brought over. He had a number from the famous Cabaret Kennels of Miss Monkhouse. Later, Dr. Jackson of Fort Worth, Texas, imported Cabaret Courtcard, who became an American champion. Courtcard would probably be measured out today. Ch. Nigel of Welfield and Stock-Dal is another that can be found in many pedigrees. Sidney Stockdale imported this dog as well as Ch. Welfield Guardsman and Ch. Jason Widdington. Nigel was the greatest of these three.

Ch. Astwood Qui Vive was imported by Hugh Chisholm of Strathglass Kennels. He also imported Mesra Dilema and Ch. Moonmageic of Chasfield. All of these can be found in old pedigrees behind the dogs of today. Long Last Kennels of Lorraine Donahue did some important importing. The great Am. &

Eng. Ch. Colonsay Blacksmith, who did much for the breed in England and in the United States, was one of the dogs Mrs. Donahue imported. She also imported Washakie Bolehills Barbara and Am. Ch. An English Rose of Colonsay.

A great liver dog imported from England was Am. & Eng. Ch. Colonsay Storm. Storm came to this country via Mexico. His first owner on this continent was Dalmex Kennels of Mexico, but he was later purchased by Dr. Josiah Harbinson of Ard Aven Kennels. Storm was a magnificently balanced dog, well marked with very dark liver spots, and he moved well and had a commanding appearance in the ring. He was a true coach dog.

The Prescotts of Tandem Acres and the Garrett of Garrett's Ice Cream Dals were also among those who imported some English stock. The Hayeses of Coachmaster Kennels also imported from England, and Little Slam Kennels of Lita and Bill Weeks imported three Ascotheath dogs from the kennels of Mr. and Mrs. C. D. Cudd.

The year before she died, Mrs. Bonney imported Ch. Duxfordham Yessam Marquis. He appeared at the DCA Specialty in Chicago in 1966.

The foundation dog of the great Williamsdale Kennels was Am. & Can. Ch. Elmcroft Coacher, who was imported in dam. This dog sired twenty-seven champions and had great influence on the breed. In addition to all the good things he did for Dalmatians, he also left a very straight left stifle in many of his descendants. Williamsdale imported a number of other dogs, including Am. Ch. Colonsay Tantivey Claudia, Am. Ch. Penny Parade of Williamsdale and the famous Igor of Key of Williamsdale, also an American champion. This latter dog was to be a great sire as Coacher had been before him. He sired many champions, but his prepotency as a stud did not measure up to that of Coacher.

Igor produced many champions. However, Igor did not help the breed as his largest contribution to his get was made in the area of his less desirable features. Coacher, on the other hand, made a great contribution. He marked his progeny with good shoulders, heads, fronts and excellent movement, and his good points are to be found even into the third and fourth generation. His poor angulation, however, unfortunately has also come down through the ages.

In the late 1970s Benito Vila imported a top winning dog from England, Buffrey's Jobe, a liver. Jobe had produced winning get in England. He finished his championship in the United States in short order. In this country he was used mostly on Montjuic dogs, although he was not limited to them. He is the top producing sire in the United States, having fifty-eight champion get.

At the present time there is a great deal of exporting of dogs going on from the United States. Some unethical people feel that this is an opportunity to get rid of the culls. Others, realizing that people overseas are trying to better their stock, are willing to ship good specimens of their breed. Dog shows are such a new popular activity in so many countries that it behooves us to send only the very best. The name of the breeder remains on the dog forever and regardless of the language involved, the name can be read in the catalogs.

Judges from the United States are invited to judge everywhere. If you sell a poor specimen overseas and it is shown in the country where it was sent, your name as breeder will be seen in the catalog and your reputation as a breeder will be diminished in the eyes of the U.S. judges who see it. If, on the other hand, you ship a good dog to a foreign country your name as a breeder will be enhanced because of this dog. Fortunately, Dalmatian breeders seem to be exporting good dogs. Some of the dogs return to the United States to be campaigned and it is good to know we helped the breed in another country.

Many dogs have been imported from Canada. One Canadian kennel, now no longer active, can account for the foundation stock of several very successful breeders in the States. The kennel was Kay Robinson's Willowmount. Looking into some fairly recent pedigrees we find many references to the Willowmount prefix.

SHOW-QUALITY DALMATIANS

When the Standard became effective in January 1963 it carried a requirement on size. The ideal Dalmatian is to be from nineteen to twenty-three inches at the withers. A Dal standing over twenty-four inches is disqualified. At the Wisconsin Kennel Club show in January 1963 the judge, William Kendrick, called for a measurement in the ring on the first Dalmatian to be questioned on size. According to the measuring committee, the dog was under twenty-four inches and was allowed to remain in the ring. Mr. Kendrick did not put the dog up as it was, he said, too tall for his taste. Many of the spectators were surprised that the dog was not measured out. It was never shown again.

When breeding Dals it is difficult to know what to expect in the way of numbers in the litter. There are litters of one puppy on record and also litters of more than twenty. Most litters average eight dogs.

Choosing the show puppies from the litter is a difficult task. Check the litter at five weeks and again at eight weeks. Old-time breeders have taught us that at those ages the puppies are most nearly like they will be at maturity. After eight weeks, do not look at the puppies except as pets until they are almost a year old. During those months some parts of the pups grow in peculiar fashion. Sometimes they are too high in the rear; other times you begin to wonder what happened to their hind legs. And heads—ugh! As the bones grow, and they grow at different rates of speed, the dogs can look dish-faced, Roman-nosed, too broad in skull, too narrow in skull, you name it. But if the head was okay at eight weeks, it will probably be a good head at maturity.

Pigment is another worry for the Dal breeder. A good rule of thumb is the outside-inside theory. Eye rims that are not filled will probably fill by maturity if the color starts in the corners. Noses that have color on the edges will probably fill. Noses that have pink corners probably will not. There is no hard and fast rule to cover this, but experience has taught us that the probabilities are as stated.

Patched puppies should be neutered or put down. Mrs. Bonney, the true

Am. & Eng. Ch. Buffrey's Jobe

Part of a Pryor Creek litter

Mrs. Dalmatian of the United States, did not put down patched puppies that were otherwise sound. She gave them to people without papers. She said that people who received a dog as a gift hardly ever asked to have the registration on the dogs. She also made it quite clear that the patched puppies were not to be used for breeding.

Dalmatians have certain characteristics that are quite different from most other breeds. For instance, the puppies are born white. The spots appear at about the time the eyes open. Shadows of the spots can be seen on the skin while the whelp is still wet; as the days pass the shadows become more pronounced until they are truly spots. Some of the dogs continue to spot out for a year or so. Others get all their spots at one time. Frequently these latter puppies seem to be too heavily marked for the show ring, but as the puppy grows, it grows into its spots. Other dogs will start to "tick out" when they reach about five years of age. This, of course, is undesirable. But it happens.

There are many tales of uninformed first-time breeders destroying whole litters of puppies because they were all white at birth, feeling that the bitch must have been bred by some unknown dog and the puppies were all mongrels. Alas, too many of these tales are true.

Occasionally a puppy will be born with a slight touch of color on an ear, a toe, across an eye or perhaps with a tiny spot on the nose. These, to the experienced breeder, are the sign of good pigment.

At one time, in England, the Dalmatian was interbred with the white Bull Terrier, supposedly to help broaden the chest and deepen the brisket of the latter breed. Many knowledgeable people say that the deaf gene in the Dalmatian came from this mixing of the breeds. The Bull Terrier people bemoan the fact that some of their choice specimens carry some spots. These are severely faulted in the show ring if they occur behind the head. Stand behind a group of Bull Terriers sometime. You can see the shadow of spots on their skin showing through the fur when the light is right.

In the 1850s James Hinks of Birmingham, England, decided to work with crosses between the Bull Terrier and the white English Terrier to produce a true Bull Terrier. Before his experiments there was no true Bull Terrier. As the name suggests, the Bull Terrier is descended from the Bulldog but not the type of Bulldog seen today. The early Bulldogs were long-tailed and resembled present-day Boxers more than any other breed. They were used for the cruel sport of bullbaiting. The dog frequently suffered from goring by the bull. In an attempt to get a more intelligent, agile and determined dog, various terriers were introduced to the Bulldog breeding. The results were called the Bull and Terrier. But about then the sport of bullbaiting was outlawed. The dogs were then put in the "pits" for dogfighting. Over a period of time the dogs developed their own type, similar in appearance to the Staffordshire Bull Terrier.

Then Mr. Hinks started his work. The white English Terrier he used is now extinct. These dogs were said to be similar in appearance to the modern Manchester but were, of course, white. Mr. Hinks used Dalmatians in his experiments and eventually produced an all-white strain, which he named Bull Terriers. At first his dogs were not accepted by the fighting fraternity, as there was a feeling that they wouldn't have the aggressive ability of the old Bull and Terrier. A fight was arranged and Mr. Hinks's bitch demolished a well-known old-type fighter and was so little marked that she was able to compete at a show the next day. Thus the Bull Terrier was accepted.

DEAFNESS IN DALMATIANS

We do know that many white Bull Terriers have been left with latent spots on the skin and sometimes the spots develop on the body, thus making it undesirable for them to be shown. Color on the head of a Bull Terrier is permissible. This entire experiment dealt with white Bull Terriers. The colored one came later. Since a deaf gene can be a color-linked gene with white animals, it is felt by some that the deafness in Dalmatians came from this experiment.

The deafness found is characterized by the deterioration in the organs of Corti, that membrane stretched across the eardrum of the dog and named for the scientist who discovered it.

In any event there is deafness in Dalmatians. Some unscrupulous people try to sweep this fact under the rug. We have heard people say, ''I have never had a deaf puppy in my kennel.'' To us this means that they have disposed of the puppy as soon as they found it was deaf. When someone says that they have never produced a deaf puppy, we raise our eyebrows. Either these people have not bred any Dalmatians or have had no more than one or two litters. Deafness occurs in the breed. It would be better to admit the deficiency and keep good records on it and see if it can be stamped out by selective breeding. This is a difficult project, of course, but it could be done. Alaskan Malamute fanciers are hard at work getting rid of dwarfism. All studs are test bred before being used as breeding stock. We could probably devise some way to do this with deaf dogs.

A study made at the University of Chicago in the late 1950s indicated that the histology of deafness in a Dalmatian is the same as that found in a child born of a mother who experienced German measles during the first trimester of pregnancy. Other studies show that the organ of Corti is missing in deaf Dalmatians. Some Dalmatians lack an eardrum altogether and, of course, cannot hear.

All Dalmatian puppies should be tested for deafness. At about four weeks, after the ears have opened, the puppies should be observed and tested. There are various ways of doing the test and other breeders, your veterinarian and possibly an ear, nose and throat physician should be consulted. Stamping on the floor, clapping your hands or blowing a whistle are all useless activities. Puppies who are deaf compensate for the lack of hearing to the extent that it is sometimes almost impossible to detect. However, the puppy who continues to sleep when the food pan arrives and doesn't stir until all the other puppies are scrambling for the goodies is the one to watch. The yelper is another. There are times when a deaf puppy will sit and howl at the world while the rest of the litter is quietly sleeping. It is giving vent to frustrations. Watch it. It may be deaf. All of these points are possibilities. None is definite proof.

Testing at four weeks, again at five, and then again at six weeks should determine which puppies are hearing puppies and which are not. Reports have been made, however, that sometimes a pup that can hear at six weeks suddenly goes deaf at three months. We have never experienced this phenomenon, but others have reported that it has happened.

DALMATIAN CHARACTERISTICS

Another unfortunate characteristic of the Dalmatian is shedding. Contrary to popular belief, short-haired dogs are harder to clean up after than the long-haired varieties. The hair of a Dalmatian (and of Labrador Retrievers, Boxers and other short-haired breeds) seems to have a barb on its end. It sticks onto furniture, clothing and even your skin! And the white hair shows up on all dark materials. Brushing your dog's coat each day helps but does not entirely clear up the problem. If you are squeamish about seeing dog hair around your home, do not get a Dalmatian. If you are willing to excuse this problem, you will have a great dog as your pet.

Dalmatians seem to have a sixth sense. We know of a Dalmatian that was purchased by a family to be a companion to their children—four active, rambunctious boys. The fourth child was a cerebral palsied child who had difficulty walking and talking but who wanted to romp and play with his older brothers. The Dalmatian was seven weeks old when it went to live with this family. It grew up being the center of attention, playing football, baseball, racing up and down next to bicycles and enjoying all the normal activity of small boys. However, when the handicapped child touched its collar it stood very still, walked very slowly with the boy and was as gentle as it could possibly be. When the boy released its collar, the dog was off and running with the gang, so to speak. The parents of these children were both physicians and were delighted to know that the dog was aware of their child's problem and could adapt to it.

The occasional bad bite in Dalmatians is always shocking to the breeder because, of course, the careful breeder would not have used an animal with a bad bite in his breeding program. Since it is found so rarely it is almost certain to be a recessive characteristic that pops up in an occasional specimen and shocks the breeder. We have found bad bites on both coasts and in between. As we now know, some of the "greats" of the past carried bad bites and are probably responsible for the inheritance. All of this points to knowing more than the names on the pedigree and the show records when we are planning a breeding.

Because color in animals is not always constant, there are two things that happen that breeders and exhibitors should be aware of. One is bronzing and the other is blackening. Bronzing starts in the shedding of the coat and means that the black or liver hairs lose their color somewhat, so the spots become rust-brown in tone, darker in the black, lighter in the liver. How bad the bronzing can be is difficult to determine and many times it can be almost impossible to decide whether the bad color is bronzing or faulty pigmentation in a particular dog. Should the change of color completely disappear after the shedding and the spots become clear black or clear liver, it was only a question of bronzing.

Blackening is another problem in color that Dal breeders have to face. Blackening is the opposite of bronzing and occurs only in the liver variety. The liver color darkens, particularly on the back, so much so that the dog, at a quick glance, appears to be marked with both black and liver spots—to be a tri-color. In the show ring it is sometimes difficult for judges to determine whether or not this process is taking place. Dogs have been disqualified for being tri-colors because the blackening in the spots has given an appearance of black on the back and light liver on the head, sides and extremities. An informed owner will wait until the dog has completed its shedding and the colors have cleared before applying for reinstatement.

While discussing color it might be well to explain the genetic combinations that occur in the breeding of Dalmatians. The black color is dominant, the liver color is recessive.

The letters BB represent pure for black. The letters Bb represent a black dog carrying the liver gene. The letters bb represent a liver dog. According to some geneticists, a dog that is BB can *never* produce a liver puppy, even if mated to a liver. A dog that is Bb can produce either black or liver offspring. A dog that is bb is always liver.

The usual rule of thumb in breeding shows that a BB dog mated to a BB bitch will produce only black puppies. A BB dog bred to a Bb bitch will produce only black puppies but 50 percent of the litter will carry the liver gene. A Bb dog and a Bb bitch will have a litter with 25 percent of the litter BB, 25 percent bb and 50 percent Bb. The genetics rule also says that a bb dog bred to a bb bitch will always produce liver offspring. There are cases on record, however, where two livers have produced black offspring. This is exceedingly rare. When breeding a Bb dog to a bb bitch 50 percent of the litter will be liver-factored blacks (Bb) and 50 percent will be liver. Because these are percentages and the litters are not always divisible in this way, it really takes a large number of dogs and a large number of litters to determine the accuracy of this formula.

According to Dr. Robert H. Schaible, a geneticist at the University of Indiana, the so-called tri-color is actually a bi-color, as there are only two different colors involved, usually black and tan. The white part of the pattern in the Dalmatian results from an absence of color rather than from the presence of a third color. Pigment cells are absent from the white regions of the Dalmatian and the tri-color Sheltie, as determined by electron microscopy. Dr. Schaible says, "The absence of pigment cells in the white regions of both breeds is due to one of the mutant genes at the piebald locus. The occurrence of tan spots on the muzzle, feet, which is objectionable in Dalmatians, is due to the effect of the bi-color gene."

Dr. Schaible classified the color pattern of a Dalmatian showing both black spots and liver spots in two different ways because he feels there are probably two different genetic mechanisms involved. One of these patterns he calls a "mosaic pattern": a black-spotted dog showing one or more liver-colored spots. The other he calls the "variegated pattern": a liver-spotted dog showing one or more black spots. The mosaic pattern is the most common. Explaining it, Dr. Schaible reports that the genetic locus for brown (liver) may be located near the end of one pair of chromosomes. The terminal portion of the chromosome bearing the allelic gene responsible for normal (black) pigmentation is deleted (broken off and lost). The recessive gene for brown which remains on the intact chromosome is then free to be expressed in all pigment cells that descend from the cell in which the loss of chromosome tip occurred. The descendant cells could form a brown spot.

Dr. Schaible has reported that studies of cases of mosaicism in mammals have offered no evidence that mosaicism or variegation is genetically transmitted. In other words, this type of marking is not passed from one generation to the other. Early prints of Dalmatians show a definite tan marking on the cheek.

Another color variation found in the Dalmatian is in the eye. Many people object to the occasional blue eye. In fact, in many countries the blue eye is frowned upon. Since it is in the genetic makeup of the dog it would take centuries of selective breeding to breed it out. Most geneticists do not know how it is inherited. No experiments have been carried out to breed single blue-eyed dogs to double brown-eyed dogs and find the ratio of blue to brown in the offspring. What does a double blue-eye bred to a double blue-eye produce in pups in eye color? Is the blue eye color dominant or recessive to the brown or is it a multiple allele? We need answers to these questions before doing anything to outlaw the blue eye. To date, there is not a shred of evidence that blue-eyed Dalmatians produce more deaf puppies or tend to be deaf themselves. It is true in other mammals that blue eyes and deafness are paired, but in the canine this fact has yet to be established.

11

Progress in the Breed

T HE 1980s was a time of great expansion and growth in the Dalmatian Fancy. The number of dogs being bred, registered and shown has increased unbelievably. In addition, there have been a number of breakthroughs in solving some of the problems of the breed.

Every dog breed has genetic problems, and the Dalmatian is no exception. Fortunately, compared to other breeds, the Dalmatian's problems are relatively few in number and affect only a minority of the Dal puppies born. Two are serious in terms of their prevalence—bladder stones and deafness. Serious breeders within the Dalmatian Club of America are working to accumulate specific statistical information that might lead to the solution of both problems.

Perhaps the most important improvement that has been made is in testing. Before scientific methods were developed for testing for deafness we had to depend on the reliability of home methods—some of which were tried and true as far as they went, while others were hit or miss. One test was to take a puppy into a bathroom and flush the toilet. If the puppy reacted to the sound of the rushing water, it was assumed that the puppy could hear. No one has been able to prove whether or not there was a possibility that vibrations were reaching the pup through its feet. Another method was to take a puppy into the kitchen, allow it to smell some good smells that were quite new to it and then, being careful not to cast a shadow, hold a pie tin over its head and drop a handful of cutlery into it. If the dog could hear, it would spread-eagle at the sudden noise and then race for cover. If it couldn't hear it would just keep on smelling the good smells.

BAER TESTING

A truly scientific method was introduced to the breed because Ken Nagler took a litter that he co-owned with a friend to the School of Veterinary Medicine at the University of Pennsylvania for an evaluation. This champion-sired litter, whelped November 27, 1982, had ten puppies. Using the conventional testing methods it had been determined that five of the puppies were deaf.

Having heard that the school might be interested in litters that had deaf puppies, Ken took all ten puppies, the dam and the granddam to Philadelphia. The school had done studies of deafness in white mink and white cats. The results had led to speculation that a high rate of deafness might occur if one or both of the parents were deaf in one ear. Such unilateral deafness might not be noticed.

The Brainstem Auditory Evoked Response (BAER) test was performed by Dr. Jerry Northington and other staff members in the school's neurology department. The results indicated that five of the puppies were indeed deaf in both ears, that three others were deaf in one ear and that the dam was deaf in one ear. The granddam had bilateral hearing. Later, the sire was tested and he did not show a normal hearing response. He was over nine years old and appeared to have an ear infection at the time. There is a possibility that he had only unilateral hearing.

The Nagler litter was the first full litter of Dalmatians tested at the University of Pennsylvania; only individual dogs had been tested previously.

The testing procedure developed by Dr. Northington involves amplifying the electric current generated when a sound is induced in the ear. Tiny electrodes are inserted under the skin in standardized locations on the anesthetized animal. One is placed just below the ear, another at the top of the skull and a third, a ground, is placed elsewhere on the body. The signal is amplified and displayed on an oscilloscope. The trace from a deaf ear is dramatically different from that of a normal ear.

Dalmatian fanciers first learned of this giant step forward at the world congress of Dalmatians hosted by the DCA at the time of the AKC Centennial show in Philadelphia in 1984. Since this experience BAER testing has become widespread, with many veterinarians throughout the country being able to do the testing. This may be the single greatest step toward eliminating deafness in the breed. All the years previous to this, breeders have used animals that might have had unilateral hearing. These dogs have continued the problem in the breed. If everyone used BAER testing and eliminated all but bilateral hearing dogs from all breeding programs, the problem of deafness could become a minor occurrence. As Dr. George M. Strain of the School of Veterinary Medicine at Louisiana State University wrote in an article in *The Spotter*, "First, if you breed to a unilateral sire or dam, you are likely to get a greater percentage of hearing impaired puppies. If the deafness problem is to be successfully reduced and hopefully eliminated some day, these breedings need to be eliminated."

Many people used to pretend that such a problem did not exist. Now that everyone is aware of BAER testing and able to have their dogs tested scientifically, there is no excuse to use partially deaf dogs in a breeding program. It is hoped that all breeders will adhere to this precept.

Studies are being made by the DCA Research Committee through its Research Subcommittee on Deafness. These studies are based on information provided through results of the BAER testing. Ivan Gignac and Sheila Wymore, both of Arizona, are co-chairpersons of the Research Subcommittee on Deafness. Local clubs have helped establish networks of cooperative breeders who are having their litters tested and the results reported. The Research Subcommittee on Deafness has recruited associates with scientific backgrounds to help in the analysis of the data collected.

INSEMINATION

Another great advance in the breeding of Dals and all other breeds was the further development of artificial inseminations, whereby frozen semen could be shipped—thus eliminating the need to subject the bitch to the stress of a plane ride when undertaking a planned breeding. Fresh-chilled or cooled semen (the terms are used interchangeably) is used in another method of artificial insemination.

In this system the semen is simply cooled and shipped, and it must be used immediately. Certain things are added to the semen to keep it motile. This method also requires a quick drive to the airport after collection and a scheduled flight that will suit the purposes of the breeder. Carol Schubert of Watseka fame has been working in this field for a number of years. She is responsible for the first Dalmatian litter whelped with the use of frozen semen. Many people have had great success using frozen semen, as have those who use cooled semen. The AKC will accept the registration of puppies whelped via the use of either type.

Several organizations in the United States work with both frozen and cooled semen and are well prepared to handle either type of collection and shipping. Special training is given to veterinarians by the various companies in the use of frozen or cooled semen.

The use of the frozen or cooled semen should lead to some interesting breedings. To date there has been no indication that the United Kingdom will allow frozen semen to be shipped into their country (the law prohibiting dogs to enter that country without a six-month period of isolation, while designed to prevent the spread of rabies, might also exclude the importation of semen) or that the Kennel Club of England will allow dogs whelped from this method of insemination to be registered. Frozen semen is accepted in Australia and New Zealand.

COLOR CONFUSION

There has always been difficulty in understanding the patch. Judges coming into Dals from other breeds have always been apprehensive about the patch

Puppies from the first frozen semen litter of Dals.

Puppies from the first cooled extended semen litter.

because it is a disqualification. Breeders know that a patch is present at birth on the all-white Dal puppy. However, few judges are in attendance when a litter is whelped and so have little or no understanding of the problem.

Tri-colors and spotting patterns (often referred to as "lemons" and "oranges") are another source of confusion in the show ring. Sometimes liver will bronze or fade, and not all the spots take on the same intensity of color at the same time. Blacks and livers alike can sunburn. Judges are apt to disqualify dogs that are perfectly legal entries because of a lack of understanding.

The DCA's Judges' Education Committee, under the leadership of Cindy Ingalls, decided to tackle the weighty problem of color in Dalmatians. Other committee members included Georgia Nichols, DiAnn Plaza, Sharon Podleski and Patti Strand. In 1988 they produced a videotape, *A Review of Color in the Dalmatian*, showing the different color patterns that can occur in the Dalmatian, using drawings and live dogs. Covered are tris, patches, dark ears and run-together spots. The tape also explains the genetic makeup of the differently colored dogs.

Special thanks were accorded Joanne Nash, Meg Hennessy, Bob Skibinski and Judy Bible for their help in the production of the video. This tape is available for purchase through the Dalmatian Club of America. All students of the breed should have a copy in their library.

BLADDER STONES

Progress on the elimination of bladder stones has moved more slowly. The Dalmatian is unique among canines in having a high level of uric acid in its urine. This leads to the formation of urate crystals that may cause urinary blockages. This occurs more often in middle-aged males than bitches. Attempts to breed this problem out have failed because all Dalmatians carry this genetic defect. Searches as early as 1940 in both Britain and the United States were unproductive. Each large-scale survey ended with the conclusion that high uric acid levels are always found in Dalmatians.

In 1973 Dr. Robert H. Schaible, a geneticist at the University of Indiana, began a crossbreeding experiment using a champion Pointer bitch of appropriate size. His goal was to breed dogs of Dalmatian type and temperament but with normal canine low uric acid levels. He secured the approval of the DCA board of directors. He bred the Pointer to a purebred Dalmatian and continued backcrossing to purebred Dalmatians, each time selecting for Dalmatian characteristics and low uric acid. He brought two puppies, a dog and a bitch, from his fifth-generation backcross litter to the National Specialty at Lexington, Kentucky, in 1980. They seemed typical Dalmatian puppies and were admired by DCA members and others attending the specialty. Dr. Schaible spent two days at the show site explaining his project to exhibitors, breeders and others and made presentations to the DCA board of directors and the Regional Club Council.

When the American Kennel Club received the request to register the two fifth-generation backcross puppies, it asked the Dalmatian Club of America for its position. The DCA board responded that it supported Dr. Schaible's research and his request for registration of the two offspring. On February 7, 1981, the AKC board granted registration of the two fifth-generation backcross puppies as Dalmatians.

Despite the fact that the DCA board of directors supported the AKC's decision, the backcross registration immediately became a dominating, controversial issue among DCA members. A majority vote of the membership opposed the registration. As a result, on August 11, 1981, the AKC placed a hold on any registrations of offspring of the fifth-generation Dalmatian/Pointer cross. This seemed to put an end to the only known means of breeding registerable Dalmatians that would be free of this genetic problem.

Several interesting things have happened since that time. While the registered male backcross has never been bred, several Dal breeders have continued the project using descendants of the bitch, Stocklore Stipples. She was bred twice, once by Dr. Schaible in Indiana and then by Holly Nelson, DVM, and Joanne Nash in California. The project is now in its ninth generation with about half of the progeny retaining low uric acid levels. Backcross Dalmatians cannot be registered with the AKC or compete in conformation at AKC shows. Some have received ILP numbers and have successfully competed in obedience.

The Dalmatian Club of Northern California passed a resolution and sent it to the American Kennel Club, the DCA and all regional clubs. The resolution read:

> Resolved, the membership of the Dalmatian Club of Northern California has reviewed the Dalmatian Backcross Project and supports this effort to provide an option to correct a genetic problem in this breed, and urges the American Kennel Club to rescind the hold on registration of the descendants of the registered backcross bitch, Stocklore Stipples.

Other help may be on the way. Three important dog-related organizations, the American Kennel Club, the Morris Animal Foundation and the Orthopedic Foundation for Animals, are providing $750,000 for a five-year study conducted by geneticists at the University of Michigan and veterinary specialists at Michigan State University. While there is no guarantee, the possibility exists that new molecular genetics techniques might enable scientists to examine genes directly under high-powered microscopes, identify defective genes and determine whether they are dominant or recessive.

It is expected that, by the end of the first five years, these scientists may find genes for about 400 diseases. According to the Morris Animal Foundation, once this technology is in place, a small blood sample will be enough to test a dog for the presence of the specific gene and to determine whether it is recessive or dominant and whether the dog is a carrier or affected. This would eliminate the need for test matings to find out if a dog carried problem genes, especially for recessive traits where carriers show no symptoms.

If the study is successful it will provide dog breeders with a valuable tool. The new test will allow them to avoid breeding to a carrier dog, or to select nonaffected and noncarrier offspring for future breedings. Skillful use of genetic testing could virtually rid a breed of a harmful genetic trait in a few generations. This would, of course, require complete cooperation of breeders, which could be achieved through a mass educational program by the breed's parent club.

Since there is no guarantee that in five years the Michigan study will produce the expected results, it is important that the DCA examine its options on the bladder stone problem and move appropriately, as it has on deafness. Uric acid acting on the epithelial tissue causes bladder stones. Reducing the tendency of Dalmatians to produce uric acid could also reduce the frequency of bladder stones and the related pain suffered by some of our Dalmatians.

HIP DYSPLASIA CONTROL

Although the Dalmatian is not among the breeds that routinely turn up with hip dysplasia, there is enough of it to cause conscientious breeders to have their dogs X-rayed and OFA certified. While this is no guarantee that the get or produce of a certified dog will not have hip dysplasia, it does give some indication of the probability of this occurring.

From January 1974 through July 1990 there were 950 Dalmatians evaluated by the Orthopedic Foundation for Animals. Only 6.8 percent of those were dysplastic. The phenotype distribution in breeds of dogs with 100 or more evaluations shows that 8.7 percent of the Dals were rated excellent, 66.3 percent scored good, 17.9 percent rated fair, 0.4 percent were borderline, 5.6 percent were mild and 1.1 percent were moderate. No Dal rated severe.

12

Showing the Dalmatian

WHEN PREPARING your Dalmatian for the show ring, you will want to groom the dog properly. Usually the whiskers are clipped and any scraggly areas around the tuck-up, the "pants" and cowlicks are trimmed away. The idea is to present as smooth an outline as possible. If you have not trimmed your dog, don't worry so long as it is clean. Many Dals are shown untrimmed and unclipped in the rough area. But there are few more unpleasant sights than a dirty Dalmatian in the show ring.

It is a good idea to carry a tote bag equipped with a damp sponge and a towel, among other things, so that you can clean off any extraneous dirt picked up from travel or exercise pens. The short coat will respond to a quick sponging and toweling. This is one of the plus values of the Dal as a show dog. Be sure the visit to the exercise area has produced results. The dog will show better and will not embarrass you in the ring. You should be at the show approximately one hour before your scheduled judging time so that you can check in with the ring steward, get your armband and observe the judge in the ring, his movement pattern and how he goes about examining the dog. Of course, if yours is the first dog in the ring the first thing in the morning, the judge will explain what he wants you to do. Be sure to carry out all the judge's instructions to the best of your ability.

If your dog is absent (has been "pulled" or is just not being shown that day), report this to the ring steward so that the poor soul is not searching all around the ringside for the missing dog. Watch the ring steward so that you will be on hand when your class is called. There is nothing more annoying to a ring steward than the exhibitor who has picked up an armband, stands close by but in conversation with other exhibitors and ignores the time to enter the ring. It happens at every show, in almost every breed. The ring stewards are exhausted by the end of the day because of nonheeding exhibitors.

When you enter the ring, take your dog to the position the steward points out to you. It may be the other side of the ring, or it may be just inside the gate. The judge will have instructed the steward where he wants his dogs set up. Set up your dog and wait for further instructions from the judge. If you are first in line and the judge asks you to lead the class around the ring (and this is done counterclockwise) make sure all the handlers in the ring are ready to take off when you do. It is bad manners and looks silly for a single entry to whip about the ring when the rest of the class is just preparing to do so.

After the dogs have been moved together, the judge will examine each entry and move it individually. Be sure to move your dog on a loose lead. Practice at home before the show so that your dog will move with you at a good pace, a pace you have determined in practice as the one that shows off your dog's movement to best advantage. Practice having your dog walk into a show pose so that when you return to the judge after your individual gaiting your dog will show himself to be the winner you know it is. If you are in the line, remember to allow space in front of you so that you are not running up on the dog in front of yours. Remember, you are the only one who can determine this space; the dog in front cannot.

When you move your dog in the ring do not give the command "Heel!" This is an Obedience command. When you move your dog in the show ring it is not heeling. In fact, a dog that moved in the Obedience ring the way dogs are moved in the show ring would fail the heeling exercise. Find another word such as "Show!" or "Gait!" or just "Let's Go!" Remember, there are some breed judges who have little or no interest in Obedience and when they hear an obedience command they are turned off. This shouldn't be true, but unfortunately it is.

Most people prefer a show lead. It isn't necessary, however, to use one. Some people use a simple choke chain, the one with tiny links, and others use a martingale-type lead, one that gives a little more control of the dog than the plain nylon show lead. Make sure it fits well up about the ears from around the neck. In any event, practice with all these leads and find the one with which you and your Dal are the most comfortable. Do not "string up" your dog on any lead. Showing in a relaxed fashion will put your dog at ease and it will show naturally.

The subject of dress is also of importance. Do not wear anything that will flap, such as a loose jacket, vest or coat. Any clothing flapping at the dog as you move detracts from the dog. Women should never enter the ring in high heels, which are dangerous and noisy on hard surfaces at indoor shows. Flat-heeled shoes with rubber soles are best for either sex. And choose your color with care. A checked skirt or pants will not give your dog a good background. Solid colors of red, blue, green or even black are much better. If you are showing a liver

Dalmatian you may choose green or brown, as they probably show off the dog to best advantage. Some people use colored show leads to emphasize the color of the dog. A red lead on a black-spotted dog is very pretty. A green or brown show lead on the liver-spotted variety is most attractive. A white lead is always in good taste.

When people start becoming involved with Dalmatians there is a tendency to make every accessory a spotted one. Some have worn polka-dotted dresses to show their dogs. This is a poor idea, as the spots on the dress detract from the dog. The dog is being shown, not the handler. Some enthusiastic people have had their automobiles painted white with black spots. A newspaper photo of a young man in a convertible with his Dal in Rhode Island during the 1950s attracted a great deal of attention all over the United States as it made the wire services. At the present time some have spotted their station wagons and one enthusiast went so far as to paint his house white with black spots.

When Harland and Lois Meistrell were doing a great deal of training of Dals, they painted their fence on the inside of the yard to match the dogs. It was a trompe l'oeil sort of thing and it was difficult to distinguish the dogs from the fence. Photos of a dog going over the broad jump against the fence also made the wire services and caused interest and amusement all over the nation.

We must remember when showing that the dog is the spotted wonder, not the handler. Do nothing in the ring to detract from the dog. Even a dangling leash can be annoying to the judge. As you move with your dog the movement of the end of the leash can catch the eye of the judge and so move his attention away from your dog momentarily.

If you are so fortunate as to be placed in a class, anyplace, say something to let the judge know you understood his placement. Signal with a nod, a wave or a "thank you." Then move to the proper ring number immediately. Stand so that the judge can see your armband and can mark his book properly.

Ring manners are important. They are nothing more than good manners in any given situation. Remember that showing dogs is a sport and good sportsmanship should prevail.

13

Obedience

THE WORKING DALMATIAN is a joy to behold in the Obedience ring. Many people feel that the Dalmatian is a difficult dog to train. The true problem is not with the dog but with the handler. You must be smarter than your dog to do well in obedience. The Dalmatian is as easily trained as a Poodle or a Golden Retriever if the handler will take the time to study his dog and learn its own particular idiom. This is platitudinous in itself, as most dogs have their own set ways of doing things and you have to learn what these are.

Once you and your Dal click, there will be few problems in training. A Dal is quick to learn and retains lessons well. As with most dogs, doing something twice the same way is a habit. If, in training, the handler will take the time to make sure that the dog *cannot* make a mistake, à la the Pearsall method of using gadgets to help, the dog will work well and without goofs.

THE EARLY YEARS

When the sport of Obedience was introduced into this country in 1933 by Mrs. Whitehouse Walker, former owner of Carillon Kennels, Standard Poodle breeders, many people became interested in it. Before this time Obedience training had long been known and practiced in Europe. Dogs were used in police work and the armies had also made use of canines as guard and sentry dogs.

The American Kennel Club adopted Obedience in 1936 and almost immediately the Dal people jumped into this phase of the sport. The first UDT dog was Io, owned by Harland and Lois Meistrell, who trained and worked Dals in obedience from the inception of this side of the sport, winning frequently. The first Ch. UDT Dal came from the Cleveland area and was named Ch. Duke of Gervais. The interesting thing about these early UDT dogs in this country is that they were both ten years old at the time their training was started. Who says you can't teach an old dog new tricks?

Of course the exercises were different back then, and so was the scoring. In those days a tracking test was required in order to obtain the coveted UD. Now a successful Tracking Dog can earn a Tracking title without any other Obedience title. At the present time we have a number of UDT Dalmatians and a number of Ch. UD Dals.

Another exercise that has since disappeared was the "speak" on command. On signal from the handler the dog was required to bark and continue to do so as often as the handler gave the signal, the judge determining when to stop the "speaking."

The DCA added Obedience classes to its specialties almost as soon as the AKC added Obedience to its jurisdiction. Among the early exhibitors were the Meistrells. They seemed to win at the DCA shows with regularity, as did Kenneth Naumer with his Dal Checkers, who became a UDT dog.

Among the early afficionados of both sides of the sport, Obedience and conformation, were Mrs. Wilbur Dewell, Mrs. Lee Ramsey, Mrs. Paul Moore and Mary Munro Smith.

Perhaps there is something in the physical and mental makeup of Dalmatians that makes them eager to work at an older age. In March 1977 an eight-year-old Dalmatian bitch owned by Harry Lockhard competed in the Los Angeles Schutzhund Club trial and was awarded NASA AD, or endurance test. Her name is Der Heidelberg of Linfield, CDX, PGE, AD. The test required the dog to go twelve and a half miles in two hours and still be able to do some Obedience work, including jumping a forty-inch jump. Heidi was the first Dal to earn this degree in either the United States or Canada.

Other well-known Obedience dogs in the early years were Ch. Whiteside Sioux Oros, UD, and Tihera, UDT, an unregistered Dal from English breeding. These dogs were trained by the Meistrells.

When the war broke out a number of dogs were needed for Dogs for Defense. The Long Island Kennel Club was active in this effort, and in cooperation with the Long Island Dog Training Club and some other training groups they organized a group of amateur trainers to train guard dogs. Lois Meistrell was among those trainers.

Although many of the clubs continued to hold their shows annually, much of the dog activity was slowed down because of the war effort. When the K-9 Corps was formed by the armed services, Harland Meistrell was tapped to assist in this project and Dogs for Defense became a supplier of suitable dogs to the K-9 Corps.

Mrs. Bonney of Tally Ho Kennels gave a Dalmatian called Hector. The Meistrells trained this dog for the corps and he was so quick to learn and so

Lois Meistrell with Whiteside Sioux Oros, UD.

Dalmatians were used as war dogs.

A bevy of Quaker's Acre dogs.

intelligent that he acquired two legs on his CD and seven points toward his championship before going on active duty as a guard dog for the army. He spent the war patrolling an oil refinery in New Jersey. When he returned to Mrs. Bonney after the war he was still an affectionate dog. All thoughts of his finishing his championship had to be discarded as his shoulders were completely "loaded" with muscle. He did, however, manage to get his third leg on his CD. He did not have much difficulty in returning to civilian life except that he objected to anyone holding any object in hand. All gardeners and staff members at Tally Ho had to be warned to drop rakes and hoes until Hector had passed by. Newcomers were always treated as enemies by Hector until they were introduced to the dog and he was convinced that they were acceptable.

At one time Quaker's Acre, Mary Munro Smith's famous kennel in Florida, held the record for the most champions with Obedience titles in the United States. Ch. Quaker's Acre Ditto, CDX, a Velvet Frank son out of Quaker Oats Pirette, was Mrs. Smith's first Obedience dog. He qualified for his CD in three consecutive shows, earning a High in Trial (HIT) in two of them. At the same time he was being shown in conformation. He earned his CDX in three consecutive shows with all scores above 195. At one show he was HIT and Group I, quite an accomplishment.

In a different section of the country we find the Sullivans pioneering in the field of Obedience, while showing in the breed ring. Again the connection with horses is clear. Bob Sullivan was a trainer at the Aksarben Stables in Omaha in the years before World War II. The stable dogs were two liver Dals named Whiskey and Soda, and Bob admired them very much. During the war Bob was in the service and while stationed at Fort Knox the Sullivans purchased their first Dalmatian, Maggie. She was an unregistered bitch. After the war the Sullivans moved to Tulsa and purchased Duchess of Dal Downs. This was the foundation of Dal Downs Kennels. Duchess came from the Surbers in Ohio. Bob trained her through her CDX.

In those years it was difficult to find Obedience Trials in the area, but the Sullivans kept trying. They bought a bitch, Pamela of Dal Downs, from Mrs. Kane's Dal Dale Kennels in Illinois. Pam was trained and made it through to UD. She was the first UD dog of any breed in the state of Oklahoma. It was difficult to obtain the UD for Pam because very few trials had the required three dogs competing in the Utility class.

Cyde Beebe, owner of Ch. Rovingdale's Impudent Ingenue, after winning two Bests in Show with her, allowed the Sullivans to have her. Imp received her CD in 1957. The Sullivans earned innumerable CDs and CDXs on Dalmatians. In the early 1960s they established Sandstone German Shepherds and accumulated nine CDs, three CDXs and one UD, plus two tracking titles in German Shepherds.

But the Dalmatians came back to their rightful place with the Sullivans. In 1972 they bought Dal Downs Dicie of Shadodal. Bob completed her Obedience titles and Marge finished her championship. She was the first bitch to be a Ch. UDT in the history of Dalmatians in the United States.

DUAL-RING DALS

People ask what makes a good Obedience dog. Actually, if you take time to think about this, the qualities needed to succeed in the Obedience ring are exactly the same as those needed in the show ring. You need a dog properly constructed if you are planning to have it jump, run and retrieve. A dog with straight shoulders is going to resent jumping after a short time. Landing on straight shoulders will pound its back teeth and it will begin to resist the command to jump. A dog with good shoulder layback is built to receive the landing; the construction of his forearm, upper arm and shoulder will cushion the landing and prevent pounding. Its rear should be a good one, too, to give it the proper spring needed for a jump.

Of course, not all dogs in Obedience Trials are worthy of the conformation ring, but it would be better if they were.

Notice the number of dogs that are competing in both rings. A dog that is properly trained for Obedience is easier to handle in the show ring. Don't walk into the show ring with your dog after one or two lessons in an Obedience class and wonder why the dog sits. It is too soon to show in the breed ring after starting an obedience program. And don't tell your dog to heel in the breed ring. The movement required in judging conformation is not heeling. If a dog were to do the heeling exercise in Obedience moving as it does in conformation, it would probably fail.

After a few weeks your dog should and most probably will recognize the difference in collars and leashes. These are intelligent animals. They know.

ADVANCED DEGREES

The interest in Obedience competition is so keen today that the American Kennel Club has now introduced an Obedience Trial Champion (OTCH) title. In order to win this title a dog must have won 100 points in competition toward it. The number of points available depends upon the number of dogs competing, as in the conformation point system. The dog must have been awarded a Utility title before it starts accumulating Obedience championship points.

In addition to the 100 points, the dog must have won a first place in straight Utility or Utility B with a minimum of three dogs competing, must have won a first place in Open B with at least six dogs in competition and a third first place must have been won under the conditions of the first two. There must have been three different judges officiating over the wins.

After winning an OTCH title the dog may continue to accumulate points and the dog having the highest number of points at the end of the year will receive recognition from the American Kennel Club by being published in the *Gazette*. The dog will also receive an award from the Quaker Oats Company that is presented at the Obedience cocktail party sponsored by the Association of Obedience Clubs and Judges, at the time of Westminster in New York.

Ch. Dal Downs Dicie of Shadodal, UDT

In addition, the Gaines Dog Food Company has for several years sponsored the Obedience Classic. Dogs are required to have accumulated scores above a certain level to be eligible. Three shows are held in two days—a red, white and blue show. The scores are tallied and averaged and the top dog becomes just that, Top Dog, for the year. Regionals are held in various sections of the United States in preparation for the Classic itself.

Earning a UDT title is something to be proud of and earning a UDT and a championship is even more of an accomplishment. To date, four Dals have acquired the dual titles. The four Dalmatians with Ch. UDT are Ch. Duke of Gervais, owned and trained by Maurice Gervais in 1946; Ch. Dal Downs Dicie of Shadodal, owned and trained by Bob and Marge Sullivan in 1976; Ch. Cal-Dal Chocolate Chip, owned by Jon and Karen Mett; and Ch. Spotted Dapper Dan, the most recent to join these special ranks, owned by Edward J. and Mary Ann Murphy. He received the final title, UDT, in 1979.

Obedience buffs will tell you that getting a 200 score is almost an impossibility and a dog that has earned a 200 is always looked upon with awe. In California Jere Bates showed a dog named Monti's Mister Mickey, UD. Mister Mickey not only scored 200 in Utility, but he acquired a total of nine 200s. This was accomplished during the 1960s and covered virtually the same exercises that are in use today.

After Mr. Meistrell's death, Mrs. Meistrell established a memorial award offered through the Dalmatian Club of America for a number of years. The Harland Meistrell Memorial Trophy winners include Princess Cinder Babe, CDX, owned by Irene Brink; Belle Monti's Little Freckle, UD, owned by Sandra Hodson; Cinders Chief, owned by R. F. Noonan; and Belle Monti's Mister Mickey, owned by Jere Bates. The only records on the Harland Meistrell Memorial Trophy winners show that three of the four dogs were from California.

The first Dal to score a perfect 200 points in Obedience was Lady Jane, owned by Naomi Radler, winning Novice B at Garden City, New York. The next day, Monty, owned by Mr. and Mrs. Melvin Lord, scored 200 at a trial in Oakland, California.

Ch. Tally Ho Black Eyed Susan, CDX, was the first Dal champion to attain an Obedience degree. Susan was owned by Mrs. Bonney, who turned her over to the Meistrells for training. When war broke out the bitch was returned to Tally Ho, as the Meistrells were deep in training dogs for wartime duties.

Obedience continues to claim the attention of a great many Dal breeders and exhibitors. More of the regional Dalmatian clubs have qualified for Obedience classes at their shows. The entry may not be large to start, but it will build. Despite the fact that many all-breed trainers are of the opinion that Dalmatians are difficult to train, many of those in Obedience competition are winning and winning well. Dals have an idiom all their own. They are probably showing their English heritage, as they resent being told to do something. Ask them nicely and they will comply. This seems to be the difference between the training in this country and in the United Kingdom. Most of our training started with German immigrants who came to this country after World War I, having served in the German army. They were quite strict in their training methods. But in England the gentle approach has always been the rule and, in the end, their dogs seem to be better trained than ours. It may take a little longer to perfect the training, but it is a better training. The really successful Dalmatian trainers in this country use the gentle touch.

All dogs deserve Obedience training whether for home or for competition. The Dalmatian is no exception, and most love to do the exercises. On the fun side, many of our dogs are allowed the privilege of serving in a team for the scent hurdle races. This is strictly fun. The dogs and the handlers enjoy it, and the audiences from coast to coast go wild with enthusiasm.

The idea of teams in Dalmatian Obedience work is not new, although many will be surprised to learn this. In the early years of Obedience in the 1940s, there was a team in the New England area composed of Lois Meistrell, Virginia Lindsay (later Prescott) and Wendell Sammet.

On the West Coast the Coach 'n Four Dalmatian Obedience Club was founded in 1953 by a group of breeders from the San Fernando Valley. At first it was called the Dalmatian Forum. It proposed to study genetic and obedience problems. In January 1955 the members applied to the AKC for recognition as an Obedience club. From this group they formed a drill team that performed at many places in the southern California area. The initial performance was at the DCSC's futurity match. It is too bad that this club has dropped from the Dalmatian picture.

In the early 1950s three young teenagers developed a complete act with their Dalmatians in the northern California area. They were Mary and Nancy Harbison and Trudy Caddel. Only one of the Dals had had Obedience training and one of them was past six years of age before the vaudeville-type training was started. These young ladies trained their dogs to roll barrels separately and together, climb ladders, walk tightropes, stand on broom handles elevated at least four feet from the ground and perform a variety of other entertaining feats.

Dalmatians were used frequently in circuses because of their colorful appearance and their ability to perform circus-type exercises.

At the present time Obedience among Dalmatian fanciers is at its very healthiest, competition being keen and exhibitors having fun. At the 1977 National Specialty show, the Chicagoland Dalmatian Club's show and the Steel City all-breed show—a three day weekend—exhibitors, spectators and judges alike were all dazzled by the performance of a seven-month-old pup in the Novice ring. Dominique's Rusty Nail, owned by Elaine Newman from the Atlanta area, racked up scores of 195, 198 and 197 to earn his CD title and the Dog World Award for his performances. Rarely does one find so young a dog so willing and such a happy, eager worker. This dog completed his UD work in October 1978.

To date there is just one Dalmatian Obedience Trial Champion, known to the Fancy as OTCH Candi's Skagit Belle, owned by Rebecca Jean and Rex Alan

Four generations of obedience-titled Dals

Coachman's Capricorn, CD

Heiloh's Comely Cricket, UDT

115

Auer and bred by Candice L. Jones. Belle's sire was Jaybar's Dally Dalrymple and her dam was Candi's Miss Freckles. Becky Auer finished the OTCH title on Belle in the summer of 1981. The Auers then moved to Guam and Belle was no longer in competition.

There are several other Dals who are getting close to the coveted 100 points to qualify as an OTCH. The point scale for the OTCH is always printed in a show catalog just before the entries.

OBEDIENCE IN RECENT YEARS

Some of the people in Dalmatians who are most interested in Obedience are also breeders, and many of the top breeders got their start in the Obedience ring. Most breeders firmly believe that any dog deserves at least a basic course in Obedience, if only to make it a better canine citizen. Anyone who advises that a dog should not be given Obedience training while it is being shown in the breed ring does the world of dogs a disservice. It is wiser to wait until the dog is steady in the "stand" exercise before rushing into both breed and Obedience. The "stack" can be accomplished by the "stand for examination," one of the basic exercises in the obedience ring.

Prominent among the breeders who are also deeply involved in Obedience is Jim Ham of Sterling Heights, Michigan. Not only is Jim a breeder of Dalmatians, he is also involved in Border Terriers. He is an Obedience and a breed judge as well. Jim and Helen Ham started their career in Dals by purchasing a pet as a birthday present for their five-year-old son. This dog's career spanned nine years. The dog became Am. & Can. Ch. Biscuit Bugatti, Am. & Can. UDT— the first Dal to complete these titles. The Hams have done some breeding and exhibiting in both breeds in which they are interested and plan to continue to do so.

When you keep eight Dalmatians plus a Beagle in the house they had better be obedient dogs or pandemonium will result. This is the pattern at the Murphy household, Touchstone Dalmatians. Cathy, who is Obedience editor of *The Spotter*, is also a licensed chief tester for the American Temperament Test Society, Inc. She believes that if a dog is not trainable and of good temperament, it cannot be a good pet no matter how pretty it may be. Using this philosophy, Cathy and her son, Dan Mazalic, have finished a number of dogs and put Obedience titles on them as well. One of their dogs, Ch. Touchstone's Yosemite Sam, UD, TT, had three HITs at Specialties and several Bests of Breed (BOB) from the classes when he was being campaigned for his championship. In 1984 this dog was rated number one in the Shuman system, in the top ten in all systems and number six in the DCA top ten.

Many people remember Dan as an outstanding junior showman. He went to Westminster for the final competition three times and won his class there one year.

Am. & Can. Ch. Biscuit Bugatti, UDT

Ch. Touchstone's Wheeler Dealer, CDX, TD

Over the years the Touchstone dogs have accumulated more than fifteen champions, one Canadian champion and around forty Obedience titles. This is quite a record for a kennel that breeds one litter a year.

Another kennel that feels that Obedience is very important is the Dapper Dan Dals of Ed and Mary Ann Murphy. They show in both breed and Obedience and feel that such a balance of the two sides of the sport is essential for a good dog. Their Ch. Spotted Dapper Dan, UDT, Can. CDX, was the fourth Dal in the history of the breed to earn these titles, all owner handled. He won both of his majors at Specialty shows and in limited showing became a multi-BOB winner. He lived to be fifteen years old. His enthusiasm and intelligence inspired the Murphys to continue to show in both rings, and they have done so with great success.

Although fate dealt Gilda Tucker of Owens Cross Roads, Alabama, a blow from which she was sure she would never recover, she has managed to come back to her beloved sport of Obedience. Her Touchstone's Hello Holly, UD, was the victim of a hit-and-run driver in front of her new home, with Gilda witnessing the entire scene. This bitch had a remarkable career in the ring. Shown eleven times in Novice, Holly had eleven scores, nine placings and two HITs. That same year she won the Dog World Award in Open and the following year completed her Utility title. The latest hopeful is Ch. Hollytree's Copper Chelsea, CDX, co-owned with Mavis Barr.

One hundred one Dalmatians earned Obedience titles in 1989, some winning more than one for a total of 141 titles. The number of Dalmatians competing in the Obedience ring seems to increase with every passing day. There are many people involved in both sides of the sport.

Jon Mett is well known for his dogs in both Obedience and in the breed ring. He is also an Obedience judge. In 1989 his dog M & M's Hobo of Bearded Oaks, UD, co-owned with Susan Brooksbank, won the Highest Combined (HC) score, which included a first in Utility for some OTCH points. The dog has close to fifty of the coveted points as of this writing.

Sue MacMillan has both Obedience-titled dogs and a tracking title on one of the Paisley dogs, either owned or co-owned by her.

The top Obedience winner for 1989 was Lidgate's Charles of Seaspot, CDX. This dog is owned by Linda and Jim Fulks and Mark Sachau. In gaining his Open title the dog also won a Dog World Award (three legs without a failure and scores over 195). Catherine Cookson's Dals garnered three CD titles and a UD. Sharon Harvey won a CD and a CDX on Admiral Chelsea Magee in one year and managed to make the top ten averages in both levels.

Tracking has become an activity for some of the Obedience people. Jeannine Navratil acquired a TD on her dog, Touchstone's Winning Colors; Elaine Dotson's Benjamin Franklin Adair, CD, became a TDX; and Libby Simendinger's Libby Fireplace Popcorn also added a TDX to her CDX. It is not necessary to have a CD on a dog to earn a TD. A dog may have the TD long before it competes for the CD title.

Kathryn Braund's Rough Rider Dalmatians are still very much involved in Obedience. Kathryn is the author of a series of books on Obedience training as well as coauthor of a book on the Portuguese Water Dog. The Braunds are breeders of this interesting breed as well as Dalmatians. Rough Rider Dals and Porties are to be found all over the United States in both breed and Obedience rings. Kathryn has always stressed the importance of training for both rings.

Ch. Spotted Dapper Dan, UDT

14

The Dalmatian: Hunter, Herder, Coach Dog

ALMOST EVERYONE who has been around Dals has noticed the manner in which they stop and hold up one front foot. This is undoubtedly a carry-over from their Pointer forebears. Dals will point in the field.

So many people feel that it is difficult to train a Dalmatian to do anything. In each case where we hear a tale of woe, we are usually able to trace the problem to the fact that the trainer has spoiled the dog, has not been firm with the dog or has expected the dog to catch on without getting through to it what is wanted.

Dalmatians are easily trained, and it isn't necessary to train them at an early age. As we have reported, the first champion UD Dalmatian in the United States was ten years old before his owner started training him in Obedience.

The Fulkses of Medford, Oregon, train their Dals for hunting. Because of the Dal's natural flushing abilities, the Fulkses have been most successful using them on pheasants. They have also used the dogs on doves. A hunting Dal has no aversion to water. Dals will retrieve a bird that falls in the water as quickly as they will retrieve on land.

Walter Back of Zion, Illinois, was using Dals in the field fifty years ago. Kathryn Braund's husband, Buzz, is a hunter and has used their Dals on his hunting trips. There are others who have found that the Dal can keep up with

Watson demonstrating steady to flush and shot

The send

The retrieve

Delivery to hand

Water retrieve

Trixie the Jungle Dog

Shorthairs, Wirehairs, Pointers and any of the retrievers. The Dalmatian is a well-rounded dog.

Walter Back, in speaking of the Dalmatian as a hunting breed, says, "They are intelligent dogs, have great stamina, common sense, are alert, have good noses and are aggressive enough to make good field dogs." He also points out the advantages of the Dalmatian coat in the field. Because it is short, burrs and stickers do not adhere to it, and if the dog gets wet, the coat dries quickly.

Walter counsels that it usually takes two to three years to develop a good hunting Dal. Field trial enthusiasts will tell you that it takes two to three years to develop *any* field dog.

In choosing a Dal for hunting you must pick one that is interested in the sport. Some Dals have little or no interest in birds, game, varmints or whatever. A Dal that is interested in hunting birds can be trained. But developing a hunting partner requires a training program—instinct can go just so far.

Dalmatians are generally flushers rather than pointers, although they do fancy themselves as pointers. It is easier to train them as a flushing dog than as a Pointer.

A theory as to why the dogs were relegated to the stable and thus developed an affinity with horses is that these dogs were more difficult to train than setters, retrievers and spaniels. Pointers and setters were easily trained to handle their chores in the field. And this is not to say that training a Dalmatian for field work is especially difficult. Training a Dalmatian for field is slightly different from the usual training for hunting dogs.

In England the gun dog was the all-important member of the squire's retinue. The Dal, resembling the Pointer, was thought to be a Pointer and was treated as such. Apparently, lacking imagination, no one took the time to make the discovery that the Dal is a better flushing dog than a Pointer, and so the dogs were sent to the stables where they became companions of the horses and developed their own thing—coaching.

In addition, Dals make excellent herding dogs. They have been used as cattle dogs in various areas of the United States. They nip at the heels of the steers who are recalcitrant about returning to the barn. Several reports have indicated that Dalmatians have also been seen sheep herding.

Although we are all aware that Dals are versatile dogs, few of us have ever thought of them as "jungle dogs." Irishman's Lady Trixie, owned by Glenys and Tom Keith, is just that. Tom has been in the U.S. Navy for almost thirty years and for most of that time has been a member of an elite group of commandos known as the Navy Seal (Sea, Air and Land) Team. He had four tours of duty in Vietnam and his specialty is jungle warfare, weapons and explosives.

When Trixie was six months old Tom took her with him to the Seal Camp at A.P. Hill in Virginia, where he would conduct courses on machine guns, low rockets, mines, etc. Needless to say, loud noises, tracers and explosives do not bother Trixie. She proved herself to be a great hunter, killing squirrels and groundhogs and once almost had a wild turkey. She ended that hunt with a mouthful of tail feathers.

Later the Keiths were stationed in Puerto Rico. Trixie finished her championship there but continued her sorties with Tom into the jungle, where she became camp guard, chief rat killer and scout dog for platoons going out on night ambushes. She also accompanied groups on their sneak beach attacks in small rubber Zodiacs and would swim to shore when the command was given. She has also flown in a Black Hawk helicopter. Trixie is a true jungle dog, able to go through heavy cover and to complete the tasks assigned.

This remarkable Dal has also done well as a dam, having produced several litters that had some top winning produce.

Trixie with Seal platoon

15

Foundation Kennels

FORTY YEARS AGO there were a number of well-known kennels and breeders who have since virtually disappeared from the scene. A few of their lines are being carried on by other fanciers, and there are a number of kennels that have been in existence all this time and are continuing to breed and exhibit.

At the end of World War II there were Dalmatians bearing the prefixes of Windholme, Gedney Farms, Edgecomb, Cress Brook, Tattoo, Toad Harbor, Hackney Way, Fyrthorne, Rabbit Run, Tally Ho and Braintree. There were others, of course, but dogs from these lineages seem to have lingered longer in pedigrees than any of the others. Whiteside Sioux, Roadcoach, Reigate, Kingcrest, Coachman, Tioga, Dalmatia, Dalquest, Green Starr, Albelarm, In the Valley, Four-in-Hand, Quaker's Acre, Pryor Creek, Williamsdale, Tomalyn Hill, Dal Duchy, Blackpool, Crestview and Long Last had also either been in existence before or started up about then. Some of these kennels are no longer in operation. In many instances the owners passed away and the kennels were dispersed. Coachman, Tioga, Dalmatia, Green Starr, Albelarm and Long Last are still producing fine Dalmatians. Long Last was the prefix used by the late Lorraine Donahue. Mike and Chris Jackson inherited Lorraine's stock and are continuing to breed Long Last dogs, as is Esquire Kennels.

In the early 1950s a number of new breeders and kennels were added to the list. In 1955 there were 172 members of the Dalmatian Club of America. In 1971 the membership totaled 179. At that time *The Spotter* was turned into a magazine instead of a brief news bulletin. The only way to receive the magazine was to be a member of the DCA.

Ch. Tally Ho's Sirius

Ch. Beau of Hollyroyde

DCA membership currently totals more than 1,000. This is quite remarkable when you consider that at its founding the club was limited to fifty members. The membership was opened in 1937, however not much happened during the war years. No new members were named until 1941. Until about 1970 there was a slow but steady growth, which has since ballooned to enormous numbers for a breed that until recent years ranked about thirty-second on the AKC list. It is predicted that the breed will reach the top ten during the 1990s.

It would be impossible to cover all the breeders and exhibitors in a book such as this. The DCA publishes a directory of its membership. Not all Dalmatian breeders are members of the DCA, however, and not all DCA members are breeders, but people interested in the breed can use the directory to locate Dalmatian fanciers in their geographic area. The members are listed by state, and many newcomers to the breed have been able to locate breeders in this way. Some of the kennels and breeders who have been around for a number of years include Dauntless, Enchanted, Sugarfrost, Canalside, Bellringer, Spottsboro, Rolenet, Little Slam and many more. A few of the prominent early kennels are described in the following sections.

TALLY HO

A very important kennel of the past, one that contributed a great deal to Dalmatians in this country, was Tally Ho, Mrs. L. W. Bonney's famous kennel. Mrs. Bonney started in Dalmatians when she was a young girl. Her home, located in Flushing, New York, had been the family estate for three generations. In the late 1930s, with the coming of the World's Fair, Mrs. Bonney decided that her home no longer had a "country" feel to it and she selected some ninety acres at Oyster Bay as the site of her new kennel and moved to it in 1938. She named the estate Sunstar Hill. By this time Mrs. Bonney was also well known as a breeder of fine Chow Chows and later became involved in Poodles.

Her kennels produced numerous champions and is one of two kennels to have owned a three-time National Specialty winner, Ch. Tally Ho Last of Sunstar.

Mrs. Bonney had a breeding program that followed closely one employed by many other great breeders of the world. This policy provides for the use of a distinct outcross every few generations. Mrs. Bonney felt that in this way a line would never really wear itself out. She made numerous trips to the British Isles, going every two years until the outbreak of World War II, and she imported many good dogs. Her last import was the impressive Duxforham Yessam Marquis. Mark was Mrs. Bonney's last champion, as she died in January 1967.

She was known worldwide as an excellent judge of Dalmatians, Chow Chows and Poodles. At her last assignment, Steel City Kennel Club in Gary, Indiana, she awarded Best in Show to a Dalmatian, Ch. Rockledge Rumble, owned by Gloria Schwartz.

As secretary-treasurer of the Dalmatian Club of America for more than fifty years, Mrs. Bonney was on top of all matters pertaining to the breeding, showing and judging of Dalmatians. If anyone ever deserved the title "Mrs. Dalmatian," Mrs. Bonney did.

FOUR-IN-HAND

One of the most influential early kennels was Leo Meeker's Le Mel, later renamed Four-in-Hand. Mr. Meeker, who lived in California, imported the very best of English bloodlines and established a breeding program on the West Coast that has yet to be equaled.

As a child Mr. Meeker had had Dalmatians and in the mid-1920s he decided to exhibit in the California shows. He found the entries very low and the quality of the specimens on exhibit poor. He purchased some dogs from the famous Cress Brook Kennel in Michigan and some from Ruth Kane's Dal Dale Kennels in Illinois. He then imported a bitch from Mr. Wardell, the English champion, Queen of Trumps. She finished in the United States easily.

Later he imported a fine dog, Four-in-Hand Mischief. This dog became an American and Canadian champion. He was shown from coast to coast and established the record for Best in Show wins for a Dalmatian. His show record includes fifty Bests of Breed, thirty-five Group Is, eight Group IIs, two Group IIIs and one Group IV with a mighty eighteen Bests in Show.

WILLIAMSDALE

A kennel established in 1938 and closed in 1976 is probably the one that has had the most influence on Dalmatians throughout the United States. That kennel was Williamsdale in Cincinnati, established by Charles Williams. He employed Martin Milet as kennel manager and handler. Together they imported a great many dogs and bred many great dogs.

In 1955 Mr. Williams sold his kennel to Martin Milet, who continued to breed and show dogs until his death in 1969. The kennel continued under the management of his sister-in-law, May Milet, until the end of 1976. Because of illness Mrs. Milet discontinued the kennel.

Although most people import bitches for foundation stock, Milet imported two great studs, Am. & Can. Ch. Elmcroft Coacher and Ch. Igor of Kye of Williamsdale. The former was imported from England in dam by Ray McLaughlin of Stratford, Ontario. After the dog had finished his Canadian championship Milet bought him and brought him to the United States where he completed his American championship with all majors. An outstanding sire, he accounted for twenty-seven champions, quite a record for the late 1940s and early 1950s.

Igor sired sixteen champion get. While a great dog and a fine sire, he didn't

Ch. Four-in-Hand Mischief

Ch. Four-in-Hand Blackberry

Ch. Elmcroft Coacher

Ch. Igor of Kye of Williamsdale

seem to have the prepotency as a stud dog that marked Coacher's get, although he sired Ch. Williamsdale Rocky, a National Specialty winner.

In the days when handlers were permitted to judge specialty shows Milet was tapped to judge the DCA show in 1957. He had won the breed at the Specialty with his homebred Ch. Williamsdale Rocky in 1953.

Mr. Milet didn't limit his imports to males, of course. He brought in a number of dogs from England and Canada. His great brace of imports was made up of Am. & Eng. Ch. Penny Parade of Williamsdale and Ch. Colonsay Tantivey Claudia. Other imports included Eng. & Am. Ch. Beau of Hollyroyde.

The foundation bitch of this kennel was Her Majesty of Williamsdale. Although she was never shown, she was a great brood bitch and produced a number of champions.

REIGATE

Reigate Kennels played a great part in the world of Dalmatians during the years it was active in breeding. Mary Leigh Lane and George Lane and their sister, Billie Close, did much to keep the Dalmatian in the winner's circle. Some of their greats include Ch. Reigate's Bold Venture, Ch. Reigate's All Clear, Ch. Reigate's Remus, Ch. Reigate's Native Dancer, Ch. Reigate's Double Trouble, Ch. Reigate's Flag Drill, Ch. Reigate's Miss Springtime, Ch. Reigate's Count Fleet, Ch. Reigate's Regimental, Ch. Reigate's Lothario, Ch. Reigate's Dress Parade, Ch. Reigate's Souvenir and several Reigate dogs that were not finished as champions but contributed a lot to the breed, including Reigate's Tracery, Reigate's Daltina, Reigate's Flora Temple and Reigate's Star Pilot. All these names pop up in extended pedigrees of many of the dogs of today.

Mrs. Lane was great to talk to about Dals. If someone said that a particular bitch or dog did this or that, Mrs. Lane replied, "Must have such-and-such a dog behind her." And careful check of the pedigree would reveal that Mrs. Lane's conjecture was correct. When the Lanes died, their kennel was closed, and thus the dog world lost a wonderful part of it, Reigate Kennels. Few, if any, domestic Dal pedigrees are without at least one Reigate dog in the background.

ROADCOACH

In Dalmatians there are a number of breeders who started out "way back when," some before World War II, and are still in the Fancy. One such kennel is Roadcoach in Dover, Massachusetts. No one can remember Dalmatians without a Roadcoach Kennel in the picture.

Mary Powers's family owned a stable of fine horses. Through the horses Mary met Alfred Barrett, who later became her husband. Together they established Roadcoach Kennels. Looking through pedigrees one is impressed with the

Ch. Reigate's Bold Venture

Ch. Roadcoach Tioga Too, CD

number of times the prefix Roadcoach appears. Although the kennel was established in the 1930s the prefix was not registered with the American Kennel Club until 1945.

So many of the New England breeders started with a purchase from Roadcoach that it is impossible to name them all. The Barretts both became breed judges and both passed on the entries of the National Specialty twice. After Mr. Barrett died, Mary continued on alone. During the 1950s the Barretts also became interested in Poodles and the Roadcoach prefix has become one to reckon with in that breed.

Dalquest, Marjorie Van der Veer's kennel, Dalmatia, Wendell Sammet's establishment, the Sittingers and many others were all helped by Mrs. Barrett and Mrs. Bonney in the start of their kennels.

COACHMAN

Mr. and Mrs. William Fetner established Coachman Kennels in St. Louis in the late 1940s and registered their prefix with the American Kennel Club in 1951. Here is another kennel that had an interest in horses as well as in dogs. And the interest in both continues.

When Jean and Bill Fetner were married, Jean had a Dalmatian that she had acquired from the Kingcrest Kennels of Dr. and Mrs. George King. They purchased several Dalmatians without a great deal of success until they found Chips—Ch. Fobette's Frishka, CD, the foundation of Coachman breeding. Chips is behind every dog they have ever bred.

Ch. Fobette's Frishka was a magnificent specimen of the breed and although she was not campaigned she managed to gain four Group Is and earned her Companion Dog title with Jean Fetner handling.

Coachman breeding has produced some of the top winners of the Dalmatian world. Four DCA Specialty winners came from this kennel: Ch. Coachman's Classic in 1958; Ch. Coachman's Callisto in 1964; Ch. Lord Jim in 1970 with Best of Opposite Sex going to Ch. Coachman's Carte Blanche, a father-daughter combination; and Ch. Coachman's Canicula in 1973. Callisto is also one of the three Dalmatians to win the Group at Westminster. A note of interest: Jean and Bill did not own any of these winners at the time of the win, the only Fetner name of ownership being on Carte Blanche, who belonged to a Fetner son, Jay.

Coachman Kennels, which was located in St. Louis for more than forty years, has moved to a magnificent estate in Rocheport, Missouri, on the Missouri River. Coachman Kennels in Dallas is still in the hands of Dr. Chris and Phyllis Fetner and they continue to breed and to show fine Dals.

Jean and Bill still have some fine dogs and continue to show and to breed. They can be very proud of their dogs. Many people speak with pride of having ''Coachman bloodlines'' in their Dals.

Ch. Fobette's Frishka, CD

Ch. Coachman's Carte Blanche

Family portrait

Ch. Fobette's Fanfare, CDX

Ch. Coachman's Chuck-a-Luck

PRYOR CREEK

Pryor Creek, the Treen prefix, owes much to its association with Coachman Kennels. Ch. Fobette's Fanfare, later CDX, was acquired from a Louisville dentist. Pepper, as he was known, had been previously owned and finished by the Fetners. He became the foundation stud of Pryor Creek, using a carefully worked out inbreeding program. This dog seemed to have prepotency in pigment, as he never sired a dog with an unrimmed eye or an unfilled nose. Through a selective breeding program the great Ch. Coachman's Chuck-a-Luck was produced.

A son of Pepper and a daughter of Pepper out of different bitches were bred to produce a suitable bitch to be bred back to Pepper. This second mating did not produce a great show winner and producer. It did, however, produce Rosie, Pryor Creek's Yaupon Rose, who was a delightful bitch to live with. Rosie preferred hunting or fishing to most activities, but she was quite willing to have puppies.

When the Treen family found that it had to move back to the Milwaukee area because Mr. Treen's employer so decreed, the number of dogs in the kennel had to be decreased. Rosie found a good home with the Smiths in St. Louis and she was left there on condition that she be bred to Coachman's Clotheshorse. This dog was an excellent coach dog whose mother had stepped on him when he was a tiny puppy. The resulting injury to his foot gave him a peculiar gait and he could not be shown. He did a fair amount of siring of excellent puppies, however. When the litter arrived Mr. Fetner chose a male as a stud puppy and sold it to the John Blairs as a pet. This pet, Brewster, Ch. Coachman's Chuck-a-Luck, became a winner in the show ring and accounted for twenty-seven champion get. Brewster died at age twelve from bloat. He had returned to the Treens as a beloved member of their household after his show career had finished. He was the first Best in Show Dalmatian to sire two Best in Show sons.

Pryor Creek has a modest record of show successes, having produced over the years both Group winners and Best in Show dogs. The breeding program was limited and the showing program has been negligible. Most of the winners from Pryor Creek breeding have had other prefixes.

Pryor Creek became interested in Dalmatians after a dog of another breed had an argument with our son and Joe lost the debate. It seemed imperative to get a puppy far removed from the breed we had had so that our three-year-old child would not grow up with a great fear of dogs. After careful study and consideration we decided on a Dalmatian. Not being expert in the breed we chose a bitch that was much too dark for the show ring. A year or so later we found our foundation bitch, Ch. Saint Rocco's Polka Dot, CD. We were living in Wisconsin at the time and then we were transferred to Houston. We remember quite well that even on the great Texas circuit in 1952 only one other Dalmatian was entered at the shows. He was an Ard Aven dog and was handled by Porter Washington. He won.

Later we found competition at some of the shows in Dallas and Fort Worth, but it wasn't easy to find points in Texas in Dals in those days. Eventually, we worked hard and built up entries. Now the Dalmatian entry at most Texas shows accounts for a major, and at the specialty show of the Dalmatian Organization of Houston in the fall of 1978 there were 101 entries!

We acquired Ch. Fobette's Fanfare and through him built a good breeding program. After about five years in Texas we were again transferred, this time to southern Illinois, near St. Louis. We established our kennel there and continued to exhibit and breed, both sparingly. In 1959 we were returned to the Milwaukee area, where we have been ever since. Our breeding days are over; our schedule does not lend itself to breeding. It is impossible to carry on a program when you are not at home.

What about our son's fear of dogs? He was completely cured and both he and his sister, Esme, Jr., became excellent junior handlers. Joe was invited to compete at Westminster, unfortunately at the time we were moving north, so he was unable to go.

ALBELARM

For more than forty years the prefix of Albelarm has been a winning one in the breed. The name of Isabel Robson is well known both as a competitor and a judge. Not only has Mrs. Robson been a breeder of champion Dals, she has known when to buy from outside her line to get a winner.

Her introduction to Dals came through her association with horses. When she was a teenager she had hunters with a friend in Southern Pines, North Carolina. Her friend had a pair of Dals and when there was a litter she insisted that Isabel take the pick of the litter. This was during the war years, so showing the dog was not considered. Later she bought a daughter of Ch. Nigel of Welfield and Stock-Dal. This was the foundation bitch for Albelarm. Dr. Byron of Lorbyrndale Kennels sold her Lorbyrndale We Hail. She showed him to his title, owner-handled. Then We Hail was bred to the Nigel bitch to produce the A litter. Albelarm has used the alphabet system of naming dogs ever since, and has passed the Z!

Ch. Albelarm Attention was the first homebred champion. For several years Mrs. Robson continued to breed and show Dalmatians. She finished many champions and bought several top dogs. She imported Eng. Ch. Cabaret Charivaris and won WB at the DCA National Specialty with her in 1952. She also imported Tantivvey Georgina, who won the Open liver bitch class at the same Specialty. Charivaris won her championship easily, but Georgina was never shown again as Mrs. Robson was too involved in showing horses to show dogs every weekend.

Later the Robsons imported Pateshull Pucelle, a liver. In the early years of breeding Mrs. Robson had two homebred Group-winning bitches: Ch. Albelarm Bewitched and Ch. Albelarm Joker.

A list of the dogs owned and/or bred by Albelarm that finished their championships reads like a history of the breed of the country. Along with numerous Albelarm prefixes we find Reigate, Willowmount, Blackpool, Colonial Coach, Coachkeeper, Quaker's Acre and Green Starr.

Ch. Colonial Coach Son of York managed to rack up 150 Bests of Breed. Ch. Coachkeeper Blizzard of Quaker's Acre, a liver dog, was the Robsons' first Best in Show winner. Ch. Coachkeeper Windsong of Quaker's Acre, also a liver, was a top winning bitch in the breed for several years. Ch. Green Starr's Shamrock won three Bests in Show.

Albelarm campaigned Ch. Green Starr's Colonel Joe, who not only won the National Specialty four times but compiled a great show record along the way with thirty-five Bests in Show.

WILLIAMSVIEW

Williamsview has been active in Dalmatian breeding for a long time. Owner William Hibbler has been a serious breeder all through the years since his kennel was established in 1939. During the war years, some of the breeding was curtailed but it resumed after the war was over. He has never campaigned a dog, but has finished eighteen of his dogs. His breeding is behind many of the newer kennels.

In looking at his dogs Bill Hibbler stresses the importance of correct type, overall balance and soundness. He is a member and past president of the Dalmatian Club of America.

DALMATIA

This kennel is a good example of the "turnover" in the sport of showing dogs. In the fall of 1972 Wendell Sammet, well-known handler, entered a Dalmatian at one of the large eastern shows. He entered his dog in the Bred by Exhibitor class and thereby caused much raising of eyebrows and questioning looks from the other exhibitors. Most of them had no idea that Wendell had ever had any connection with Dalmatians, as in recent years he had been showing Poodles and Yorkshire Terriers.

Wendell's great bitch, Ch. China Doll of Dalmatia, won Best of Breed at the Dalmatian Club of America's Specialty show in 1949. Ch. Colonel Boots of Dalmatia won the Specialty in 1954.

His fine male, Ch. Bootblack of Dalmatia, sired one of the all-time greats of the breed, Ch. Roadcoach Roadster. And the name "of Dalmatia" has graced a number of top animals in the breed.

Wendell was interested in obedience in the years after World War II and he participated in the road trials. He acquired his first Dalmatian from Roadcoach. From time to time Wendell breeds a litter of Dals and if any look promising he shows them. He is now actively showing for Tioga Kennels.

Ch. Bootlack of Dalmatia

Am. Can. & Mex. Ch. Coachman's Classic, CD

KORCULA

When the Garvins' pet Collie died, their son Charles, not yet in his teens, asked to have a different breed. He wanted a Dalmatian. The family bought a pet, which turned out to be Ch. Korcula Salona, CD, the top winning bitch in the United States for several years. She won more than 100 Bests of Breed, six Group Is and was the top winning Dal Bitch for five straight years. In 1968 she was Best of Opposite Sex at the DCA national under Isabel Robson. In 1972, coming out of retirement, she won the Pittsburgh specialty show under Joe Faigel. The Veteran Bitch class at the DCA national was hers for three straight years in 1973, 1974 and 1975. She died in 1975 of bloat. She is still the top winning owner-handled bitch in the history of the breed.

Korky was also outstanding as a producer. She was responsible for the foundation stock of other newer kennels, including Eleanor Hilen's Indalane Dals. One of her daughters was Ch. Korcula Midnight Lace, which established the Korcula-Midnight line. Notable among these Dals are Ch. Korcula Midnight Margie, Ch. Korcula Midnight Hannah, Ch. Korcula Midnight Cannonball and Ch. Korcula Midnight Moonstone.

All this started with a pet Dal who was trained in Obedience before she ever saw the inside of a conformation ring. Charlie Garvin also became a top Junior Showman with Korky and won the Leonard Brumby, Sr., Memorial Trophy at Westminster. This is the only Dal who has participated in such a win.

The Garvins have finished forty-eight champions to date. At the present time their claim to fame is Ch. Korcula Midnight Star Bret D, known as Charley. This dog has been ranked in the top ten in Best of Breed wins and in the list of specialty winners and is tied for number seven in Best in Show wins, with eight so far. He also won the Kal Kan Pedigree Award three years in a row. Charley is the only Dalmatian Best in Show winner whose sire and son are also Best in Show winners, and he is the only Dal champion whose sire and dam are both DCA National Specialty winners.

ALTAMAR

When Maria Johnson moved from St. Louis to southern California she took with her the makings of a fine kennel. Her foundation dogs were all Coachman breeding. With this start she had the joy of winning the National Specialty with her beloved Tack, Ch. Coachman's Classic, in 1958. This dog also won the Dalmatian Club of Southern California specialty show twice, in 1956 and 1958, by which time he had added Mexican and Canadian titles to his name. In fact, a challenge trophy was offered for Best of Breed at this specialty in Tack's name and Maria Johnson retired the trophy! She won the specialty with Ch. Altamar's Aristos in 1966, with Ch. Altamar's Acheson in 1972 and with Ch. Altamar's

The great Ch. Korcula Salona, CD

Ch. Coachman's Canicula

Ch. Korcula Midnight Margie

Ch. Korcula Midnight Star Bret D

Ch. Colonial Coach Cheshire

Ch. Colonial Coach Devonshire

Adastar in 1976. Obviously, Tack was the foundation of the Altamar kennels of Maria Johnson.

Tack also brought fame to the Dalmatian breed in quite another way. When Dodie Smith's classic, *One Hundred and One Dalmatians*, was purchased by Walt Disney, Maria was contacted to help the studio in its drawings of Dalmatian puppies and grown dogs. Tack was the model for the hero dog, Pongo. Puppies at Altamar were used by the Disney cartoonists for the various dogs in the film, one of the animated feature-length productions of Walt Disney Studios. The story of the production of this movie is half a book in itself. Suffice it to say that Maria and her Dalmatians, all from the goodness of her heart and a fondness for the breed, helped the studio immeasurably. She went on TV programs with her dogs to publicize the movie when it was released. Everything the studio needed to learn about the dogs, Maria supplied. During the sketching in preparation for the actual animation, Disney artists came to the Johnson home and observed and sketched the puppies. Other times Maria took her dogs to the studio so they could be sketched. Tack posed for many publicity stills. It was a great experience for Maria and the dogs.

Almost all of Maria's breeding has been on the line with Coachman stock. Her foundation bitch went back to Four-in-Hand Mischief. She has imported several English dogs and has used them on occasion to introduce some feature she was looking for, but mostly her breeding and type is Coachman. We continue to see fine Altamar dogs in the show ring occasionally.

COLONIAL COACH

One of the oldest registered kennels still active in Dalmatians is Colonial Coach, located in Wauconda, Illinois. Bud and Laura Knowles founded the kennel in 1946 in Des Plaines, Illinois.

In 1964 Laura fell ill and was unable to continue to operate the kennel. Natalie and Ron Fleger took over for the Knowleses. Laura died in 1965 and the kennel was moved to Wauconda. Bud Knowles passed on in April 1979.

The Flegers have retained the high standards of breeding that the Knowleses had established. Some of the great dogs from this kennel are Ch. Colonial Coach Devonshire, Ch. Colonial Coach Cheshire, Ch. Colonial Coach Brouette and Ch. Colonial Coach Son of York, to name a few.

GREEN STARR

Green Starr is one of the oldest Dalmatian kennels in existence. This kennel was started by Dr. David Doane. He had known a Dal while he was interning and resolved to have one of his own as soon as he could. He kept his resolution. David and his wife, Margie, continue to breed fine Dalmatians.

Although Ch. Green Starr's Colonel Joe was not bred by the Doanes, he was of their breeding. The Doanes are the breeders of Ch. Green Starr's Shamrock, the top winning bitch for several years. She was owned by Isabel Robson of Albelarm Kennels.

There have been many other champions bearing the Green Starr prefix that the Doanes have bred and shown to their championships. They were the breeders of Ch. Green Starr's Undergraduate, a liver bitch that was acquired by the now defunct Pennydale Kennels of Arthur and Muriel Higgins. Undergraduate was a top winner and left a legacy in her produce.

LABYRINTH

Spanning a number of years we find the breeding of Labyrinth Kennels, Chris Dyker's Dals. Shortly after the war Christine became interested in Dalmatians when her then husband-to-be owned a bitch named Reveille Girl. When he moved into an apartment he placed the bitch with good friends, Teresa and Nick Nichols.

Labyrinth's foundation bitch Dot along with her daughters have been responsible for some nineteen champions in the United States. There are also Bermudian, Brazilian, Canadian and South African champions from this breeding.

Notable offspring from Labyrinth are the winning litter brothers, Ch. Tuckaway Bold and Brave, Ch. Tuckaway Gallant Man and Ch. Tuckaway Jason James. These dogs were sired by Ch. Coachman's Canicula, who was Best of Breed at the 1973 National Specialty. Mrs. Dyker is cobreeder of these dogs with Dr. Remmele, who owned Canicula. All these dogs have been Group winners.

Mrs. Dyker is continuing to breed on the same bloodlines and to show top Dalmatians. She is also a judge of Dals and Poodles and has had the honor of judging at the National Specialty show of the Clube Dalmata do Brasil as well as the DCA National/Specialty.

WATSEKA

To win the National Specialty must be one of the greater thrills in the life of any breeder-exhibitor. To win the National Specialty *three times with the same* dog must be the consummate thrill. This feat was accomplished by Don and Carol Schubert with their great dog, Ch. Panore of Watseka. Panore was named Best of Breed by Dr. David Doane at the National Specialty held in California in 1972. In 1974 he again won the breed at the national show in Waukesha, Wisconsin, under Winifred Heckmann. A short while later the dog was retired. In 1977, Panore was entered at the National Specialty in Crete, Illinois, as a

Ch. Labyrinth of Tuckaway Julep

Ch. Labyrinth Sleigh Belle

Ch. Colonial Coach Carriage Way

Ch. Tamarack's Tennyson v Watseka

Ch. Panore of Watseka

Ch. Labyrinth Oscar Madison

151

Veteran Dog. He won the Veteran Dog class judged by Isabel Robson. Best of Breed competition was judged by Alfred E. Treen. The dog looked superb and the longer the judging went on, the better he looked. He won.

Watseka has produced numerous champions and established a fine line of dogs. Panore sired Dylan, who in turn sired Ch. Tamarack's Tennyson v Watseka, a Best in Show winner and winner of the 1983 DCA National Specialty. This was a bittersweet win for Carol Schubert, who handled the dog for owner Allen Sheimo, as Don had passed away in June of that year.

Due to physical problems, Carol has curtailed the breeding program at Watseka, but she is still very much involved in the breed. She has been representing a firm dealing in frozen and cooled sperm for the last several years and has had a great track record in this field. Tennyson is the sire of the first Dalmatian litter produced by frozen semen.

INDALANE

Indalane Kennels in Dayton, Ohio, belong to Eleanor Hilen, who has finished a number of dogs. Her most outstanding dog was Ch. Tuckaway Traveler Indalane, who was also a top-quality stud dog. Not only has Traveler sired numerous specialty- and Group-winning dogs, but he also was one of the first Dalmatians to earn a Temperament Title (TT). Since serious breeders consider temperament to be one of the most important characteristics of a dog, this was a pioneering step. Indalane continues to do serious breeding. Mr. Hilen collects old fire engines, a fitting hobby to accompany breeding Dals.

A remarkable line of dogs was established from Am. & Can. Ch. Coachman's Chuck-a-Luck (Brewster). This dog was the sire of Ch. Lord Jim, who sired a litter that produced Ch. Count Miguel of Tuckaway and Ch. Tuckaway Traveler Indalane, both of whom were productive sires. Count Miguel is the sire of Ch. Fireman's Freckled Friend, who is the sire of Ch. Korcula Midnight Star Bret D, who is the sire of Ch. Snowood Superstition Bret D—both Best in Show dogs. Following the direct line from Brewster, Count Miguel is the only one without an all-breed Best in Show to his credit, but he did win Best of Breed at specialty shows.

Traveler sired fifty-four champion get and Count Miguel sired forty-nine. The fact that littermates sired more than 100 champion get, without taking into consideration Best in Show wins, is extraordinary in itself.

MELODY

A decision to purchase a Harlequin Great Dane puppy is the reason Melody Dalmatian Kennels are in existence! Jack White (Dr. John V. White, Jr., DVM) had asked his father for a puppy. While looking for a suitable Harl to buy, Jack

Ch. Count Miguel of Tuckaway

Ch. Melody Dynamatic, a Best in Show liver dog

came across a litter of Dalmatians and fell in love with them. Since his father was making the purchase, Jack had to be content with a puppy of pet quality. This bitch was Calculator's Miss Sincerity and, while Jack was not aware of it, she came from show stock. Her background was Green Starr.

While stationed in Texas during his service days, Jack attended his first dog show. He was enthusiastic over the dogs and the competition. A breeder advised him not to breed Sindy, as she was lacking in some nose pigment. Being a novice, Jack ignored the advice, bred Sindy and founded a kennel. One of the bitches from the first litter was Ch. Melody Sweet, CD, an outstanding Dalmatian. Another champion produced in this first litter was Patrick Larabee. Ch. Long Last Ripcord, a son of Ch. Colonsay Blacksmith, a great import from England, was the sire of this litter. In a later litter Sindy produced two well-known liver bitches, Ch. Melody Crimson and Clover, CD, and Ch. Melody Up Up and Away, CD.

After Jack finished his military service he moved to Colorado and attended veterinary medical college.

While Sindy was actually the foundation bitch for Melody Kennels, the Whites' best-known bitch is Sweet. Sweet went on to win six Group firsts and various wins at regional and national Specialties.

When Jack and Beth were married Beth had Collies, but she soon became interested in the Dals. They are both interested in conformation and obedience and nearly all of their own champions have a CD, but other interests—cattle and Appaloosa horses—take too much of their time for them to train for advanced titles.

DOTTIDALE

Amy and Elli Lipschutz's interest in the breed was practically inherited from their father, who used to run for blocks following the horse-drawn fire engines with the Dals flying at their heels when he was a boy. They acquired their first Dalmatian in 1947 when they were children. Their interest has never flagged.

Their greatest Dal was Ch. Dottidale Jo Jo, who, in 1967 was the top winning liver Dal in the United States, rated number four in the Phillips ratings. He won the Breed at the Kennel Club of Philadelphia, Eastern Dog Club, Westchester and Greater Pittsburgh Dal Club. He also won the Veteran Dog class at the Dalmatian Club of Southern New England specialty in 1970 and the Veteran class at the DCA National Specialty in 1971.

He has also acquired a record as a sire. In 1969 he sired Dalhalla's Thunderbolt and Dottidale's Cedelia. Thunderbolt was named Best of Breed at Westminster in 1972.

Jo Jo's daughter, Dottidale Elizabeth, is another of this kennel's outstanding Dals. For three years in a row, 1975, 1976 and 1977, she was the winner of

Ch. Melody Ring of Fire

Ch. Melody Sweet, CD

Ch. Melody Up Up and Away, CD

Ch. Dottidale Jo Jo

Ch. Bellringer's Sundance

the Veteran Bitch class at the Southern New England Specialty and she captured the same win at the DCA show in 1976.

Most of the Dottidale dogs are owner-handled in the ring and they continue to produce good specimens, usually placing or winning each time they are shown. Dottidale is now located in Kentucky.

PILL PEDDLER

Pill Peddler is the prefix used by Alberta Holden for her dogs. Alberta and her husband, Dr. Eugene Holden, have been breeding Morgan horses and Dalmatians for many years. Much of Mrs. Holden's breeding stock is from the now inactive kennel of the Lloyd Reeveses' Rabbit Run. Mrs. Reeves, who winters in Florida and spends her summers in New England, is no longer active as a breeder but has retained her interest in the breed. Mrs. Holden, with judicious use of other lines, such as Dalquest, Roadcoach and Tuckaway, has developed a very fine breeding program and had great success with her dogs. The Holdens have now closed the kennel in New Hampshire and moved to the South, where they continue breeding Dalmatians successfully.

PAISLEY

Paisley Dalmatians was really founded on Obedience interests. Sue Mac-Millan (then Sue Reinarz) had trained the family Beagle in Obedience and decided she would like a smart-looking, flashy dog for Obedience and breed competition. She acquired a Dalmatian after learning of the remarkable record of Belle Monti's Mister Mickey, the Dal with so many high scores on the West Coast. She acquired a lovely liver bitch from Blackpool, Ch. Blackpool's Red Nora. This bitch finished her championship with several Bests of Breed over specials and won four consecutive High in Trial awards from the Novice class. The two times she was shown in Canadian Obedience Trials, she won HSDT. When she achieved her CDX she was bred. Unfortunately, Sue lost her in whelping the litter.

Probably, the most famous of the MacMillans' dogs is Pooka, Ch. Melody Up Up and Away, CD. This lovely liver bitch has more than forty Bests of Breed and more than twenty-five Group placings. Twice she was among the top ten Dals. When Paisley Dalmatians was revived Sue wanted to continue with liver Dals and worked with Jack and Beth White of Melody Dals in Colorado to get the bloodlines required, hence the Melody prefix.

Paisley Dalmatians have continued to prosper, with many champions produced and many obedience titles earned. Sue MacMillan and her daughter, Jessica, are found in the show rings in many sections of the country. With Ch.

Melody Up Up and Away, CD, as a foundation for the line, the MacMillans have managed to establish a type of Dal that is recognizable as Paisley.

The most prominent member of their "stable" at this time is Jocko, Am. & Can. Ch. Paisley Peterbilt, who is also an Am. & Can. CDX and TT. He is also a multiple Group winner, a specialty winner, DCA Award of Merit winner, and an all-breed and specialty High in Trial winner. Jocko has also received a Dog World Award in Obedience and a Temperament Title and he is the sire of fourteen champion get.

CROATIA

What a change there must have been in the lifestyle of the Johnsons when they made the switch from Chihuahuas to Dalmatians!

Audrey and Forrest had bred and shown Chihuahuas for about ten years when they decided to go into Dals. They had admired the dogs for some time, having been attracted to the breed by their flashy appearance.

In the summer of 1967 while visiting relatives in Massachusetts they found two puppy bitches in a litter and had them shipped to Iowa. Two Dal puppies in a house accustomed to Chihuahuas and an occasional Miniature Poodle was too much, so they sold one of the pups and kept the other. Unfortunately, Lady did not turn out to be show quality, nor was she a brood bitch. So she was sold and new stock was introduced into the picture. The Johnsons named their Dalmatian breeding "of Croatia."

Their first homebred champion, Mr. Diamond Chips of Croatia, finished his championship under a year of age with a Group I and a Group IV from the classes. He finished with all majors and was always Best of Winners. He was named Best Puppy at the National Specialty in 1970. His first litter sired at Croatia was out of Ch. Crown Jewel's Nadana Topaz. Her sire was Ch. Crown Jewels Black Diamond and her dam was Ch. Crown Jewels Black Agate. This litter produced four champions.

The Johnsons are founders of the Davenport Dalmatian Club and are very active in dog activities. They are also members of the DCA and the Chicagoland Dal Club. Mr. Johnson has served as president of the DCA, and as trophy chairman and show chairman for the National Specialty. He is also a judge of Dalmatians and Poodles.

SHAWNEE

Ch. Jameson of Shawnee has won two specialty shows two times each! He was named Best of Breed at the Chicagoland specialty show in 1974 and 1975 and he won the same award at the Dalmatian Club of Detroit specialty show in

Ch. Melody Joleen of Croatia

Ch. Mr. Diamond Chips of Croatia

the same years. In addition, he accumulated forty-three Bests of Breed, including the Westminster Kennel Club in 1975. He was always owner-handled.

Jamie is owned by Bill and June Dahn of Ohio. In 1965 the Dahns decided that it would be nice to have a dog for companionship and protection. They were sure they wanted a purebred and studied books that they found in libraries and pet shops. They were having difficulty finding a Dal so they contacted Maxwell Riddle, then the pet editor of the *Cleveland Press*. He gave them the name of Elizabeth Doyle, a local breeder. In May 1966 they acquired a bitch, Brigadier's Jubi of Shawnee. Brigadier was the prefix Mrs. Doyle used on her dogs. Jubi is a combination of June and Bill. The Dahns lived on Shawnee Street, thus the name came into being.

The Dahns, through Mrs. Doyle and Betty Kilfoyle, another Dalmatian fancier, became interested in the emerging Western Reserve Dalmatian Club and in showing their dog. They soon found that Jubi was not going to be a champion, so they decided to breed. They chose Ch. Koko's Mr. Copper, a liver, for a sire. The resulting litter gave them Ch. Marvelous Maggie of Shawnee, CD. She finished on her second birthday, having picked up the Obedience title along the way. Maggie was bred to Ch. Lord Jim and Jamie was pick of that litter. Jamie has sired numerous champions of record.

JAMAR

Jack Austin of Canton, Ohio, and his wife Marcella have JaMar Dals. Jack and Marcella have had Dals for a number of years but confined most of their activity to the Obedience ring. When they decided to go in for conformation showing they acquired Pacifica's Maid of the Mist as their foundation bitch. They finished her easily.

She had a single litter that produced Ch. JaMar's Magic Lady of the Mist, Ch. JaMar's Minnie Dixie Belle and Ch. JaMar's Dusty Boots. Lady was bred to Ch. Blackpool Ironstone and produced Ch. JaMar's My Gypsy Rose. All of the breeding has been linebreeding on the Blackpool lines.

Jack Austin had the distinction of being chosen in 1977 to judge the first futurity in the history of the Dalmatian Club of America. He drew an entry of eighty-eight, which will stand as a record for a first-time event.

He and Marcella are quite active in the all-breed club in their hometown and have served in various capacities at the Western Reserve Dalmatian Club. For many years Jack was president of the Canton Humane Society. He served as president of the DCA and is now a popular Dalmatian judge.

DELTALYN

A pet Dalmatian that did not have enough quality for the show ring led Bob and Judy Rivard to buying a quality bitch. Someone referred them to Crown Jewels in Chicago and they bought an eight-week-old bitch who later became Am. & Can. Ch. Crown Jewels' Delta Diamond. They also bought a twelve-week-old male from Alberta Holden's Pill Peddler Kennels. Delta Diamond finished in August 1972 and the male, Am. & Can. Ch. Delta Dals Mr. D, finished in July 1973.

They bred Delta Diamond to Ch. Coachman's Canicula, producing two champions in the litter, Ch. Deltalyn's Mystic Brandy and the Best in Show dog Ch. Deltalyn's Decoupage. Decoupage, or Cooper as he is known, finished owner-handled at fourteen months, having taken nine points from the Puppy class. In 1975 he was the number three Dal and in 1976 he was number two. Both years he was the number one owner-handled Dal in the United States.

In addition to the Best in Show win at Vacationland Kennel Club, Cooper had at least ten Group Is and numerous other group placings. He was also Best of Breed at the Dalmatian Club of Southern New England in 1975; at the Western Reserve Dalmatian Club in 1975 and 1976, and the spring specialty show of the Dalmatian Organization of Houston. He was Best of Breed at Westminster in 1976.

Bob and Judy are very active in Dalmatian affairs, having served the New England club in various capacities. Judy spent a number of years as editor of *Coaching Lines*, the bulletin of DCSNE. They are conscientious breeders and careful trainers and their Cooper has contributed much to the future of the breed. Bob, who serves on the board of governors of the DCA, is also a judge of the breed.

DYMONDEE

The Lesters, with their Dymondee Kennels, have been active in the breed for about twenty years. Fred and Joan were given a Dal puppy and started a career in Obedience with it. While at the shows they watched the breed judging and saw Dals with a great deal more quality than their pet, Duke. Their first conformation dog, Dutchess, earned a CD in the United States and her championship in Canada.

Colonial Coach Chess was given to Joan as a Mother's Day present and the breeding program began. Joan was able to acquire Ch. Poco Chimney Sweep (Tibit), the dam of Ch. Range Trail Maple Creek Maham, Ch. Range Trail Maple Creek Flagg and Maple Creek's Someone Lovely, all sired by Am. & Can. Ch. Coachman's Chuck-a-Luck. Later Flagg came to live at Dymondee, as did Ch. Kale's Checquered Coachman, sired by Ch. Roadking's Rome—a Best

Ch. Deltalyn's Decoupage

Ch. Jameson of Shawnee

in Show son of Chuck-a-Luck. The bloodlines at this kennel are mostly Coachman and Colonial Coach.

MONTJUIC

Benito Vila and his wife, Teresita, have been involved in the breed for more than twenty years. Instead of breeding on a simple pedigree, the Vilas breed only to offspring of certain dog families. This change in breeding plans occurred when they imported a top winning liver dog from England, Ch. Buffrey's Jobe. After using the dog on several bitches, they discovered that if the bitch had descended from The Ace of Fyrthorne, a well-known American sire in his day, the puppies were most desirable. If the bitch's background did not trace to The Ace of Fyrthorne, the puppies were not as desirable. Having made this discovery, the Vilas concentrated on breeding to bitches of the proper background. The same formula worked on those specimens sired by Jobe, whether male or female. The subsequent breedings were successful only when the mate was of the proper family. This is not quite the same as linebreeding, although it is a definite approximation of it.

Of Spanish descent, the Vilas name all their dogs with Spanish names and pronounce the names in the Spanish way. Montjuic is an old Catalonian battle cry. The first top dog from this kennel was Ch. Imam de Montjuic. When six months and two days old he went Best of Breed over a well-known special. He continued his winning ways by taking BOB at several specialties and at all-breed shows. He was used extensively as a sire of the Montjuic dogs and can be found in their pedigrees.

LOTZADOTS

Among the breeders in the Chicago area we find DiAnn Plaza and Lotzadots Kennels. Their start in Dals was through a bitch, Lady Lotzadots, who had had two other homes before coming to live with the Plazas. She turned out to have such a lovely temperament that their veterinarian suggested she be bred. By this time Ray, DiAnn's husband, and her daughter, Linda Richmond, had become interested in the breed. After careful study the bitch was bred and produced two champions.

The Plazas continue to breed, carefully selecting the stud for the bitch, and are very active in the Chicagoland Dalmatian Club.

CHESHIRE

Cheryl Steinmetz entered the world of Dalmatians illegally. She was training a Poodle in Obedience and at a show borrowed a Dalmatian from Mary and

Ch. Tioaga Commander Joe

Ch. Pill Peddler's Christmas Holly

Ch. Iman of Montjuic

Am. & Can. Ch. Cheshire's Northern Lights

Claudia Blair to show in Junior Showmanship. Cheryl, fifteen years old at the time, was unaware of the requirement that the dog belong to her or a member of her family. Later Cheryl purchased a Dal from the Blairs, Round Tower's Hickory Smoke, Am. & Can. CD. A few years later Cheryl found a bitch to her liking, Ch. Paisley's Star of Kirkland, CD.

Cheryl has continued to breed and exhibit. Her most memorable bitch to date was Ch. Cheshire's English Ivy. Ivy was a winner in the show ring, a fine producer and a favorite dog wherever she lived. Her biggest win was Best of Breed at the Chicagoland specialty. She so far has produced Ch. Cheshire's Breakdancer, Am. & Can. Ch. Cheshire's Northern Lights, Cheshire Katlin of Kipling, CD, Ch. Alfredrich Bay Colony Hytime and Ch. Harmony of Cheshire T. Redrock—quite a number for a bitch to produce in seven years.

SNOWOOD

Snowood is the kennel prefix chosen by Meg and Mike Hennessey of Elgin, Illinois. They had had a foundling Dal and an unwanted pup before and these had proved the breed's worth in the stable. Meg is an avid exhibitor of horses.

When they decided to get a "good" dog and show it, their lives changed. Showing dogs is a time-consuming activity and requires hours of preparation. Since the Hennesseys are also breeders, they spend a great deal of time with the Dals. In a few years they have managed to produce several Sweepstakes winners and Group-placing dogs and a Best in Show dog, Ch. Snowood Superstition Bret D, a grandson of Ch. Fireman's Freckled Friend, making him a third-generation Best in Show animal. His sire is multiple Best in Show winner Ch. Korcula Midnight Star Bret D.

FIRESPRITE

Ray and Norma Baley decided they should have a dog for their children, so they obtained a Dal. Knowing nothing about the breed, they set out to learn. They attended matches offered by the Chicagoland Dal Club and finally joined the club. A few years later, by this time into the swing of showing and knowing what to look for in a litter, Norma joined the DCA. She served the Chicagoland club in many capacities including president, leading the club on to bigger and better things. She has served the DCA in a number of capacities including two full terms as president. Her breeding is known all over the United States, as she has been very careful in her selection of studs and dams. One of her top dogs was a liver, Ch. Firesprite and Coachlyte Gigolo, who was a top stud dog as well as a superb showman.

Ch. Folklore 'n Firesprite William Tell and Ch. Firesprite's Trixi Dixi, CD

FOLKLORE

Robert and Diana Skibinski purchased their first show-quality Dalmatian from Norma Baley's Firesprite Kennels, co-owning the dog with her. This was Ch. Firesprite's Trixi Dixi, CD. Using this as their foundation bitch they have successfully bred several champions. Sired by Am. & Can. Ch. Saratoga's Missouri Outlaw, this bitch produced two champions in one litter, Ch. Folklore 'n Firesprite William Tell and Ch. Firesprite 'n Folklore Flirt. Tell has amassed a fine show record and is becoming known as a sire. It is interesting to see what two breeders working together can produce. Third- and fourth-generation litters are now seeing the show ring from this combined effort.

WOODBURY

The old adage says that two heads are better than one, so it stands to reason that two generations are better than one. In the Woodbury Dalmatians we have Sue and Ernie Schuenaman and Sue's parents, Bob and Fran McCrary, hard at work breeding for better Dals with every litter. Woodbury was Mrs. McCrary's maiden name. Most of the dogs' names have a touch of the Confederacy in them. Woodbury dogs are well known throughout the nation, as they have bred specialty show winners and Group winners.

CAVALIER

Dr. Michael Manning purchased a family pet and trained it for Obedience. Because his father was a fire fighter there was only one breed to consider, the Dalmatian. Seeing some of the dogs in the breed ring led him to purchase another Dal and breed her. He went to the Melody Kennels of Beth and Jack White in Colorado, and later bred to the great liver dog, Ch. Melody's Dynamatic. He later developed a line using the Strands' Cadillac of MGR as the foundation sire. Dr. Manning has finished approximately twenty champions and put titles on them in both the United States and Canada.

Believing that exercise is very important to developing a good moving Dal, Dr. Manning rides horseback about six miles each day and takes the dogs with him for the exercise. He starts them out as early as they will follow the horse. The puppies are not allowed to go the full route, but by the time they are mature they have developed great musculature and move as a Dal should—and they are able to follow the horses all the way.

MARICAM

Mariann Witherspoon of Maricam Dalmatians has been breeding for a number of years, but no dog she has bred gave her as much pleasure as her Ch. Maricam's Saucy Susy, CD. Susy had a remarkable show career, starting with a Best in Match win when she was just twelve weeks old. This pattern continued to her second Award of Merit win at the 1988 DCA specialty show, won from the Veteran Bitch class. She won her first Award of Merit from the Veteran Bitch class at the National Specialty in 1985. She was a multi-BOB winner, a Group placer and she won the breed at two specialty shows. Most of these wins came after the age of seven. Her veteran year was 1988, so to speak, as she won every Veteran class she entered, including a Best Veteran in Sweepstakes at the Detroit specialty. Her last Best of Breed win was in April 1988 at the age of eleven years and nine months. Susy was always owner-handled by Mariann.

COACHWAY

Walter and Marie Johnson have been exhibiting Dalmatians for some thirty years. Their Coachway prefix has accounted for a number of champions both in the United States and in Canada. They were active in the formation of the Cambridge Minnesota Kennel Club, the all-breed club near their home, and are active supporters of the Greater Twin Cities Dal Club. They have acquired a young male puppy and are looking forward to campaigning him in the near future.

Walter's greatest claim to fame is his wonderful record keeping and statistical work. For many years he supplied *The Spotter* with statistics for the feature "Top Spots" and volunteered other rankings of interest, all of which found their way into the magazine. Marie was a member of the DCA for many years, but Walter never joined. In grateful appreciation of all his wonderful work, the DCA made him an honorary member—the first in the history of the club.

ROBBSDALE

Tim Robbins is another well-known breeder who was in high school when he became involved in dogs. His first bitch was a pet he had received as a graduation present. He was able to finish one of the pups from a litter whelped by this bitch, handling it himself.

He started going to shows with other members of the then organizing Baytown Kennel Club and talking to Dal people he met there. He learned to handle dogs and showed a number of breeds for other people, most notably Italian Greyhounds.

Looking for quality he purchased a bitch from Crown Jewels in Chicago, finished her and bred her three times. The first two litters were whelped while Tim was still a college student. He traveled to a number of shows with handlers on weekends. Through this experience he not only became a handler but a good and careful breeder as well.

Tim helped organize the Dalmatian Organization of Houston and has served as its president. He is quite active in the DCA and is the current editor of *The Spotter*.

Multiple Best in Show winner Ch. Farga de Montjuic

Handler Bill McFadden with eleven of the champion Dals he has shown.

16

Present-Day Kennels

WHEN Ch. Green Starr's Colonel Joe retired, he had amassed the finest record ever known in the breed. However, records are made to be broken. It is doubtful that a human will ever run as fast as a mile a minute, but the running records are getting faster and faster if only by tenths of seconds at a time. The same is true of dog show records. Colonel Joe's record fell to Ch. Fireman's Freckled Friend, known as Spotty.

SPOTTY'S STORY

It is always wonderful to have a winning dog, but to start at the top is a great thrill—although it does tend to color the rest of one's show activity. Spotty is a true Cinderella dog.

Rob and Sharri Peth of St. Louis bought a Dalmatian for their children. The Dal was chosen because Rob Peth is a fire fighter and obviously he had to have a firehouse dog. They knew absolutely nothing about the breed. The puppy was not only unfinished in pigment, but it was also deaf. The Peths didn't realize it was deaf until it was hit by a car. They immediately looked for a replacement and were fortunate enough to find Paula Moore, a Dal breeder who was living in St. Louis at the time. She had received a stud fee puppy from Joan Lester of Dymondee Kennels. After explaining some of the finer points of the bitch to the Peths, she sold them the puppy, who became Dymondee's Dot to Dot, call name Seagrave.

While attending a charity fund-raiser the Peths saw a drill team demonstration put on by the members of the St. Louis Dal club. They didn't know why, but they knew that these dogs were different from their Seagrave. Then they saw a son of Ch. Count Miguel of Tuckaway. This dog looked like their bitch; it had the same type head, shoulders, etc. Since they were unable to find Paula Moore, who had moved away from St. Louis, they called Joan Lester and asked her about breeding to Count Miguel. Joan told them it would be good linebreeding and to go ahead. They did and had a nice litter of pups. One of these pups caught their eye immediately, but a friend had asked to have a pup if they ever bred Seagrave, so this pup was saved for him. In the meantime the friend found another dog that suited him, and so Spotty was the "leftover" puppy in the litter.

When Spotty was fourteen months old the Peths learned of the specialty show to be held by the St. Louis Dal club. They had three weeks to prepare. Turning to Joan Lester again they were told to see if Bill Busch, a handler from Cape Girardeau, Missouri, would take Spotty. Bill said yes and took the dog for training. At the specialty the dog won a third place in his class. The next day at the all-breed show he was Best of Winners and Best of Opposite Sex and the Sunday show found him BOW again. In the next two weekends the dog finished his championship with two more majors and a Best of Breed over specials. One year later he won his first Best in Show.

Spotty won a total of forty Bests in Show and was Best of Breed at four National Specialties. He also won the Non-Sporting Group at Westminster under Emil Klinckhardt in February 1985, making him the fourth Dalmatian in history to accomplish this win.

As a show dog Spotty is unsurpassed. As a sire he has broken records, too. He has at least five Best in Show get, two of which are bitches. His grandchildren are making a mark for themselves as well.

As often happens many bitches were sent to him for breeding, and the results were not always perfect. It is a shame that people cannot decide on a stud dog for their breeding program by studying the dog, the bitch and the bloodlines rather than breeding to the current top winner who is not always suitable for the bitch in question.

Spotty is the product of linebreeding. Am. & Can. Ch. Coachman's Chuck-a-Luck is behind him on three lines. This dog was the product of carefully planned intense inbreeding and his descendants are among the top winners in the breed.

An interesting sidelight on the Peths, who have continued to breed and to show their dogs with some success, is that Rob Peth is the breeder of record on only two champion Dals. One is Spotty and the other is his daughter, Ch. Fireman's Becky Newsham, also a Best in Show winner.

CANALSIDE

Helene and Pauline Masaschi named their kennel Canalside because it is located on the canal that separates Cape Cod from the mainland. They have enjoyed many wins over the past few years. Their first big win was with Ch. Pacifica's Boston Bandit, who won the first specialty of the Dalmatian Club of Quebec. The dog was an American, Canadian and Bermudan champion.

They showed another Dal, Ch. Coachman's Chocolate Soldier, and then acquired Ch. Coachman's Hot Coffee from Jean Fetner of Coachman Kennels. Hot Coffee won Best of Opposite Sex at the DCA National Specialty twice, once handled by the well-known handler, now judge, Jane Forsyth and once handled by Helene. Hot Coffee also won Best of Breed at the Dalmatian Club of Southern New England (DCSNE) under Mary Klein and won the Non-Sporting Group at the all-breed show that day. She has several other specialty wins to her credit, including going BOS from the Veteran Bitch class at the DCSNE show. Hot Coffee holds the distinction of being the only bitch to win Best of Breed at Westminster two times, in 1982 and 1984.

More recently the Canalside pride and joy is Samantha, formally known as Ch. Godins To Be or Not To Be. Not only is this bitch a Best in Show and Group winner, but she also was Best of Breed at the DCA National Specialty in 1989. She presents a beautiful picture in the ring, and we can expect much more from her.

TIOGA

Many Dalmatian fanciers say, "Once a Dal fancier, always a Dal fancier." Hope Smith (Mrs. Walter Smith), who had some outstanding dogs in the past with her Tioga Coach Kennels, has returned to the breed with some top show specimens. Using Wendell Sammet as a handler has been a splendid choice, as Wendell is also a Dal breeder. Together they have been able to put a number of good dogs in the ring, including Ch. Tioga Maggie Thatcher and Ch. Tioga Queen Anne's Lace, mother and daughter. These two bitches are very similar in type and have done their share of winning. Lace started her show career by winning Best Junior in Sweeps at the Dal Club of Southern New England specialty show and has continued her winning ways.

In addition to having some fine bitches, Mrs. Smith has also bred some quality dogs.

ERIN

In 1976 Sharon and John Lyons decided they wanted a good quality Dal, so they attended the National Specialty show at Norwich, Connecticut. There they met Jean Fetner of Coachman Kennels and purchased Coachman's Paisley Candybar. This liver, known as Hershey, finished in style and produced eleven champions. One of the puppies was Ch. Coachman's Hot Coffee, who became

Ch. Lord Jim

Ch. Tioga's Queen Anne's Lace

a multi-Group, multi-specialty winner, including being chosen Best of Opposite Sex at two National Specialties.

The Lyonses have had some very successful dogs with good wins at Specialty Shows in the past fifteen years. Both are working at the other side of the ring as judges these days.

MADHURASON

Dalmatian fanciers feel there is no other breed, and the feeling is enhanced when someone who has had quite a show career in another breed switches to the spotted dogs. Anne Fleming started breeding quality Dals about thirteen years ago. Earlier she had been a successful breeder of Doberman Pinschers, and records show that she was quite successful in that breed.

Her liver dog, Am., Can., Mex. & Int. Ch. Madhurason's Tanfastic, has won two Bests in Show. A bitch, Ch. Madhurason's Harewood Home, finished by going WB and BOW at three specialties. These are just the latest important animals in Anne's kennel.

Two Madhurason dogs were featured in the *AKC's World of the Pure-Bred Dog* (Howell, 1983). Now that she has found the wonders of this breed, we hope Anne stays with it.

HOPI KACHINA

Breeding sparingly, never more than one litter a year, Ray and Cathy Nogar have had a great deal of success. Over the years, they have had approximately two dozen champions, most of which they bred and showed in the Bred by Exhibitor class. At least half of these champions are liver. Living as they do in the Southwest where there are not many shows each year, they have managed to follow a breeding and showing program that could be used as an example for others to follow. They have a type in mind and that is all they are looking for, both in a stud dog and in the produce they keep.

They bred the only Dalmatian that has achieved both a championship and UDTX, Ch. Hopi Kachina Indian Summer, a liver-spotted bitch. Indi is also a talented coach dog and appears at the National Appaloosa Horse Show in that capacity. Indi has had but one litter, which produced Ch. Hopi Kachina Mosairu II, CDX, TDX. He had some Group placements when shown in conformation.

SUMMERHILL

Although Edith Gladstone's interest in Dals began when she was a teenager, she became a show buff later in life. She started out in her teens with a dog

Ch. Hopi Kachina Mosairu, TDX, CDX

Am. Can. & Bda. Ch. Spatterdash Coal Tar Tobyson

Ch. Blackpool Bullshott

Ch. Blackpool Crinkle Forest

named Hawthorn's Black Pepper, CDX, who was out of Mrs. Paul Moore's Hollow Hill breeding. Edith put Obedience titles on her and had her ready for Utility, but college intervened. Pepper won the Dog World Award for excellence in Obedience, earned several High in Trials and was high scoring Dal at the DCA specialty in New Jersey in the 1950s.

Edith later returned to her interest in Dals and purchased Ch. Albelarm Starr of Summerhill. Sired by Colonel Joe out of Ch. Coachkeeper Windsong of Quaker's Acre, he managed to amass an enviable record in the show ring. By this time Edith was married to Nelson Gladstone and together they continued to breed and show dogs. One of their top bitches was Ch. S & P Starlet of Summerhill, CD, who ranked as the number one bitch in 1982 and 1983. The Gladstones' dogs were tightly linebred on Green Starr, Quaker's Acre and Coachman lines.

In 1986 the Gladstones were fortunate to import from England Ch. Knightstone Huntsman, a tightly linebred Washakie dog.

SPLASH O' EBONY

With the proliferation of Dal breeders throughout the United States it is remarkable that some people have been able to produce some excellent winning dogs with a very limited breeding program. A case in point is Debbie Nierman of Dallas, Texas. Debbie purchased her first Dal in 1979, and although she finished the dog she had a better idea of what she was looking for and so was happy to purchase a foundation bitch from Sue Schuenaman of Woodbury Kennels. This pup became World, Int., Las Americas, Mex. & Am. Ch. Splash o' Ebony's Woodbury Jaki.

ATLANTIS

About twenty-five years ago the Hoover family decided that their two boys needed a dog, and so John and Emily Hoover acquired a Dal for Todd and Scott. Unfortunately, the dog turned out to be deaf. Another dog was purchased from Fred Klensch.

In about 1975 son Todd became listed as cobreeder and owner, as he had spent a great deal of time studying the breed and choosing the pups to show from the litters. Todd's interest in Dals is still ongoing, as is his mother's. Although the travel schedule demanded by their jobs is an arduous one, they continue to do some breeding and place their good dogs with trusted co-owners so that they can continue their bloodlines.

BARKER'S BEST

In the Detroit area we find Betty and Loy Barker with their Barker's Best Dals. The Barkers started with a pet Dalmatian in 1964. Shortly after acquiring

Ch. S & P Starlet of Summerhill, CD

Ch. Splash o'Ebony's Jubilation

Am. & Cuban Ch. Quaker's Acre's Young Bess

Ch. Maricam's Saucy Susy, CD

their Chocolate Chip Miss they attended the Detroit Kennel Club show. Watching the Dal judging and seeing the Dals on the bench, Loy announced that his dog was as good as any there. His statement was challenged by another exhibitor who dared them to get the dog in the ring and prove the statement! The Barkers accepted the challenge and have been breeder-exhibitors ever since. Chocolate Chip Miss acquired a CD and a Canadian championship.

The Barkers have been active in the Dal Club of Detroit and Betty served as show chairman for the 1986 National Specialty, which was held in the Detroit area.

TATTERSALL

When Beth Hallman bought her first dog she was determined to have a Dalmatian. The only place she could find one was in a pet shop. Although this bitch, Lady Arabesque Christabel, was of poor quality, Beth managed to put a CDX on her without any trouble. While showing in Obedience, Beth would watch the breed being judged and realize the difference in quality between her dog and those in the show ring. She wrote to Jack and Beth White of Melody Kennels and asked for a dog. She acquired Ch. Melody Cat Ballou and she was off and running. Next she contacted Carol Schubert of Watseka and acquired Ch. Johnnie Walker of Watseka.

Later, after Beth married Bobby Hallman, they established Tattersall Kennels in Texas. Her foundation bitch was Tattersall Wedgewood Cameo.

ESQUIRE

When a good breeder passes on and there is no one to continue that breeder's breeding program, it is wonderful to find that new people are ready to pick up the threads of the program and to continue. The Altmans, who live in the Pacific Northwest, bought a pet Dal and then discovered the great hobby of showing. They bought a liver bitch, an outcross of Long Last and Hopi Kachina, and started Homespun Dals. They have been able to finish some of her produce, but they feel that their biggest triumph was buying a puppy from Esquire Dalmatians, a kennel that is carrying on Long Last.

Not only do the Altmans train their dogs for conformation, they also put Obedience titles on them and now are considering tracking.

MERRY GO ROUND

Prominent among the breeders in the Pacific Northwest are Rob and Patti Strand with their Merry Go Round Dals. In the slightly more than twenty years they have been involved in the breed they have handled numerous dogs to their championships and the sires they have bred have produced more than 100 champion get. Working carefully and using selective breeding, they have established their own line and it is breeding true. Their triumphs have included many specialty wins, Group wins and several Bests in Show. Their current champion sire is Am. & Can. Ch. Merry Go Round, XKE, a multi-Best in Show and specialty show winner.

JAYBAR

Jaybar Dalmatians of southern California contributed to the success of Merry Go Round Dals. Barbara Niemeyer founded Jaybar after she learned of the world of dog shows. Her first dog was a rescue dog, but her interest in quality Dals was sparked by the beauty of the dogs found at shows. She determined to breed one that could be shown to its championship. Her Ch. Dandy Dan of Coachmaster, a liver, was the sire of twenty-one champions. His sister, Bobby's Suzanne of Birch, became the dam of three champions—one of whom, Ch. Karastella Cadillac of MGR, became one of the top producers in the breed. Ch. Jaybar's Black Label was a Group winner. Mrs. Niemeyer is now a Dalmatian judge.

PROCTOR

Serving on the Board of Governors of the DCA has not stopped the breeding program of Eva Berg and her husband, Ken. Using the prefix Proctor they have finished more than thirty champions. Their foundation study was Ch. Merry Folks of Tallara and their foundation bitch was Ch. Paisley of Proctor, a daughter of Ch. Melody Up Up and Away, CD, one of the top producing bitches in the breed and the daughter of another top producer, Ch. Tamara of Watseka.

In addition to their breeding program, the Bergs are committed to the obedience ring and many of their champions are also Obedience titlists.

RAMBLER

Rambler Dalmatians, owned by Jim and Joanne Nash, was started when the Nash family decided they wanted a puppy in their lives. It had never occurred to them that they would become deeply involved in breeding and showing dogs. Although it has been less than twenty years since they purchased their first Dalmatian, they are probably the foremost breeders in the northern California area today.

The Nash family is also involved in Obedience and in temperament testing.

Am. Can. Ch. Merry go Round, XKE, Best in Show winner

Am. Can. Mex. & Inter. Ch. Madhurason's Tanfastic

Many of their champions have at least a CD in Obedience (some are currently working in Utility) and a TT to prove their excellent temperaments.

The list of dogs they have bred and finished is too extensive to list here. They credit help from Fred Klensch, the Dahlstroms, Mark Sachau, Sue Mac-Millan of Paisley, Gladys Cox, Marsha Knight and many co-owners. Rambler Dalmatians has provided foundation stock for many kennels across the United States.

ROYAL OAKS

It is heartening to know that the breeding program and careful planning of an established kennel will be carried on when the owner and guiding hand is no longer here to do so. The Tallara Kennels, with breeding based on Leo Meeker's great Four-in-Hand stock, is being carried on by Eric and Ardith Dahlstrom under the Royal Oaks prefix.

When the Dahlstroms moved to a rural area in northern California and had no way of attracting puppy buyers, they entered into an arrangement with Jim and Joanne Nash (Rambler), and their co-ownership agreements have produced some top winning and top producing get.

All the Royal Oaks dogs are OFA-certified and BAER tested. Only bilateral hearing dogs are used in the breeding program.

SPOTTSBORO

Spottsboro Dals of Donna McCluer has been in existence since 1972. With a limited budget for breeding and showing, she has managed to get two dogs in the list of all-time winning dogs that runs in *The Spotter* each year. The dogs, oddly enough, are father and son! The top winner of the two is Ch. Spottsboro Rebel Streak, who tallied 219 Bests of Breed. His son, Ch. Spottsboro Sungold Streaker, CD, scored 84 BOBs.

Donna is also active in Obedience and tracking. Her dogs spend much time at photography studios, where they are used in advertising photos.

JO DAL

Jo Dal Dalmatians is another successful kennel in California. Mae and Jo Mellinger are busily engaged in breeding good Dals with good temperaments. They started in Dals in 1962, but the bitch they acquired had no interest in showing. The Dalwood owners, Carol Haywood and Peggy Rudder, later asked to breed the bitch because their foundation bitch had had to be spayed and they were about to lose their line of breeding stock. This bitch was able to produce several champions for Dalwood.

With the show bug still biting them, the Mellingers acquired a dog from Crown Jewels and a bitch from Colonial Coach. From them they bred a specialty show winner. Later the bitch produced Ch. Jo Dal Drummer Boy Hapi Dal, who was an all-breed Best in Show winner.

HARMONY

Harmony is the kennel name of Jan and Doug Nelson, who now live in Evergreen, Colorado. The kennel was founded in 1971 when they were living in the Minneapolis area. In 1975 they acquired their first Dalmatian. Their foundation bitch was Ch. Paisley's Harmony Bouquet, CD, TT, a liver sired by Ch. Long Last Living Legend out of Ch. Melody Up Up and Away, CD, the famous Pooka. This bitch had an enviable Specialty career in 1978, going Winners Bitch in St. Louis, Best of Winners in Chicago, Reserve Winners Bitch at Davenport and New York and winning first place in the Open Liver class at the National Specialty.

The Nelsons' first Harmony litter was produced in 1977. From that point on they have continued to breed sparingly, with temperament and soundness being emphasized. Since they also wish to demonstrate the intelligence of their dogs, most of them have Obedience titles as well.

TUCKAWAY

In the Kentucky area we still have Tuckaway, the Dal kennel of Sidney Remmele, DVM. The second generation is now involved, as Sid's daughter, Julie Rian, is breeding and showing Dals under the Tuckaway name. This is a help to Dr. Remmele, as his popularity as a judge of numerous breeds keeps him very busy.

PEPPER PIKE

Shirley and Joe Newmark have been involved in Dals since the early 1970s. They established their kennel, Pepper Pike, in 1972. Early on their main interest seemed to be in Obedience, but all their dogs were also shown in the breed ring. Perhaps the most famous of their dogs was Ch. Glenn Oaks Favorite Son, a liver Dal, a son of Ch. Jameson of Shawnee. He has sired a number of champion get and managed to garner seventy-two Bests of Breed in his show career. Their Ch. Colonial Coach at Pepper Pike, CD, was a HIT, a specialty BOB and a Group winner at an all-breed show, all in 1979.

SARATOGA

Just west of St. Louis one finds Saratoga Dalmatians in St. Charles, Missouri. This kennel was established in 1972 by Denver and Georgia Nichols. Thinking they were buying a pet, they were soon stricken by the show bug. The original dog was Georgia's Peach Blossom, CD. A little later they purchased Toga, Saratoga of Santana, their foundation bitch. She finished her championship, added a CD and then started producing for them. Other champions from Saratoga are too numerous to mention, and many more can be expected as the Nicholses are continuing a fine breeding program.

CULURIEN

Kennel names often have fascinating stories behind them and Culurien Kennels is no exception. The word is pronounced Koo-LOO-ree-en, and it was taken from Tolkien's *Lord of the Rings* and translates to "song of gold." This is the kennel name used by Sue Sommerfield, who is deeply immersed in Dalmatians—aided and abetted by her mother, Fay, and her father, Stan.

When Sue arrived in her family there was a Boxer who was two years older than she and who became her babysitter. He lived more than fifteen years. Later Sue opted to get a Dalmatian because she liked the personality and temperament of the breed. She obtained from Billie Ingram her first Dal, Brio Breeze's Shining Star, CD.

Sue has been working as a trainer at Olde Towne School for Dogs in her area of Virginia and has been doing some handling for other people. One great win as a handler was going WB at the 1984 Centennial specialty show with Ch. Cal's Dal's Diamond Liver Lovely, owned and bred by Bill and Natalie Johnson.

OVATION

There are numerous people involved in Dalmatians who had wanted a dog as children but were denied that privilege. Among those is Charlotte Katz with her Ovation Dalmatians. Charlotte really didn't know what kind of a dog she wanted, she just wanted a dog. When she married she found that she could have a dog and decided that a Dal would be the best kind. She found, through trial and error, Jackie Esworthy and her Cynjac Dals. Cynjac's Pepsi Generation was the name of her first dog. Shortly thereafter a career change took these two Marylanders to Minneapolis.

An Obedience instructor sent Charlotte to conformation classes held by the Minneapolis Kennel Club. There Charlotte met Sue MacMillan of Paisley Dalmatians, who became her mentor. After successfully breeding Pepsi to a Paisley

Ch. Saratoga's You Can Have It All

Ch. Rambler Singular Sensation

dog and having the good fortunate to have three of the litter finish, the Ovation dogs were once more to transfer location.

Because of her association with Sue, Charlotte learned to read and evaluate pedigrees. She has had continued success with her breeding program of perhaps one or two litters per year, producing specialty, Sweepstakes and Group winners.

PARADOX

Lynne Baum grew up in the household of a professional handler and a Boxer breeder, so her interest in dogs and dog shows has been with her always. When Lynne was younger she showed a Whippet and a Doberman in the Junior Showmanship classes.

When Lynne became an adult she acquired a Dal and finished it the following year. This was Ch. Tujay's Polkahontas. Lynne put a CD on her shortly after she finished. She acquired another Dal from Sheila Wymore. She has done some breeding with Donna McCluer's Spottsboro dogs. At present she has Paradox Enchanted Toi, CD, and Paradox Peerless Panda, CD. All of Lynne's dogs are shown in both the breed and the Obedience ring. She is hoping for a great future with her dogs.

CARDHILL THIDWICK

Lizabeth Hancock was an Obedience buff through and through. She had a lovely Dal, Coachlake London Lady, CD, and was planning to continue in Obedience with her when her father was transferred with the military to Germany. When they came home Lady was too old to jump for the required exercises in the advanced classes. Lizabeth acquired from Carol Diehl another Dal, also an Obedience dog. But then she decided she might try her hand in conformation. She co-owned a bitch with Carol, bred a litter and finally whelped her first homebred champion, Ch. Cardhill Thidwick Cleopatra. Lizabeth has continued to breed and show and has not neglected the Obedience side of the shows either.

COACHMASTER

Breeding to the great Ch. Roadcoach Roadster gave the Coachmaster Dals a great start on winning and producing. Bob and Shirley Hayes bred their bitch, Black Baby of Tarzana, to the great winning Dal and produced a great winning bitch, Ch. Coachmaster's Roadette. Roadette in turn became a great producer for the Hayeses. She was bred to Ch. Colonial Coach Carriage Way and produced the winning bitch Ch. Coachmaster's Bernadette.

Among other wins, Roadette was Best of Breed at the Dalmatian Club of Northern California from the Veteran Bitch class at eight and a half years of age in 1971. She was named Best Brood Bitch at the southern California specialties in 1970, 1971 and 1972. Six of her produce from two litters were show winners. Bernadette finished her championship in Mexico as well as in the United States and won numerous Groups and Bests of Breed here.

The Hayeses have continued to breed and have produced a number of champions, including Ch. Coachmaster's Impresario, who was sired by Ch. Rickway's Topper, sire of Carriage Way, Ch. Dandy Dan of Coachmaster and a specialty winner, Ch. Coachmaster's Tycoon, owned by the Sachaus. They now live in Minnesota.

HAPI-DALS

Hapi-Dals is another California kennel that has been breeding Dalmatians for a number of years. Ralph and Margaret Schools are the guiding lights of these dogs. Over the years they have finished about twenty champions. The foundation stud was Ch. Blackpool Lancer, a son of the great winning bitch Ch. Blackpool Crinkle Forest. This dog sired a number of champion get, including Ch. Cal Dal Chocolate Chip, UDT, the second male in Dal history to have both a championship and a UDT title. He was owned and handled by Jon Mett. Many of the Hapi-Dals are behind some of the winning dogs of the present time.

CARAVAN

The Heriots, who own Caravan Dals, completed a long distance move from the Washington, D.C., area to Iowa City, Iowa. They reported that they were unprepared for the friendliness that greeted them in dog circles in that area of the country. They started out with Snowcap and Green Starr stock and have finished several champions and bred a few litters. They were fortunate enough to win a Group with their homebred bitch Ch. Caravan's Campaign Promise and were delighted to receive notes and cards of congratulations from their competitors.

The Heriots are now living in Winston-Salem, North Carolina.

COACHKEEPER

In the Houston area a breeding kennel that has produced a number of champions is Coachkeeper, which belongs to the Romeros. Among the champions they have produced we find Ch. Coachkeeper Quaker Queen, Ch. Quaker's Acre Coachkeeper, CD, Ch. Coachkeeper Mocha Mist, Ch. Coachkeeper's Pamela Sue, Ch. Blizzard of Quaker's Acre, Ch. Gale Storm of QA and Mex. Ch. Coachkeeper's Prince of La Mancha. The names indicate the background of these fine animals.

BESPECKLED

Dog affairs are a family activity at the home of Nan and Ken Nagler. Nan is the handler in the conformation ring and Ken and daughter Susan are the trainers in the Obedience ring.

Some years ago Nan decided she wanted a dog. She knew she wanted a Dalmatian, as she had seen one in the neighborhood and felt that it was the most beautiful animal she had ever seen. The Naglers purchased a puppy that became Lightning Sparks, UD. He was mostly Never Complain breeding, Emily Lennartson's stock.

The UD title on the dog started Ken on obedience work to the point that he is now a judge of all obedience classes. Their second Dalmatian was Ch. Princess Lois of Loki, UD. Lois was mostly Reigate and Byrondale breeding. A male out of Lois that finished his championship and UD title was Ch. Charcoal Chips, UD. They also owned Ch. Bespeckled Becky, UD. The Naglers are now using the prefix Bespeckled on all their breeding.

It is difficult to imagine achieving a championship and a UD on a Dalmatian, but the Naglers have had three, and several dogs which have had CDs and CDXs.

ROLENET

Doing a favor for a friend introduced Bob and Lenore Liggett to the world of Dalmatians. For some time the Liggetts had been showing Boxers in the Texas area with little success. One day, Mrs. Chester of Shiloh Dalmatians asked Bob to handle a Dal for her at a show. Bob agreed to help her out and so found the Dal to be a great breed.

Mrs. Chester with pleased with Bob's handling and consulted him on finding a stud for her bitch. Together they wrote to numerous kennels and finally decided to use Ch. Blackpool's Bullshot. Mrs. Chester gave Bob a bitch from the ensuing litter.

Through this breeding the Liggetts became acquainted with the Peterses of Blackpool Kennels. Later Bob acquired a fine animal from the Peterses, Ch. Blackpool's Ironstone. Stoney was the foundation stud of the Rolenet Dalmatians.

The Liggetts continue to breed and show fine specimens. Bob serves as treasurer of the DCA.

Multiple BIS winner Am. & Can. Ch. Godin's To Be or Not To Be. Samantha has tied the record for most BIS wins by a bitch.

Ch. Bespeckled Becky, UD

LIMESTONE

Cincinnati is now the home of Limestone Kennels, owned by Cindy Ingalls. Her top dog is Am. & Can. Ch. Limestone Zara Padaric. He sired a fine dog out of Am. & Can. Ch. Camosun's Kate Dalrymple, a liver that was sent to Brazil. Other dogs in her kennels are Limestone Nell of Raintree, a liver, Benjamin of Bay Colony, also a liver, Limestone Lexington and Limestone Counterpoint, all of them winning Dalmatians.

Cindy has done some fine work for the breed as leader of the Judges' Education Committee.

ROAD RUNNER

In Florida, where many people have moved either to escape the dreaded northern winters or for retirement, the outstanding breeding kennel in Dalmatians is Road Runner, owned by the Gambles of Fort Meyers. Their first great dog was Ch. Richard the L. H. Roadrunner, CD. Richard finished by winning the Group at the Augusta Kennel Club. He has done his share of siring and some of his get are doing very well in Colombia, Venezuela and Brazil. The Gambles were helped on their way by the advice and counsel of Mary Munro Smith and Bob Einig, who used to handle for them.

Another of their winning dogs is Ch. Range Trail Bunker Hill. They also have Ch. Pill Peddler's Roadrunner Jane, Ch. Roadrunner's Love Bug and Ch. The Roadrunner's Mickey Finn. Mrs. Gamble is now a judge.

OTHER BREEDERS OF NOTE

Other West Coast breeders who are showing and breeding with success include the Barnetts of Drumhille, Patsy Wallace Jones with Chalkhill Dals, Ed and Carol Petit with their Hansom Dals, Dalwood Dalmatians and Irene Brink and the Cinder Dals. Fred Klensch and his Pacifica Dalmatians produced a Best in Show winner, Ch. Pacifica Pride of Poseidon, as well as a specialty show and a Best in Show winner, Ch. Beaumont of Pacifica. Few kennels produce two top award winners.

Dalwood Dals, owned by Georgiann Rudder and Carol and Diane Haywood, have produced a number of very fine dogs but they are proudest of their Dalwood's Knight Edition. He finished in the United States and then went to Mexico City for four international shows, returning home with the International, Mexican and world show titles, winning Best of Breed at all four shows and a Group I, II and IV.

In the Phoenix and Tucson areas we find Van Dals and Tucwinn. Van Dals owes its fine reputation to Crestview foundation stock. Three champions were

194

produced in one litter sired by Ch. Crestview Thunderstar out of Dono Perro del Punto, CD, Ch. Van Dals Raisin in the Sun, Ch. Van Dals Puddin Pie, CD and Ch. Van Dals Whipper Snapper were all handled to their titles by Bonnie Van der Vort, who also handled Ch. Crestview Rogue to Winners Dog at the DCA specialty in 1978 in California for his owners, Jim and Vi McManus.

At Tucwinn, Sarah Simaan has been the handler most of the time. She is the daughter of Constance Simaan, the breeder and owner of Tucwinn dogs. The foundation stock for the breeding kennel is Melody and the breeding program is built from linebreeding to the Melody status.

In Wyoming we find the Jalonens with Khaseyno Kanines, and in Nevada we find Coachwyn, owned by Karen Barthen, who has been successful with Ch. Coachwyn's Chevy and Ch. Coachwyn's Color Me Candid.

Famous imported Ch. Nigel of Welfield

The famous Ch. Snow Leopard

17

Around the World
with the Dalmatian

ALTHOUGH the breed's place of birth may be uncertain, there is no doubt that the coach dog was adopted and developed by the British. England became the Dals' mother country.

UNITED KINGDOM

Early writers put the Dal in Great Britain more than 400 years ago. Also used to symbolize the Church of Rome when Oliver Cromwell was in power (1653–1658), by 1665 the Dal was coaching on English roads. By 1790 a likeness was carved on wood by Thomas Beswick and published in London. Previously referred to as the Coach Dog, Carriage Dog, Spotted Dog, Plum Pudding Dog, "Spotted Dick," Danish Dog, Harrier of Bengal, Braque de Bangale, *Canis variegatis* or Little Danish Dog, the dog was called a Dalmatian by Beswick.

By 1860 classes were offered at a dog show in Birmingham. The Dal arrived as a show dog in England more than 100 years ago.

Before that the breed's job had varied. Used as a gun dog, a badger and bullbaiting dog, a coach dog, a guard dog and companion for travelers and mail, a promenade dog, a protection and attention-getting dog for elegant carriages, a "pack" or watchdog for farmers' wives going to market, a music hall entertainer, and a Gypsy trick dog, the Dal was also used as a heraldic symbol. In addition to being one of the best looking of all dogs, the Dal had intelligence, versatility and charm and was a good companion.

The British loved Dalmatians. They defined breed type and brought it closer to perfection. They drafted a Standard that later became the foundation for the Standards of all other countries. They organized clubs for the Dal's promotion and protection.

Exported from England to most of the rest of the world, the Dalmatian was received with considerable enthusiasm. The British type was used to improve the breed on the continent and overseas. Imports from Great Britain have been the foundation stock for important kennels the world over.

Agitation in England for a Dalmatian club was started by Hugo Droesse. Mr. Droesse had promoted twenty-one Dalmatian entries for the Crystal Palace Show in 1889. There had been none the year before. With the enthusiasm generated by this support Mr. Droesse wrote to the dog papers: "At the last Crystal Palace show several exhibitors and gentlemen interested in Dalmatians expressed their willingness to support a special club for the breed, and urged on me to take the matter in hand, acting in the meantime as hon. sec. pro tem. As the proposal is a most welcome one to me, and has my full approval and support, I shall be pleased to hear from anyone favorable to the object, and trust that not only lovers of the breed in Great Britain, but also those residing abroad, will communicate with me. At the same time I shall be glad to have any propositions and suggestions, in regard to the club to be formed, which are likely to be of value and good for the furtherance of the object."

As a result of this start the Dalmatian Club was founded in 1890, with W. B. Herman as secretary. A Standard was formulated that same year. It was the fourth for the breed. Previous Standards had been unofficial descriptions written by Vero Shaw in 1882, by Stonehenge (John Henry Walsh) in 1886 and a translation from *Der Hunde Sport* published in the *Fanciers Gazette* in 1889. When the North of England Dalmatian Club was formed in the Manchester area in 1903 it adopted the 1890 Standard, with only a change in the weight of bitches.

World War I almost annihilated the breed. To counteract government pressure to destroy all dogs, the Kennel Club of Great Britain stopped all registration for the duration. Added to the deprivations due to the war was a general muzzling order lasting until 1922 because of rabies brought in by imported dogs.

Without horses it seemed the coach dog was losing friends. The Crystal Palace show in 1920 had only one Dalmatian. The single exhibitor, Fred Kemp, thought something should be done about it. In 1925 a group of enthusiasts met at Crufts and from that meeting the Southern Dalmatian Club was formed. Mr. Kemp became and remained its president for twenty-two years. The Dalmatian's fortunes began to change.

The Southern Dalmatian Club grew rapidly. It soon became national in

198

Queen Victoria had a Dalmatian

Ch. Colonsay's Olaf the Red

Goworth's Victor

Am. & Can. Ch. Colonsay Blacksmith

scope. In 1930 it changed its name to the British Dalmatian Club. The All Ireland Dalmatian Club was formed in 1934.

World War II played hob with the entire Dog Fancy. Little breeding took place. "Radius shows" were instituted by the kennel club. Only dogs living within twenty-five miles of the show site were permitted to enter. When peace was achieved dog activity began again. The three Dalmatian clubs and the British breeders made a fresh start. Apparently the enthusiasm and know-how survived because when the first postwar specialty show was held on October 2, 1945, by the British Dalmatian Club there were 263 entries.

By 1947 the British Dal Club was publishing *Spots of News*, a newsletter edited by Leighton Yeomans, to keep members informed. The club engaged in many kinds of varied activities, educational and social. It developed a rescue service "dedicated to helping needy dogs to find kindly humans and happy homes." Membership in other countries grew. *Spots of News* from the start reported exported dogs becoming champions in many other countries. That same year the original Dalmatian Club phased out.

The British Dalmatian Club handbooks, which had been published from 1934 through 1938, were reinstated in 1949 and published every three years since. The Dalmatian continued to hold its own in Britain despite some economic ups and downs. The breed became better known and loved when Dodie Smith's *One Hundred and One Dalmatians* was published in England in 1956. Five years later moviegoers were charmed by Walt Disney's version of the story as an animated cartoon.

When the British Dalmatian Club leadership became concerned about a 20 percent drop in registrations in 1954, they could not anticipate the future effect of the efforts of Dodie Smith and Walt Disney. The delightful book and the animated movie had considerable impact on the popularity of the breed around the world. Mrs. Smith's book was first published serially in *Woman's Day* magazine under the title, "The Great Dog Robbery."

In commenting on this in 1977, Mrs. Cooper, editor of the British Dalmatian Club's monthly newsletter, wrote: "Obviously nobody at that time would have believed a time would come when the club was seriously asking members to try to restrict breeding, or that several hundred pounds a year would need to be spent in rescuing and rehabilitating dogs which were in need of homes."

The British Dalmatian Club continued to grow. Its Golden Jubilee Championship show in April 1975 pulled an entry of 99 dogs and 140 bitches, total number of entries 464. By 1977, when the Queen's Silver Jubilee was being celebrated, the club had 1,079 members, 887 at home and 192 overseas. It had overseas representatives in seven countries: Australia, Canada, Holland, India, Sweden, the United States, and New Zealand. There were overseas members in twenty-one countries: Australia, Brazil, Belgium, Canada, Finland, France, Germany, Holland, Hungary, Kenya, Liberia, New Zealand, Nigeria, Norway, Portugal, South Africa, Spain, Sweden, Switzerland, the United States and Yugoslavia.

Ch. The Lash

Litter of British puppies

Whether the official regulatory bodies of these far-flung nations were affiliated with the Kennel Club of Great Britain or more recently with the FCI (Federacion Cynologique Internationale), founded in 1911, or independent of either, the British Standard became the basis for judging the breed. It has been translated into many languages. While the Standard has been rewritten in some countries, particularly the United States and Canada, the Dalmatian dog remains remarkably the same around the world. This we have found to be true when judging in Australia, New Zealand, South Africa, Mexico, Canada and South America. There are some discussions about size and length and blue eyes, but the friendly, dignified, beautifully spotted dog is universally loved as a companion and guard.

Dalmatian owners in many countries gather together to form clubs to further the breed and their own enjoyment of dogs. One needs to list them to realize how many have grown up over a period of time in many parts of the world. Where known we have included the year of their origin.

GREAT BRITAIN

>Dalmatian Club, 1890–1947
>North of England Dalmatian Club, 1903
>Southern Dalmatian Club, 1925–1930
>British Dalmatian Club, 1930
>All Ireland Dalmatian Club, 1934
>Dalmatian Club of Scotland, 1970
>Northern Ireland Dalmatian Club

EUROPE

>French Dalmatian Club, 1951
>Dalmatian Club Luxembourgeois
>Nederlandse Club Voor Dalmatische Honden, 1947
>Klubben for Storre Selskapshundraser (Norway)
>Deutscher Dalmatiner Club, 1920
>Finnish Dalmatian Club
>Swedish Dalmatian Society, 1962
>Dalmatian Club of Switzerland
>Dalmatian Club of Czechoslovakia
>Dalmatian Club of Austria

AFRICA

>Dalmatian Club of South Africa, 1961
>Southern Cross Dalmatian Breeders Club
>Dalmatian Club of East Africa

ASIA

>Indonesia Dalmatian Club
>Dalmatian Club of Japan

Dalmatian Club in Australia, 1943
Dalmatian Club of South Australia, 1972
Dalmatian Club of Victoria, 1953
Dalmatian Club of New Zealand
Dalmatian Association of Queensland, 1973
Dalmatian Club of Australian Capitol Territory, 1977

NORTH AMERICA

Dalmatian Club of Canada, 1966
Club Dalmata de México, 1975
Dalmatian Club of America, 1904 (29 local clubs mentioned in chapter 5)
Dalmatian Club of Quebec

CENTRAL AND SOUTH AMERICA

Dalmata Clube do Brasil
Dalmatian Club of Trinidad and Tobago, 1958
Club Argentino del Dalmata
Club Dalmata de México AC, 1975

SWEDEN

Dalmatians are a popular breed in Sweden. The Dalmatian Club there was founded in 1962 and has about 500 members. The breed has grown from practically no dogs at all to a fairly large segment of the dog population.

In the early part of the century there were a few Dalmatians in Sweden, mostly of German and English stock. These seem to have died out.

In the early 1930s two dogs were imported from England. They were Marjo of Elk Isle and Dotty of Elk Isle. A few years later a bitch named Princess Polly and a dog named Duff were brought in from England. These four were used for breeding and all the Dals in Sweden descended from them. The breed went into a sad state, as all the dogs were inbred without any infusion of new blood to help the situation. Anna Hammarlund had a good Dal puppy from this original line. She called this dog Kief. He was an International, Norwegian and Scandinavian champion. She then imported some English bitches and established a great stock of Dals in Sweden. Kief was about the last Dal from the original stock. Mrs. Hammarlund also imported a male from America, Ch. Fleetwood Nu Boot of Dalmatia, a son of the famous Bootblack out of Ch. Fleetwood Farms China Doll. With this infusion of blood from the United States and the English imports, the Dalmatian in Sweden is now well established. Pictures of the Swedish dogs show them to be sound, well-boned and well-marked animals.

Mrs. Hammarlund is the author of a book on Dalmatians. She deals mostly with breeding the possible genetic combinations and how to handle puppies. The book, a fascinating one, is written in Swedish, of course. Natalie Fleger of Colonial Coach met Mrs. Hammarlund when she visited the United States. Mrs. Hammarlund gave her a copy of the book. Several breeders were able to find someone to translate it. We have enjoyed reading about the Swedish dogs.

ARGENTINA

In Argentina there is a very active and dedicated breeder. Andrea Paccagnella has been in Dals since she was thirteen years old. Her father gave her and her sister an encyclopedia on dogs and they fell in love with the Dal. After much begging Andrea received a lovely little bitch as a present from her father. Unfortunately, the dog turned out to be deaf. She lived with Andrea for fourteen years, however. Andrea had taught her to obey hand signals. About this time they moved to Brazil and there she learned about showing and breeding. She acquired her foundation sire and dam from Dr. Walkyria Figueiredo's kennel. Dr. Figueiredo's dogs were a combination of Watseka, Melody and Paisley breeding—all three top kennels in the United States. With these dogs Andrea proceeded to establish her own line when she returned to Argentina. She has bred ten champions, with more on the way.

Using the prefix Zagreb, Andrea has produced the top Dal in Argentina for 1987 and top bitch in 1985 and 1988. She and her sister were active in the club Argentino del Dalmata, which is inactive at this time.

MEXICO

In Mexico until recently Dalmatian breeding has been done pretty much on a hit-or-miss basis. At one time, however, there was a major kennel known as Dalmex and owned by Dr. Phillip Chancellor. He purchased a number of top winning dogs and bitches in both England and the United States in order to produce good Dals. At one time he had at least eighty dogs and produced about fourteen litters each year, all well-thought-out breedings.

One of his dogs that had won an all-breed Best in Show in the United States was declared ineligible by the AKC to win this award. This triggered a disastrous reaction in Dr. Chancellor's kennel. He discontinued all Dalmatian activity, dispersed his kennel and the careful breeding disappeared into mediocrity.

A number of other breeders were known to be producing some Dalmatians in Mexico. Among them was Mañuel Avila Camacho, president of Mexico from 1940 to 1946; the Beteta family, Ramon and his nephew Mario Ramon, both of whom were ministers of finance under different presidents; the Rivera Torres family; Manuel Buch; a Señor Jaurequi; and Luis Garcia Maurino.

Eng. & Am. Ch. Colonsay Storm

Mex. & Int. Ch. Queene Victoria de la Mancha and Mex. & Int. Don Benjamin de la Mancha

Dr. Chancellor's dog Ch. Dalmex Chicharrin won an all-breed Best in Show in Mexico in 1961. The only other all-breed Best in Show win for Dalmatians was in Mexicali in 1976 when an American-bred liver Dal, Am. & Mex. Ch. Little Slam's Jack of Hearts, won the honor.

In 1975 the Club Dalmata de México AC was incorporated. It is the official club for the breed in Mexico and presently has as members most of the serious breeders and exhibitors of Dalmatians in Mexico. It has held several specialty shows. The first show in April 1976 was judged by Robin Hernandez. The second assignment for the specialty in November 1976 was given to Dr. David Doane of the United States. Evelyn Nelson White judged the third specialty in November 1977 and Alfred E. Treen passed on the dogs at the fourth specialty in 1978.

The Mexican Kennel Club (Federación Canofila Méxicana) is affiliated with the FCI, so all the Standards used in Mexico are approved by that body.

The Mexican Dalmatians are certainly under greater influence from the Dalmatians in the United States than from those in England, Germany, Sweden, Luxembourg and other European countries. It is logical that the Mexican Standard would resemble that of the Dalmatian Club of America. The point of contention is, of course, the blue eye, perfectly acceptable in the United States and Mexico, frowned on in European countries.

The original officers of the Club Dalmata de México were Raymond F. Fitzsimmons, president; Emilio Barajas, vice-president; Rodolfo Saldana, secretary; and John Hogan, treasurer. Enrique Castillo was a director.

Mr. Fitzsimmons has been a leader in the Dalmatian community for a number of years. The National Breeders Association named him the Distinguished Breeder of the Year in 1976, a highly coveted honor.

Early in the decade there was little or no usable stock in Mexico. The La Mancha line (Fitzsimmons and Gonzales) went to the United States to improve the quality and provide a reasonably acceptable gene pool available for serious breeders. The La Mancha line has accounted for fifty-three champions and fifteen international champions, two of which are world champions. Three of La Mancha's imported dogs have achieved Mexican championships. All three are international champions and one of them has won an American championship. The third imported dog was a liver male, Ch. Coachkeeper Prince de La Mancha, sired by Ch. Storm King of Quaker's Acre out of Ch. Cinderella's Coach Keeper, and litter brother to the Best in Show Ch. Coachkeeper's Blizzard of Quaker's Acre. This dog was involved in a serious car accident that eliminated any further showing.

The Club Dalmata de México seems to be in a dormant state at the present time, although there are still a number of Dals to be found in Mexico. Raymond Fitzsimmons's business has placed him in the United States most of the time, so he is unable to lend his leadership to the Mexican club as he did in the past. This, coupled with the untimely death of Alejandro Gonzalez, co-owner with Raymond of the La Mancha Dals, has conspired to put the club on the back burner.

Ch. Duca di Mantua

Am. & Can. Ch. Countryroad Cool Million

Several Mexican Dals were shown in the spring of 1990 at shows in Mexico City, so all of them have not disappeared. We can hope for renewed interest in the breed in the future. Now that the AKC has opened the door for Mexican dogs to compete in the American shows as the Canadian dogs have always done, we can look forward to seeing more of them in the ring.

SOUTH AFRICA

The South African club was formed in December 1961 by the leading Dalmatian breeders in the Transvaal, namely Mesdames Bell, Hoggard, Peacock, Popham and Roseveare, and Messrs. Aronson, Bell and Peacock. Mr. Aronson was transferred overseas shortly after the forming of the club, but the other members built the organization into a fine group of fanciers.

Mrs. Peacock remembers the days when only three or four Dals would be entered at a show. The British Dalmatian Club offered a silver spoon to be awarded to the first Dal to win Best of Breed over an entry of at least six dogs. After a four-year struggle the target number was reached and the spoon was awarded to Mrs. Peacock's Ch. Judith of Yumbani.

The club held its first specialty show in October 1976. It was judged by Captain E. E. Adams, a Boxer breeder and a judge of a number of breeds under the Kennel Union of South Africa aegis. Chairman of the specialty show was C. E. McDonald. Serving with him were Mrs. McCallum, Mrs. J. Davies, Mrs. S. McDonald, Miss McCallum, Mr. E. Davies and Miss J. Maltman.

The Southern Cross group was originally an offshoot of the Dalmatian club, but whatever caused the divergence has been lost in the limbos of the past. Now the membership of the two groups overlaps and each club supports the efforts of the other.

At the Goldfield's Kennel Club show in 1977 there were nearly sixty Dalmatians entered, and the two clubs banded together to host a delightful dinner party for the American judges at that show.

CANADA

The Dalmatian Club of Canada is an active and cohesive group even though its membership is spread all over the provinces and there are few local clubs to help it grow. The only one in existence is the Dalmatian Club of Quebec, which was responsible for the first Dal specialty ever held in Canada.

The Canadian group suffered a terrible blow in 1989 with the sudden death of Monica Brooks. Mrs. Brooks and her husband, John, were the authors of the monumental book *Dalmatians in Canada*. Monica was secretary and John is president of the Dalmatian Club of Canada. They had both served the club in the past in numerous capacities. Monica's passing has been a great loss to the club.

An Argentine Grand Champion

Am. & Can. Ch. Alfredrich Handsome, Tall 'n Dark

Am. & Can. Ch. Countryroad Lassiter

The club holds a National Specialty each year, moving it around from East Coast to West Coast and points in between. When it is held on the West Coast and as far east as Winnipeg very few exhibitors from Ontario and Quebec manage to compete. When it is held in the eastern provinces the reverse is true: very few exhibitors form the west are to be found. And yet many of the Canadians show at the DCA shows no matter where they are held. Canadian exhibitors have chalked up some impressive wins at U.S. specialty shows, including the DCA National.

Among those who cross the border with some frequency is Sam Hart, from Hamilton, Ontario. Sam gained fame with his Am. & Can. Ch. Korcula King of Hearts. He has shown numerous Canadian dogs to their championships in both countries, supporting many regional specialties as well as the national. One bitch that he handled, Am. & Can. Ch. Canusa Kandi Kisses, was Best of Breed at three specialty shows in the United States. In addition, Sam has officiated as a Sweepstakes judge in Ohio and has done some judging in Canada.

Linda and Charles Cyopik registered their kennel, Countryroad Dalmations, with the Canadian Kennel Club in 1973. Their first litter was whelped in 1974 and their first Canadian champion finished in 1975. To date the Cyopiks of Puslinch, Ontario, have finished sixty homebred Canadian champions and twenty homebred American champions. Kay Robinson Maurer of the famous Willowmount Dals started them off. They obtained a bitch from her and following her advice produced their first Canadian Best in Show and American specialty winner, Am. & Can. Ch. Countryroad Cool Million. This dog sired thirty-five American and twenty-seven Canadian champions. He is still prominent in the bloodlines of some of today's winning dogs. Four of the Countryroad Dals— Cool Million, Cool Classic, Strike it Rich and Lassiter—have won Best of Breed at ten American specialty shows. All four held championships in both countries.

The Cyopiks continue to breed carefully and successfully. A bitch of their breeding, Am. & Can. Ch. Countryroad Cachet Roadpartner, was sired by Benito Vila's English import, Ch. Buffrey Jobee. The bitch is owned by John and Betty Pris of British Columbia. In the three months the Cyopiks showed her she earned her American title in three straight weekends, including BOW at the Pittsburgh Dal specialty. She earned enough Bests of Breed and Group placements to be the number one Dal bitch in Canada for 1989.

Alfredrich Kennels, of Casselman, Ontario, owned by Jean-Richard Millaire and Al Kay, has made a great impression on the breeding and winning of Dalmatians both in Canada and in the United States in a very short space of time.

A puppy supposedly destined to be a pet started the kennel on its way. This "pet" turned out to be Am. & Can. Ch. Evomack's Tsar of Carlsbad. He was Best of Breed at the Dalmatian Club of Canada specialty in 1980. He has sired some outstanding animals, including Am. & Can. Ch. Sunkist Singalong, dam of Am. & Can. Ch. Alfredrich Handsome Tall 'n Dark. This dog has had four all-breed Bests in Show in Canada and one in the United States—the first Canadian Dal to accomplish this. He has also won fourteen specialty shows in the

United States and sired more than twenty American champions. He has also won three Awards of Merit at DCA specialties. Chum, as he is known, will not be widely campaigned in the future but will be shown at selected specialties. He continues to sire fine puppies. His dam is also the granddam of a National Specialty winner, Am. & Can. Ch. Godin's To Be or Not To Be.

Going west we find some additional serious breeders. While they are not as active in attending specialty shows in the United States as those in Ontario or Quebec, they are nonetheless just as serious and dedicated.

Catherine Blinko came to Canada from England in 1952. At that time she had Labrador Retrievers, but her neighbor had horses and a Dal. She became interested in the Dal and when she returned to England for a visit she tried to buy a dog from Miss MacFie of Colonsay. Miss MacFie sent her a pup named Simon, registered as Colonsay Jester's Bell. It was difficult to finish a Dal at that time in British Columbia, where she lived, as there were so few of them.

A second visit to England brought a liver bitch from Maidun Kennels near Dorchester. She became Ch. Belisama of Maidun, call name Penny. Mrs. Blinko started showing her in the late 1950s. Simon remained a fine stud dog and Mrs. Blinko bred a daughter of his and Penny's, Ch. Camosun's Christmas Carol, to Ch. Double-Tree Break-in-the-Rein, Earl Libbey's fine liver dog. One of the descendants of this breeding was Am. & Can. Ch. Camosun's Bryony, a Canadian multiple Best in Show winner, Best of Winners at the DCA National Specialty in 1979 and a Group winner in the United States. She was the daughter of Can. & Am. Ch. Camosun's Fiona MacLeod, who won the first Dal National Specialty at Calgary, Alberta, under the late Joe Faigel.

Mrs. Blinko and Nilda Dorini have been good friends for a number of years and Mrs. Dorini does some of the showing and training for Mrs. Blinko. Best of Opposite Sex at the Canadian Dal specialty in 1989 was Mrs. Dorini's Horseman's Topper Too.

In Winnipeg we find Marie DuBois Gylytiuk, who is breeding and showing both in Canada and the United States using the prefix Rompford. Gina Stoski and Catherine Smith are both well-known Canadian breeders living in the Calgary area. Another notable breeder is William Thorburn in Saskatchewan. On the western coast we find Nilda Dorini, Thurley Duck and Joyce Ashley, all of whom are very active in both breeding and showing. These are but a few of the many fine breeders and exhibitors in the Dominion.

LUXEMBOURG

Although the Grand Duchy of Luxembourg is tiny in area, the Luxembourg Dalmatian Club is not. It is a very active group of people working hard to promote Dalmatians all over Europe. The guiding light of the group is Barbara Kacens, who acts as the secretary and the "responsible" editor of the *Spotted News,* the monthly publication sent out by this club. It contains information from

The beginning of Dalmatians in Japan

all over the world concerning the breed and lists the coming shows and the results of important ones.

This club published *Dalmatians in the World,* an informational book concerning all the clubs and countries in which there is any activity in Dalmatians. The club also published a Dalmatian handbook in 1978.

NEW ZEALAND

There are many Dals "down under" as well as several clubs devoted to the breed. In New Zealand there is a national club that holds specialties under the rules of its kennel club.

A guiding light in the Auckland area is Gordon Morris, a well-known breeder. He stepped into the place left vacant by the untimely death of Dr. Margaret Topping. Dr. Topping started with what she thought was a pet Dal, but she was persuaded to show her pet at one of the all-breed shows in the area—and won. She realized that she had better quality than a pet and when she "made up" her champion she was hooked into the show picture.

Dr. Topping was the leader in founding the Dalmatian Club of New Zealand. She had visited her family in Wales and attended Crufts in February 1970. She wanted a puppy from the famous Fanhill Faune, but Mrs. Woodyatt, the breeder and owner of Faune, refused to sell her one. She did advise her, however, that the Dals would succeed when there was a club. When she returned home she gathered together a few Dalmatian people that she knew and so a club was formed. Gordon Morris and Dorothy Hunt were among the founders and have continued their interest to the present.

AUSTRALIA

In Australia there is the Dalmatian Club of Australia, which formed in Sydney, New South Wales, in 1943; the Dalmatian Club of Victoria, formed in 1953; the Dalmatian Club of South Australia, dating from 1972; the Dalmatian Association of Queensland, formed in 1973 and the Dalmatian Club of Australian Capitol Territory, which dates from 1977.

Prominent among the breeders and exhibitors in Australia are Jan and Ivan Kirin, Mary Young, R. Lawson, Harry Glynn, Graham and Susan Day, Derek Johnson and John and Sonia Gattfield, to name a few.

All dog activity in Australia is governed by the Australian Kennel Control, which is a part of the Agriculture Department. All county fairs are required to hold a dog show in conjunction with the fair. If the shows are not large enough they do not qualify for challenge certificates and are considered "parades." A parade is the equivalent of our match shows. In addition to the fairs, numerous all-breed shows are held during the year.

18

The World Congress

 E ARLY IN JUNE 1979 the British Dalmatian Club voted to hold a world congress. Using the banner "Dalmatians of the world unite!" notices were sent to clubs all over the world. Invitations to speak were also issued.

The congress took place in April 1980 at the Kensington Close Hotel in London, with approximately 140 people in attendance. Special arrangements were made with the kennel club to hold a special championship show in conjunction with the congress.

Papers were given concerning Dalmatians in the United Kingdom and on the Continent, in South America, New Zealand, Scandinavia, North America and Australia. Workshop groups were assigned and people were divided into study groups toward the end of the first day. The second day was given over to sightseeing, visiting and shopping to allow the "home members" to prepare for the show the next day. The championship show was held on Saturday with the renowned Joe Braddon judging. On Sunday a paper on the work of the Animal Health Trust and a paper on the role of the dog press were given, followed by a talk by Mr. Braddon on Dalmatians as he sees them around the world. A paper on modern veterinary techniques and surgery was the final presentation. A working lunch and a general question-and-answer period ended the congress.

Representatives were on hand from Canada, New Zealand, Australia, Brazil, Holland, Czechoslovakia, Germany, France, Belgium, Sweden and the United States. Representing the United States were Dr. and Mrs. John Garvin, Penny Lincke and her husband, Mr. and Mrs. Alfred Treen, Evelyn Nelson White and Charles Colling. Mrs. White read the paper on Mexico prepared by

Raymond Fitzsimmons, who was unable to attend at the last minute. Mary Young represented Australia, and Vivian Sterns, president of the Dal Club of Canada, represented that group. Anna Hammarlund of Sweden presented a study on deafness in the breed that had been done in her country. Mr. and Mrs. Edmund Beim were the representatives of the Dalmatian Clube do Brasil. Mrs. Beim is an international dog show judge.

The feeling of unity was so great that the United States contingent returned home determined to do something to keep the contacts between national groups going. When the AKC announced plans to hold the Centennial show in Philadelphia in 1984 and to hold a world congress of kennel clubs in conjunction with the celebration, the DCA decided to issue invitations to all the Dal clubs in the world to attend another world congress of Dalmatians in Philadelphia at that time.

The second Dalmatian congress was a great success. Held in Bala Cynwyd, a suburb of Philadelphia, from November 12 through 14, 1984, it drew representatives from all over the world. A steering committee composed of the people from the United States who had attended the congress in London as well as Vivian Sterne of Canada was appointed. The Congress Committee included Mrs. Alan Robson, Mrs. Richard M. Keith, Mrs. Alvin F. Lindsay, Jr., Mrs. Nancy Reiter and Alfred Treen, chair.

At the opening reception Monday night there was an art exhibit, arranged by Helene Masaschi; a sound-slide program on the Dalmatian in art, based on the private collection of the authors and expanded by Clay A. Holland; a historical exhibit, arranged by Eleanor Hilen, and a bibliography booth, chaired by Norma Baley.

Numerous speakers presented papers, including Gwendoline E. M. Eady of England, who discussed Dalmatians in Great Britain. Gordon Morris of New Zealand spoke on Dals in the Antipodes. A paper assessing congenital deafness in Dalmatian dogs was presented by Dr. Sheldon A. Steinberg and George C. Farnbach, at which time BAER testing was introduced to the Fancy. An all-rounders impression of the breed Standard was given by Dr. Harold R. Spira, from Sydney, Australia. Three different subjects—Dalmatian colors, Swedish scientific work on deafness in Dalmatians and skin problems and cures—were covered by Anna Hammarlund of Sweden. A talk on selecting a stud dog was presented by Mary Young, from Sydney, Australia. One breed, one Standard was the topic of a talk by Sam Hart of Hamilton, Ontario, Canada. Jane G. Hayes, from São Paulo, Brazil, spoke on Dalmatians in Brazil.

Richard M. Heriot presented some introductory remarks for a panel on the management of the uric acid problem in Dalmatians. This was followed by a scholarly medical report presented by Dr. C. D. Fetner on urate metabolism in the Dalmatian. John Lowery, from York, Pennsylvania, founder of the Dalmatian Research Foundation, spoke on a dietary approach to the uric acid problem in the Dalmatian. Other panel topics included the clinical presentation of urate calculi in Dalmatian dogs, by Dr. Kenneth C. Bovee; and genetic control of uric acid in the Dalmatian, by Robert H. Schaible.

Other scholarly talks included topics such as domestication of the dog, by I. Lehr Brisbin, Jr., a population ecologist with the U.S. Atomic Energy Commission; and reproduction in the dog, by S. W. J. Seager. A hearty welcome to Centennial Week was supplied by William S. Stifel, president of the AKC.

Each person in attendance received a reference book that contained all talks given at the world congress, plus the papers of those who were unable to attend. This book included a set of hand-colored drawings prepared by Mrs. Hammarlund that was attached to her presentation of the genetic aspects of color. There were also letters of good wishes from the Dalmatian Club of South Africa, the Philippine Canine Club, the Northern Ireland Dalmatian Club, the All Ireland Dalmatian Club, the Klubben for Storre Selskapshundraser in Norway, the Dalmatian Club of Canada, the Dalmatian Club of Czechoslovakia, the Dalmatian Club of Switzerland and the Dalmatian Club of Austria.

A day of sightseeing followed the congress and on Friday the Dalmatian Club of America specialty show was held. A gala dinner dance ended the festivities, and everyone prepared to attend the two-day American Kennel Club Centennial show that began the next day.

An autotype of a Dalmatian

19

Fun Things and
Side Effects

ALMOST EVERY BREED can point with pride to celebrity owners, but the Dalmatian seems to have collected a great number, particularly in the movie community of Hollywood and Beverly Hills. Singer John Davidson acquired a puppy to accompany his Arabian horses so that his children could grow up surrounded by the same type of animals he had had as a child.

Actor Darrin McGavin went so far as to have a jogging suit made to match his dog so they will look good together as they run each day.

Glenn Ford has a number of Dals and amuses himself and his friends by training them to do a number of tricks. His Dals have appeared on national television doing their thing.

Daniel Taradash won an Oscar for the screenplay *From Here to Eternity* in 1953. At that time he was actively engaged in exhibiting his Dalmatians. While he is no longer active in the show ring he remains a member of the DCA.

The late Adlai Stevenson, former governor of Illinois, Democratic candidate for president and ambassador to the United Nations, had a Dal named Artie (King Arthur) with him in the Governor's Mansion in Springfield. A full-page picture of the governor and his dog appeared in *Life* magazine.

The great operatic basso Ezio Pinza, later known to millions for ''Some Enchanted Evening'' in *South Pacific,* contributed his two Dalmatians to the war effort in 1942.

Dalmatian postage stamps.

Dalmatian head belt buckle.

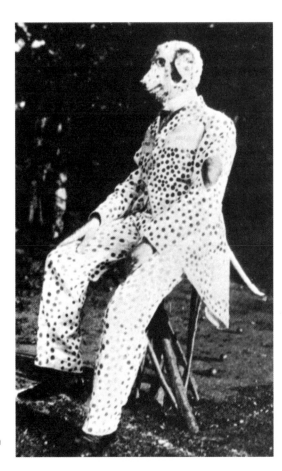

Dr. Wheeler-O'Bryen in Dalmatian fancy dress.

Jim Callea's dog is mascot of the city of Davis, CA, Fire Dept.

Dalmatians love to play frisbee.

A litter of Altamar puppies posing for Disney.

Vanity license plates attract Dalmatians.

Still photo from the movie Tucker.

We all know about George Washington and his "coach dog." The late Arthur Fiedler, that musical institution of the Boston Pops Orchestra, always had a keen interest in fire fighting, fire-fighting equipment and the like. Over the years he was made honorary fire chief of more than 400 fire departments. So when he decided to get a dog there was only one breed that appealed to him, the Firehouse Dog, of course. Mr. Fiedler obtained his Dalmatian from Roadcoach Kennels and named it (what else?) Sparky.

Sparky was a beloved member of the Fiedler household for a number of years and was sadly missed by the entire family.

In an interview on the CBS program "60 Minutes," Mr. Fiedler was asked about an analogy to W. C. Fields, who is frequently quoted as having said, "Anyone who hates kids and dogs can't be all bad." Arthur Fiedler said he didn't think it applied. He said, "I like dogs . . . and I have children of my own."

The well-known oil man from Fort Worth, Texas, E. E. "Buddy" Fogelson, husband of movie star Greer Garson, owned a fine obedience Dalmatian named Axel of Hillview, UD. Axel was shown in competition by Cal Boykin, an active kennel man from the Dallas-Fort Worth area.

In Bennington, Vermont, there is a tourist attraction known as the "lawn of dogs." The lawn was established by Millie Matteson. Her interest in antiques was encouraged by her husband. In the 1930s Mrs. Matteson saw a cast-iron statue of a Dalmatian. It was life size and stood near an iron foundry at Poultney, Vermont. It was about 100 years old then. The foundry is still in business but no longer casts the dogs.

The Mattesons bought the dog. Later on they found another Dalmatian statue that had also been cast at this foundry. They acquired this dog, too. They decided to collect cast-iron animals. They found a finely detailed life-size Newfoundland. In 1940 they found a statue of a very large dog that they thought was a statue of a Mastiff. It wasn't a Mastiff but a giant dog, breed unknown. This statue had been an important feature in a canine cemetery and had once stood on the estate of Commodore Vanderbilt before its use at the cemetery.

In the 1930s Mrs. Bonney found a pair of Dalmatian statues that she had shipped to her Sunstar Hill estate at Oyster Bay, Long Island. After her death, Mr. and Mrs. Arthur Higgins acquired the statues to flank the entrance to their Pennydale Dalmatians' home at Syosset, New York. Today, Dr. and Mrs. Doane have one of Mrs. Bonney's statues and have acquired another statue.

In Oklahoma City there is a pair of Dal statues guarding the driveway of a home in the exclusive residential area of Nichols Hills. As far as can be determined, the family always had pet Dalmatians.

Today the antique dogs have a market value of $1,500 to $3,000. The price of the statue is only the beginning. Transportation and labor to set up the animals cost almost as much as the statue itself. And these dogs must be maintained; painting each year is almost a necessity. But they seem to be so lifelike that live dogs have been known to bark at them.

Arthur Fiedler

Willy Necker

It seems natural that the hearty-eating, highly visible Dalmatian frequently turns up in dog food advertising and TV commercials. It is a little startling to know that a picture of a Dalmatian with a green collar was used to promote Fatima cigarettes in the spring of 1927.

A Dalmatian's portrait is part of the design of a stained-glass window of a church in Bolinbroke, Lincolnshire, England. The two-light window is based on a Benedictine theme depicting the seasons of the year and some of the lovely things man had cause to be thankful for. The dog was one of them. Mr. Skeat, the artist, obtained his Dal, Widdington Dannilad, from Mrs. Hayman in the early 1950s.

Mosaic panel

Ch. Fireman's Freckled Friend

Multiple BIS winner Ch. Swabbie of Oz-Dal, one of two holding the record of 8 BIS wins by a bitch.

20

Top Spots

$\mathbf{C}$H. FIREMAN'S FRECKLED FRIEND topped the Best in Show record of Ch. Green Starr's Colonel Joe in 1987 and went on to establish a new record of forty Bests in Show. He tied Colonel Joe's record of winning four National Specialties.

Best in Show records on the Dal are well known to Dalmatian enthusiasts, as each year Walter Johnson compiles the list for *The Spotter*. Records are made to be broken. Ch. Four-in-Hand Mischief's record of eighteen Bests in Show stood from 1941 to 1979, and Ch. Roadcoach Roadster's record of seventeen top awards remained untouched from 1959 until 1979. Mischief was English-bred and Roadster was an American-bred dog.

Ch. Green Starr's Colonel Joe won the DCA National Specialty four times and had thirty-five Bests in Show. He also garnered more Best of Breed wins than any other Dalmatian shown to date.

Ch. Lord Jim is in fifth place with thirteen Bests in Show, and Ch. Panore of Watseka holds sixth place with ten top awards.

The top winners in bitches are Ch. Swabbie of Oz-Dal and Ch. Godin's To Be or Not To Be, who both have a total of eight Bests. Ch. Blackpool's Crinkle Forest follows with six.

Only sixty-seven Dalmatians have won a Best in Show since this award was started in 1925.

Liver-spotted Dalmatians, once not as popular as black-spotted dogs, are now in the limelight. It is a rare entry of Dalmatians in any show without at least one liver specimen being shown. The color choice is a matter of taste. At one time people would comment, "He is a well-marked dog *for a liver*." No longer

Ch. Coachman's Callisto

Ch. Roadcoach Roadster

The most titled Dalmatian bitch in the world- Int. So. Amer. Ch. de Las Amer '87 & '88, Perv. Bi-Perv., C.R., Dom. Gua, Ch. Sundance's Touch of Trouble, Dom, Gua, CD, TT, A/D owned by Dr. Sherry K. Guldager of Sundance Dalmatians.

does one hear comments of this nature. The liver Dalmatian has come into its own and its breeders have developed spotting patterns equal to those in the black-and-white dogs. Some people feel that livers should be forgiven lack of pigment in eye rims and noses. No Dalmatian should be forgiven lack of pigment, in our estimation. This is a serious fault, for without proper pigmentation we will lose the main characteristic of the breed, the markings.

Over the years the statistics show that ten of the sixty-seven Best in Show Dalmatians have been livers. The first to achieve this honor was Ch. Colonsay Storm, an import, owned by Mr. and Mrs. P. M. Chancellor, at the Peninsula Dog Fanciers dog show, Bremerton, Washington, March 30, 1952. The judge was the late Alfred LePine. The win was over an entry of 554, a good-sized show in those days. Ch. Green Starr's Masterpiece, owned by Dr. and Mrs. David Doane, was Best at Duso Kennel Club, Narrowsburg, New York, June 30, 1956, over an entry of 323. The judge was Mrs. L. St. George. Masterpiece was also named Best at Carroll County Kennel Club, North Conway, New Hampshire, on July 29, 1956, over an entry of 220 by the late Mrs. L. W. Bonney.

Ch. The Lash, owned by Ard Aven and El Tross, beat 484 dogs at Vancouver Kennel Club, Vancouver, Washington, January 27, 1957, under judge G. D. La Monte.

Ch. Roadcoach Spice topped 553 dogs at Rhode Island Kennel Club, Cranston, Rhode Island, April 8, 1962, under Mrs. L. S. Davy. She was owned by Roadcoach Kennels and is the only liver bitch to have won a Best in Show.

Ch. Melody Dynamatic was named Best at the Colorado Kennel Club show in Denver on September 15, 1973, by judge Henry Stoecker over 1,002 entered dogs. Johnny, as he was called, was owned by Ch. E. Flock, Jr. He tied the record for liver Best in Show wins by repeating at the Buckhorn Valley Kennel Club show, Fort Collins, Colorado, March 8, 1975, under judge Herman G. Cox over 730 dogs.

Judge R. C. Graham awarded the top place to Ch. Coachkeeper's Blizzard of QA at the Susque-Nango Kennel Club, Green, New York, June 28, 1974. The dog was owned by Mrs. A. R. Robson, Albelarm Kennels, and was handled by Bobby Barlow.

Ch. Lancer's Sir Lancelot, a liver dog, owner-handled by Ron Brooks, was named Best in Show at Progressive Dog Club in Wayne County, Michigan, April 24, 1976, by judge John Honig over 1,059 dogs.

Over the years four Dalmatians have won the Non-Sporting Group at Westminster. The first to do so was a bitch, Ch. Swabbie of Oz-Dal, in 1949. Swabbie was shown extensively, handled by the well-known Jack Funk. Although she was bred several times and had one or two champion get, she is not remembered as a producer and cannot be found in many extended pedigrees. Blanche Osborne, her owner, was a registered nurse—that probably gives a clue to the meaning of Swabbie. She was a lovely bitch and because she was so good and did so much winning very few champion Dals were entered against her. As her show record piled up most exhibitors decided not to campaign their champions against her.

The second Group winner at the Garden was Ch. Roadcoach Roadster in 1956. He was owned by Mrs. S. K. Allmann (later Mrs. George Ratner). His record of show wins at that time was unheard of. Mrs. Ratner campaigned him extensively with Charley Meyer handling.

Ch. Coachman's Callisto is the third Dal to win the Group at Westminster. Bred by Coachman Kennels in St. Louis, he was purchased by Arthur and Muriel Higgins of Pennydale Kennels, Syosset, New York. Arthur Higgins handled the dog to his great win at the Garden in 1963. In fact, Arthur handled the dog most of the time, using a handler only when it was impossible for him to get to the show.

Ch. Fireman's Freckled Friend was the fourth Garden Group winner.

Ch. Fireman's Freckled Friend winning Stud Dog class at DCA National Specialty with two Best in Show get.

21

The Dalmatian Fancy's Book of Records

$\mathbf{D}$ALMATIAN FANCIERS like to challenge each other's knowledge or memory of facts or events. Some discussions appear destined to last forever. In the interest of harmony and fun it seemed worthwhile to create a book of records for the Dalmatian Fancy.

Selected events are listed in order of occurrence. Some of these landmarks are negative and reflect the need for support that earlier fanciers provided. For instance, neither England nor the United States had a Dalmatian present at its first dog show.

Records of "firsts" and "mosts" attained over the years in the United States also appear in this chapter. Additional tabulations are in other parts of the book. There is no attempt to weigh the importance of these highlights and milestones of breed history, only to gather them into a single reference resource. This in itself may be an all-breed record. It could develop into a treasury of information about the Dalmatian. If any reader has knowledge of additional highlights or achievements that might interest Dal fanciers, the authors would be delighted to learn of them.

MILESTONES

1780   First printed use of word "Dalmatian" in the English language to describe a breed of dogs was in a translation of *Natural History,* by Count de Buffon, published in Scotland.

1787   George Washington reports the purchase of a coach dog stud for Madame Moose, his wife's pet.

1790   The first English writer to use the word "Dalmatian" to designate the breed was Thomas Bewick in *A General History of Quadrupeds.*

1829   First reports that the practice of cropping ears was dying out.

1859   First dog show held in Newcastle on Tyne, June 28 and 29. Sixty entries, no classes for Dalmatians, only Pointers and setters.

1860   Practice of ear flap removal discontinued in England.

1860   Dog show classes for Dalmatians, one of five breeds scheduled, included at Midland County Repository, Cheapside, Birmingham, England on December 3 and 4, 1860. "No prizes awarded."

1861   First record of Dalmatians being shown in England at Leeds, North of England Exhibition of Sporting and Other Dogs, July 16 through 18, 1861. First prize to Caesar (2550), owned by Mr. G. Hutchinson of York.

1873   The Kennel Club founded in Great Britain.

1874   First dog show in America held at Memphis, Tennessee, October 8, 1874. No Dalmatians competed.

1877   Westminster Kennel Club held first show. No Dalmatians competed.

1880   Captain (5394) and Crib (2557) became first two Dalmatian champions in England.

1882   Vero Shaw produced the first unofficial Standard, a formal breed description under systematic headings with numerical Standard of Points in *Illustrated Book of the Dog.*

1884   American Kennel Club founded on a nonprofit basis.

1886   Stonehenge (Dr. John Henry Walsh) published the second unofficial Standard, a detailed description of the breed in his *Dogs of the British Islands,* fourth edition.

1888   First Dalmatian registered with the AKC.

1888   Canadian Kennel Club formed.

1889	Twenty-one Dalmatians entered at Crystal Palace show in London.
1890	First club formed in England to support Dalmatians. Disbanded in 1947.
1890	First official Standard published in England.
1895	The practice of cropping dogs' ears was prohibited by The Kennel Club in Great Britain.
1904	Dalmatian Club of America formed with twenty-six charter members. Membership limited to fifty.
1905	DCA elected an AKC member club.
1906	First road trial for Dalmatians at Wissahickon, Pennsylvania.
1907	Inception of Best in Show at AKC events.
1920	First official FCI Dalmatian club founded in Germany.
1924	Alignment of breeds into five groups started at AKC shows. Became six in 1930 and seven in 1983.
1930	South of England Dalmatian Club became the British Dalmatian Club.
1930	Record entry of 458 at first specialist show (limited) in England at Tattersall's in Knightsbridge.
1931	Morris & Essex Kennel Club agreed to hold classes for Dalmatians at its May 23 show.
1933	British Dalmatian Club achieved championship status in April.
1934	AKC granted permission for two preliminary Obedience Trials.
1936	Obedience Trials made a formal part of the AKC's purebred dog program. The first AKC-licensed Obedience test held at the North Westchester Kennel Club, Mount Kisco, New York, June 13, 1936. Twelve entries, no Dalmatians.
1937	Restriction limiting DCA membership to fifty lifted.
1956	Dodie Smith's *One Hundred and One Dalmatians* published.
1961	Walt Disney's animated cartoon *One Hundred and One Dalmatians* released.
1962	Dalmatian Club of America revised description and Standard of the Dalmatian February 12, 1962, approved by the AKC December 11, 1962.
1968	Ch. Fanhill Faune, owned by Mrs. E. J. Woodyatt, became Supreme Champion at Crufts, London.
1971	*The Spotter* of the Dalmatian Club of America changed from a newsletter to a magazine format.

1975   Golden Jubilee Championship show of the British Dalmatian Club held April 5 with an entry of 239.

1976   Dalmatian Club of America membership reached 516.

1977   Fiftieth specialty show of Dalmatian Club of America presented September 23 with 327 dogs entered in conformation and obedience. On September 22 the first Dalmatian Futurity was held as well as the annual Sweepstakes. The two-day event was held at Crete, Illinois.

1980   World congress for Dalmatians held in London.

1984   World congress of kennel clubs held in Philadelphia.

1984   World congress for Dalmatians held in Philadelphia.

1984   AKC Centennial show held in Philadelphia.

1989   Revised AKC/DCA Dalmatian Standard.

1991   Dalmatian Club of America membership tops 1,000.

CONFORMATION FIRSTS

The first Dalmatian registered in the American Kennel Club Stud Book was Bessie (10519), whelped October 1887. Owned by Mrs. N. L. Havey, San Francisco, California. She was recorded as white, black and tan—breeder and pedigree unknown. Bench show—second prize, San Francisco, 1888. Walter Johnson reports, "Bessie appears in Volume 5 of the Stud book but has no progeny registered with AKC. Her fame appears only in her timely registration."

First Dalmatian registered as the result of completing a championship was Ch. Hoyt (82449) in 1905. Breeder, N. R. F. Roges, New Castle, Pennsylvania, owner J. M. Schontz, Sharon, Pennsylvania.

The first Dalmatians recorded as being shown in the United States were shown at the San Francisco Dog Show, April 27–May 2, 1883. The record is in the July 1883 issue of the *American Register*. The two males were owned by Dr. E. H. Woolsey with Spot placing first and Speck second. There were two females, Nellie Dodge, owned by A. J. Kelly, placed first and Ruby, owned by H. B. Slocum, placed second.

The first Dalmatian champion confirmed by the AKC was a male. Ch. Edgecomb D'Artagnan (80503), owned by Miss M. W. Martin, Philadelphia, Pennsylvania, breeder, J. S. Price, Jr., black and white, whelped June 9, 1902. Recorded November 1904.

The first bitch confirmed as a champion was the second Dalmatian to win this honor. She was Spotted Diamond (80504), owned by Miss M. W. Martin, Philadelphia, Pennsylvania, breeder, Mr. Berkholder, black and white, whelped November 1901.

The first imported Dalmatian champion, Ch. Windy Valley Snowstorm

(87741), white with black markings, whelped May 1, 1903. Breeder W. B. Herman (England), owner Windy Valley Kennels, New York.

Tally Ho Last of Sunstar was the first Dalmatian to take the Non-Sporting Group. He came out of the American-bred class at the Nassau County Kennel Club's May 17, 1924, show.

The first all-breed Best in Show under the Group system was Ch. Gladmore Guardsman at the Valley Kennel Club, New Kensington, Pennsylvania, under Judge G. V. Glebe. He won over 179 dogs shown at the two-day event, April 27–28, 1928.

The first DCA National Specialty was won by Ch. Tally Ho Last of Sunstar at Mineola, New York, on June 26, 1926. He won it again the following year and in 1931 became the first three-time winner. This record remained for forty-six years. It was tied by Ch. Panore of Watseka in 1977. Ch. Tally Ho Last of Sunstar and Ch. Panore of Watseka each came out of the Veterans class to win their third National Specialty. Colonel Joe won his fourth from the Veterans class.

The first bitch to win the National Specialty was Ch. Tally Ho Fore Thought, at Forest Hills, New York, on May 18, 1928.

The first liver-spotted Dalmatian to win a National Specialty was Ch. Tally Ho Samson, at Florham Park, New Jersey, on May 26, 1950.

OBEDIENCE FIRSTS

The first Dalmatian entered in an Obedience class was Captain Fiske, exhibited by Louise Geddes Fiske in the Novice A class of the Eastern Dog Club, Boston, Massachusetts, February 21–22, 1937. The Obedience Test Club of New York (Mrs. Whitehouse Walker, secretary, Bedford Hills, New York) offered both cash and special prizes for Novice, Open and Utility "Obedience Test" classes.

The first Dalmatian to earn a Companion Dog title, Meeker's Barbara Worth, owned by George S. Walker, January 10, 1939.

The first male Dal to earn an Obedience title, Blotter's Boy, CD, in February 1940.

The first Dalmatian to earn Companion Dog Excellent (August 20, 1940) and Utility Dog (November 1, 1940) degrees was Io, not registered, owned by Harland and Lois Meistrell.

The first Dal bitch to earn a Utility Dog title, Spur of Victory, UD, Long Last Kennels.

The first Dal Champion to win a CD title, May 1, 1940, Ch. Byron's Penny, owned by Robert Byron.

The first and only Dalmatian recipients of the short-lived UDT title were Roadcoach Tess (N4258) and Dickie's Candy (N134720), both confirmed in the January 1956 AKC *Gazette*. Previously a dog was required to pass a "tracking test" before being permitted to use the title of "UD," signifying "Utility Dog." These tests were given in connection with what was then called an Obedience Test Trial or at another time. The American Kennel Club issued a "Tracking Test" certificate for dogs successfully passing this test. For a brief period this became a UDT title. Later Tracking trials evolved as separate events with the resulting Tracking Dog title. Now the owner of a dog holding both the UD and TD titles may use the letters UDT after the name of the dog, signifying "Utility Dog Tracker."

The first Dalmatian to achieve both championship and Utility Dog titles, Ch. Duke of Gervais, UD, owned by Maurice Gervais, December 8, 1944.

The first champion Dalmatian bitch to earn a Utility Dog and a Tracking degree, Ch. Dal Downs Dicie of Shadodal, owned by Bob and Marge Sullivan in 1976.

The first 200 score, by Lady Jane, owned by Naomi Radler at Garden City.

The first OTCH won by Candi's Skagit Belle, owned by Rebecca Jean and Rex Alan Auer in 1981.

MOSTS

The most Best in Show awards to date, 40—Ch. Fireman's Freckled Friend (NS753102).

The most BIS awards won by an English import, 18—Ch. Four-in-Hand Mischief (A204760).

The most BIS awards won by a bitch, 8 (tie)—
Ch. Swabbie of Oz-Dal (N32668); Ch. Godin's To Be or Not To Be. (NT 281700)

The most BIS awards won in a single year, 13—Ch. Lord Jim (NA619679) in 1970.

The most champion get, 58—Ch. Buffrey Jobe.

The most champion produce, 16—Ch. Melody Sweet, CD.

YOUNGEST

The youngest Dalmatian to win Best in Show was a bitch, Ch. Ser Dals Lone Star, at the age of one year, two months and twenty-seven days.

The youngest Dalmatian to finish its championship is Ch. Crown Jewels' Hope Diamond II (NA371586), at the age of slightly over seven months. Born June 9, 1965, he finished on the Florida circuit in January 1966 and was confirmed in the March 1966 AKC *Gazette*.

OLDEST

The oldest Dalmatian Best in Show winner was Ch. Four-in-Hand Athos (A424221) at the age of seven years, five months and two days.

Epilogue

Eugene O'Neill, whose plays won four Pulitzer Prizes, was called the "American Shakespeare." He wrote more than thirty plays, including *Anna Christie, Strange Interlude, Ah, Wilderness!, The Iceman Cometh* and *Long Day's Journey into Night,* which was not to be produced until twenty-five years after his death.

"The Last Will and Testament of an Extremely Distinguished Dog" is a touching tribute to the Dalmatian Blemie, owned by the playwright and his third wife, the actress Carlotta Monterey. O'Neill wrote this gem as a comfort to Carlotta a few days before Blemie passed away from old age in December 1940.

Blemie's will epitomizes the love between Dalmatians and their owners and serves as a fitting *finis* to the text of this book, which has also been written with love by its authors.

Eugene O'Neill and Blemie

The Last Will and Testament of an Extremely Distinguished Dog

I, Silverdene Emblem O'Neill (familiarly known to my family, friends, and acquaintances as Blemie), because the burden of my years and infirmities is heavy upon me, and I realize the end of my life is near, do hereby bury my last will and testament in the mind of my Master. He will not know it is there until after I am dead. Then, remembering me in his loneliness, he will suddenly know of this testament, and I ask him then to inscribe it as a memorial to me.

I have little in the way of material things to leave. Dogs are wiser than men. They do not set great store upon things. They do not waste their days hoarding property. They do not ruin their sleep worrying about how to keep the objects they have, and to obtain the objects they have not. There is nothing of value I have to bequeath except my love and my faith. These I leave to all those who have loved me, to my Master and Mistress, who I know will mourn me most, to Freeman who has been so good to me, to Cyn and Roy and Willie and Naomi and—But if I should list all those who have loved me it would force my Master to write a book. Perhaps it is vain of me to boast when I am so near death, which returns all beasts and vanities to dust, but I have always been an extremely lovable dog.

I ask my Master and Mistress to remember me always, but not to grieve for me too long. In my life I have tried to be a comfort to them in time of sorrow, and a reason for added joy in their happiness. It is painful for me to think that even in death I should cause them pain. Let them remember that while no dog has ever had a happier life (and this I owe to their love and care for me), now that I have grown blind and deaf and lame, and even my sense of smell fails me so that a rabbit could be right under my nose and I might not know, my pride has sunk to a sick, bewildered humiliation. I feel life is taunting me with having over-lingered my welcome. It is time I said goodbye, before I become too sick, a burden on myself and on those who love me. It will be sorrow to leave them, but not a sorrow to die. Dogs do not fear death as men do. We accept it as part of life, not as something alien and terrible which destroys life. What may come after death, who knows? I would like to believe with those of my fellow Dalmatians who are devout Mohammedans, that there is a Paradise where one is always young and full-bladdered; where all the day one dillies and dallies with an amorous multitude of houris, beautifully spotted; where jack rabbits that run fast but not too fast (like the houris) are as the sands of the desert; where each blissful hour is mealtime; where in long evenings there are a million fireplaces with logs forever burning, and one curls oneself up and blinks into the flames and nods and dreams, remembering the old brave days on earth, and the love of one's Master and Mistress.

I am afraid this is too much for even such a dog as I am to expect. But peace, at least, is certain. Peace and long rest for weary old heart and head and limbs, and eternal sleep in the earth I have loved so well. Perhaps, after all, this is best.

One last request I earnestly make. I have heard my Mistress say, "When Blemie dies we must never have another dog. I love him so much I could never love another one." Now I would ask her, for love of me, to have another. It would be a poor tribute to my memory never to have a dog again. What I would like to feel is that, having once had me in the family, now she cannot live without a dog! I have never had a narrow jealous spirit. I have always held that most dogs are good (and one cat, the black one I have permitted to share the living room rug during the evenings, whose affection I have tolerated in a kindly spirit, and in rare sentimental moods, even reciprocated a trifle). Some dogs, of course, are better than others. Dalmatians, naturally, as everyone knows, are best. So I suggest a Dalmatian as my successor. He can hardly be as well bred or as well mannered or as distinguished and handsome as I was in my prime. My Master and Mistress must not ask the impossible. But he will do his best, I am sure, and even his inevitable defects will help by comparison to keep my memory green. To him I bequeath my collar and leash and my overcoat and raincoat, made to order in 1929 at Hermès in Paris. He can never wear them with the distinction I did, walking around the Place Vendôme, or later along Park Avenue, all eyes fixed on me in admiration; but again I am sure he will do his utmost not to appear a mere gauche provincial dog. Here on the ranch, he may prove himself quite worthy of comparison, in some respects. He will, I presume, come closer to jack rabbits that I have been able to in recent years. And, for all his faults, I hereby wish him the happiness I know will be his in my old home.

One last word of farewell, Dear Master and Mistress. Whenever you visit my grave, say to yourselves with regret but also with happiness in your hearts at the remembrance of my long happy life with you: "Here lies one who loved us and whom we loved." No matter how deep my sleep I shall hear you, and not all the power of death can keep my spirit from wagging a grateful tail.

—Tao House,
December 17, 1940

Glossary

Angulation: Probably one of the most frequently used (or misused) terms among dog fanciers, "angulation" refers to the angles created by bones meeting at various joints, especially at the shoulder, stifle and hock; the pastern and pelvic areas may also be involved. Dogs exhibiting the correct angulations for a given breed are spoken of as being "well angulated" or "well turned."

Balance (syn. symmetry, symmetrical appearance): A descriptive noun frequently employed by dog breeders, exhibitors and especially judges to describe the pleasing, harmonious and well-proportioned blend of an animal's parts and features, resulting in a final, composite effect of total symmetry; the aim of all dedicated breeders. The verb "to balance" is used to explain the relationship of one anatomical area to another. "Balanced" is frequently applied to skull components, that is, equal length of brain case and foreface.

Barrel-shaped: Having a rounded rib section.

Bitch: A female dog.

Bite: The relative position of the upper and lower teeth when the mouth is closed. *See* Level bite, Overshot, Scissors bite, Undershot.

Brisket: This term is mostly taken as a synonym for "breastbone" or "sternum." In some breed Standards it is used in place of "chest" or "thorax." *Deep brisket, deep in brisket* (syn. well-developed brisket, well-let-down brisket, deep chest, deep in chest, deep in ribs)—A reference to a chest down at least to the elbow region; the opposite of a shallow chest. The term is another way of expressing adequate chest depth.

Butterfly nose: A particolored nose; that is, dark, spotted with flesh color.

Buttocks: The muscular area surrounding the ischiatic tubers of the pelvis. Above, the buttocks merge into the croup; below, they blend with the upper thigh region.

Coarse, Coarseness: Applied to overall construction, and especially bone, head and/or muscle properties, meaning lack of refinement, a heavier, plainer, larger or clumsier physique than desirable. The opposite of "weediness." "Coarse" may also apply to coats, implying a rough or harsh texture.

Coat: The dog's hairy covering.

Cowhocked: When the hocks turn toward each other.

Croup: The muscular area just above and around the set-on of the tail. It merges into the rump in front and technically overlies the lower half of the pelvic region, that is, from the hip joints to the buttocks.

Dewclaw: An extra claw or functionless digit on the inside of the leg; a rudimentary fifth toe.

Disqualification: A decision made by a judge or by a bench show committee following a determination that a dog has a condition that makes it ineligible for any further competition under the dog show rules or under the Standard for its breed.

Dog: A male dog; also used collectively to designate both male and female canines.

Drive, Driving power: A term used to describe hindquarter propulsion. Dogs with powerful rear action are sometimes referred to as having "plenty of drive."

Ectropion: The scientific term for exceedingly loose lower eyelids or "haw-eyedness."

Elbow, Elbow joint: The joint in the forelimb created by the articulation of the humerus (arm) above and the tibia/fibula (forearm) below.

Entropion: An anatomical abnormality caused by spasm and contraction of the muscles controlling the eye rims. This, in consequence, causes affected eyelids to turn and roll in toward the eyeball. The resultant contact of eyelash to eyeball produces a state of semipermanent irritation, indicated by squinting, excessive tear flow, etc. Both upper and/or lower eyelids may be affected, the lower more frequently. Furthermore, the problem may be unilateral or bilateral, that is, it may occur on one or both sides.

Expression: The general appearance of all features of the head, as viewed from the front and as typical of the breed.

Forechest: That portion of the breastbone that projects beyond the point of the shoulder when seen in profile.

Furrow (syn. median line, flute): A longitudinal groove, formed by bone formation and/or muscular development, running along from the center of the skull, that is, the frontal bone junction, toward the stop.

Gait: The pattern of footsteps at various rates of speed, each pattern distinguished by a particular rhythm and footfall. The two gaits acceptable in the show ring are walk and trot.

Height: Vertical measurement from the withers to the ground; referred to usually as shoulder height. *See* Withers.

Hock: The tarsus or collection of bones of the hind leg forming the joint between the second thigh and the metatarsus; the dog's true heel.

Leather: The cartilagenous lobe of the outer ear. A term most commonly used in reference to sporting breeds. Also designates the skin of the hairless front portion of the muzzle (nose leather).

Level bite: A condition where the front teeth (incisors) of the upper and lower jaws meet exactly edge to edge. Pincer bite.

Liver: A color; deep reddish brown.

Loin: Region of the body on either side of the vertebral column between the last ribs and the hindquarters.

Lumber: Superfluous flesh.

Muzzle: The head in front of the eyes—nasal bone, nostrils and jaws. Foreface. Also, a strap or wire cage attached to the foreface to prevent a dog from biting or from picking up food.

Nose: Organ of smell; also, the ability to detect by means of scent. Technically, the term "nose" refers to the external nose, its associated nasal cartilages and nasal cavity. To most dog fanciers, however, the word "nose" simply means the external portions, or even the muzzle as a whole (for example, "long nose," "short nose," etc.). Evidence of this lies in the use of descriptions like "butterfly nose," "dudley nose," etc.

Occiput: Upper, back point of the skull.

Overshot: A condition where the front teeth (incisors) overlap and do not touch the front teeth of the lower jaw when the mouth is closed.

Paddling: A compensating action, so named for its similarity to the swing and dip of a canoeist's paddle. Pinching in at the elbows and shoulder joints causes the front legs to swing forward on a stiff outward arc. Also referred to as "tied at the elbows."

Pads: Tough, shock-absorbing projections on the underside of the feet; soles.

Pastern: The metacarpus, that is, the region between the carpus (wrist) above and the digits (foot) below. The pasterns of different breeds exhibit great variations in type, strength, length and slope, depending upon usage. Description of some of the most common types follows:

Distended pastern joint—The rather unattractive knobby appearance, especially when viewed front on, of an enlarged carpal or pastern joint. Common causes include coarse bone, injury, arthritis, etc.

Down in pasterns (syn. sunken pasterns, falling pasterns)—Pasterns with a greater than desirable slope away from the perpendicular, when viewed side on. Apart from being unsightly, excessively sloping or broken-down pasterns tend to reduce exercise tolerance, as dogs so affected tire more easily than sound animals. Causes include greater than normal pastern length, tendon looseness due to prolonged rest, sickness and dietary imbalance.

Slanting or sloping pasterns—The most commonly required pastern type in the breed Standard, that is, the anatomical mean between "upright pasterns" on the one hand and "down in the pasterns" on the other.

Slope of pasterns—The angle formed by the pasterns' longitudinal axis with the horizontal of the ground. The actual ideal pastern slope tends to vary with the breed. Many terms are employed by the breed Standards to define the ideal for a given breed, including "upright," "perpendicular," "gentle slope," "steep," etc. For normal function, some degree of pastern slope is essential.

Upright pasterns (syn. steep pasterns)—Pasterns in which the longitudinal axis approaches the perpendicular. The opposite of being "down in pasterns," upright pasterns are inadequate shock absorbers. Dogs so affected tire more easily and have a slightly shorter stride than those with normally sloping pasterns.

Pigmentation: Refers to depth, intensity and extent of color or markings.

Reach: A reference to the distance covered with each stride. For example, a dog said to have plenty of reach or lots of reach is one with maximal stride length.

Ring tail: A tail carried up and around, almost in a circle.

Scissors bite: A bite in which the outer side of the lower incisors touches the inner side of the upper incisors.

Shyness: Timid, reserved behavior; shrinking from familiarity or contact with others.

Single tracking: In normal canine movement, irrespective of breed (but more readily observed in the taller varieties), the tendency is for the legs to incline more and more under the body as the speed increases. Eventually the paws, as seen by their imprints, travel in a single line. Such action is referred to as "single tracking."

Skull: The bony components of the head. A most complex and highly specialized region, the skull (including the lower jaw or mandible) is divided into two sections: (a) the brain case (cavum cranii), formed by the fusion of fourteen individual bones, and (b) the facial and palatal portion (foreface), consisting of thirty-six highly specialized bones, of which all but two (vomer and basihyoid) are paired. The term "skull" is often used by dog fanciers in reference to the brain case; this is technically incorrect. The skull as such includes the brain case as well as the facial/palatine segment of the foreface. The skull is the head's bony framework and not the head as such.

Spring of rib: A reference to the shape of ribs after their emergence from their articulation with the thoracic vertebrae. Spring of rib has direct influence upon chest capacity. The more pronounced the arch (within reason), the greater the exercise tolerance; the flatter the spring or arch, the greater the restrictions on lung and heart development and, consequently, the less the anticipated stamina. A dog with correct rib curvature and development is said to be "well sprung," "well rounded" or "well arched in rib."

Standard: A description of the ideal dog of each recognized breed; it serves as a word pattern by which dogs are judged at shows.

Stifle (syn. knee joint, stifle joint): A joint in the hind leg, formed by the articulation of upper and lower thighs. The canine stifle joint is an area of special importance to dog fanciers in that "hindquarter angulation," often mentioned in breed Standards, relates directly to the angle formed at this joint, determining such angulation or turn. This is described as "good" or "well turned" in most breeds. Only a few Standards request anatomically "inadequate" stifle angulation; animals so constructed are often referred to as being "straight in stifle."

Substance (syn. timber): Used in reference to bone, particularly leg bone, that is, a dog with heavy substance is one well developed in bone size, strength and density as related to overall structure and strength.

Throatiness: An excess of loose skin under the throat.

Topline: The line of the dog's back (top) from the set-on of the neck to the tail.

Trichiasis: A rather painful anatomical abnormality, related to entropion and caused by eyelashes erupting in abnormal, misplaced positions and directions. Some eyelashes, occasionally many, grow in toward the eyeball. Constant eyelash-to-eyeball contact results in irritation and, finally, injury. Early symptoms of trichiasis include tear secretion, sensitivity to light as evinced by squinting, etc. Trichiasis is thought by most experts to have an inherited background.

Tri-color: Three-colored dogs; white, black and tan.

Tuck-up (syn. cut-up): The appearance produced by the abdomen's underline as it sweeps upward into the flank and/or hindquarters region.

Underline: The combined contours of the brisket and abdominal floor. Known variously as "underline," "underbody," "lower body line" or "abdomen line."

Undershot: A condition where the front teeth (incisors) of the lower jaw overlap or project beyond the front teeth of the upper jaw when the mouth is closed.

Weaving: Unsound gaiting action that starts with twisting elbows and ends with crisscrossing and toeing out.

Whiskers: Longer hairs on muzzle sides and underjaw.

Withers: The highest point of the shoulders, immediately beyond the neck.

Wrinkle: Loose, folding skin on forehead and foreface.

June Harrah Bronze

Appendix

Dalmatian Best in Show Winners

Ch. Fireman's Freckled Friend (d) NS753102 black	40
Ch. Green Starr's Colonel Joe (d) NS187661 black	35
Ch. Four-in-Hand Mischief (d) A204760 black	18
Ch. Roadcoach Roadster (d) N201878 black	17
Ch. Lord Jim (d) NA619679 black	13
Ch. Panore of Watseka (d) NC1679 black	10
Ch. Fire Star's Sonny Boy (d) NS394145 black	8
Ch. Godin's To Be or Not To Be (b) NT281700 black	8
Ch. Korcula Midnight Star Bret D (d) NT88524 black	8
Ch. Rolenet's Ragtime Dandy (d) NS426849 black	8
Ch. Swabbie of Oz-Dal (b) N32668 black	8
Ch. Ye Dal Dark Brilliance (d) N350818 black	7
Ch. Blackpool Crinkle Forest (b) N706235 black	6
Ch. Ard Aven Shamus (d) N265615 black	5
Ch. Farga De Montjuic (b) NT10344 black	5
Ch. Crestview Dan Patch (d) NS45762 black	4
Ch. Coachman's Chuck-a-Luck (d) NA35983 black	3
Ch. Fireman's Becky Newsham (b) NT 163347 black	3
Ch. Green Starr's Shamrock (b) NS888421 black	3
Ch. Merry Go Round X K E (d) NT215546 black	3
Ch. St Florian Pisces Jordache (d) NT45141 black	3

Ch. FanFayre's Beau of Short Acre (d) NS612286 black   2
Ch. Green Starr's Masterpiece (d) N190812 liver   2
Ch. Madhurason's Tanfastic (d) NS977669 liver   2
Ch. Melody Dynamatic (d) NB753573 liver   2
Ch. PGR Heilou Samson, CD (d) NS485415 black   2
Ch. Rovingdale's Impudent Ingenue (b) N85612 black   2
Ch. Tuckaway's The Peddler (d) NS364368 black   2
Ch. Albelarm Starr of Summerhill (d) NS367514 black   1
Ch. Alfredrich Handsome Tall 'N Dark (d) NS991751 black   1
Ch. Arora's Lacy Britches (b) NT118445 black   1
Ch. Beaumont of Pacifica (d) NS51334 black   1
Ch. Coachkeeper's Blizzard of Q A (d) NS26557 liver   1
Ch. Coachman's Coat of Arms, CD (d) NS548500 liver   1
Ch. Colonsay Storm (d) N116860 liver   1
Ch. Calabra Star Dust of Ragusa (d) N10499 black   1
Ch. Deltalyn Decoupage (d) NS132793 black   1
Ch. Deltalyn 'n' Penwiper Kisncuzn (b) NT604840 black   1
Ch. Devlstr Syngln Rich N Spirit (d) NT276436 black   1
Ch. Driftwood's Chimney Cricket, CD (b) NS950041 black   1
Ch. Esquires Black Talisman (d) NT102938 black   1
Ch. Four-in-Hand Athos (d) A424221 black   1
Ch. Gladmore Guardsman (d) 538831 black   1
Ch. Gren's Coal Tar (d) N346971 black   1
Ch. Indalane Travelog of Tasha (d) NS867705 black   1
Ch. Jo Dal Drummer Boy Hapi Dal (d) NS7808730 black   1
Ch. Knightstone Huntsman (d) NT102800 black   1
Ch. Lancer's Sir Lancelot (d) NS181316 liver   1
Ch. Melody Ring of Fire of B B, CD (d) NB933443 black   1
Ch. Nigel of Welfield and Stock Dal (d) A773733 black   1
Ch. Pacifica Pride of Poseidon (d) NA39551 black   1
Ch. Pill Peddler's Apostrophe (d) NT251423 black   1
Ch. Reigate's Bold Venture (d) A401493 black   1
Ch. Roadcoach Post Parade (d) N146988 black   1
Ch. Roadcoach Spice (b) N492982 liver   1
Ch. Roadcoach Tioga Too (b) N31081 black   1
Ch. Roadking's Rome (d) NS21580 black   1
Ch. Rockledge Rumble (d) NA211578 black   1
Ch. Ser Dals Lone Star (b) N181352 black   1
Ch. Snowood Superstition Bret D (d) NT 276452 black   1
Ch. Strathglass Cricket (b) A638173 black   1
Ch. Tally Ho Sirius (d) A254581 black   1
Ch. Tamarack's Tennyson v Watseka (d) NS618272 black   1
Ch. The Lash (d) N227715 liver   1
Ch. Tuckaway Bottoms Up Gusto (d) NS670642 liver   1
Ch. Williamsdale Rocky (d) N81989 black   1
Ch. Williamsdale's Michael (d) A629252 black   1
Ch. Willy Overland in the Valley (d) N612551 black   1